FREDERICK DOUGLASS, SLAVERY, AND THE CONSTITUTION, 1845

OTHER TITLES IN THIS SERIES

Also available

ABOUT THE AUTHORS

Mark Higbee is professor of history at Eastern Michigan University. He holds a PhD from Columbia University. He is an author of articles, essays, and blog posts on African American history and pedagogical approaches in the history classroom. He has been involved in the Reacting to the Past community since 2005.

James Brewer Stewart is the founder of Historians Against Slavery and James Wallace Professor of History Emeritus at Macalester College. He has published a dozen books on the history of the American antislavery movement, has appeared in several American Experience historical documentaries, is co-editor of the series Antislavery, Abolition, and the Atlantic World at Louisiana State University Press, and has spoken widely about abolition on college and university campuses.

REACTING TO THE PAST

FREDERICK DOUGLASS, SLAVERY, AND THE CONSTITUTION, 1845

Mark Higbee, Eastern Michigan University

James Brewer Stewart, Macalester College

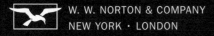
W. W. NORTON & COMPANY
NEW YORK · LONDON

BARNARD
REACTING TO THE PAST

W. W. Norton & Company has been independent since its founding in 1923, when William Warder Norton and Mary D. Herter Norton first published lectures delivered at the People's Institute, the adult education division of New York City's Cooper Union. The firm soon expanded its program beyond the Institute, publishing books by celebrated academics from America and abroad. By midcentury, the two major pillars of Norton's publishing program—trade books and college texts—were firmly established. In the 1950s, the Norton family transferred control of the company to its employees, and today—with a staff of four hundred and a comparable number of trade, college, and professional titles published each year—W. W. Norton & Company stands as the largest and oldest publishing house owned wholly by its employees.

Editor: Justin Cahill
Project Editor: Laura Dragonette
Editorial Assistant: Funto Omojola
Managing Editor, College: Marian Johnson
Production Manager: Stephen Sajdak
Marketing Manager, History: Sarah England Bartley
Design Director: Rubina Yeh
Book Design: Alexandra Charitan
Director of College Permissions: Megan Schindel
Composition: Jouve International
Illustrations: Mapping Specialists, Ltd.
Manufacturing: Sheridan Books, Inc.

Library of Congress Cataloging-in-Publication Data (TK)

ISBN 978-0-393-68063-8

W. W. Norton & Company, Inc., 500 Fifth Avenue, New York, NY 10110
wwnorton.com
W. W. Norton & Company Ltd., 15 Carlisle Street, London W1D 3BS

1 2 3 4 5 6 7 8 9 0

CONTENTS

FREDERICK DOUGLASS, SLAVERY, AND THE CONSTITUTION, 1845

 PART 1: INTRODUCTION

BRIEF OVERVIEW OF THE GAME

Frederick Douglass, Slavery, and the Constitution, 1845 is set in a time and place unimaginable today, when advocating the abolition of slavery was far more controversial and dangerous than was supporting its perpetuation: the United States of America in 1845. Its subject is the central paradox of American history: how, in a nation founded on professed ideals of equal rights and freedom, did the institution of slavery, and its underlying belief in white supremacy and Black inferiority, become so entrenched and long lasting?[1] How was slavery justified, and how was it criticized? Debates in the game focus on the intellectual and cultural clashes between the proslavery, Status Quo Faction—the entrenched, respectable and often powerful proponents of American slavery—and the Abolitionist Faction—a small but dedicated movement calling for slavery's immediate and universal abolition. They vie for the support of players who are independent of both Factions.

The question facing the country in 1845 was not the Civil War—which was then unimaginable—but whether Abolitionist critics of slavery had any legitimacy, any right to push for universal, immediate emancipation. Could the Abolitionists be suppressed outright? Must their treachery in aiding slaves running away from their lawful owners be tolerated? The many violent anti-Abolitionist mobs in the North showed that this was hardly just a "southern" concern. Few white Americans, in the North or the South, favored the equality of Black and white.

This game plays out in a series of Meetings that take place in July 1845 in New York City. The first Meeting is a literary forum on the newly published *Narrative of the Life of Frederick Douglass, an American Slave, Written by Himself,* hosted by the illustrious English author Charles Dickens. The second Meeting is a banquet honoring John C. Calhoun of South Carolina and his view of slavery as a "positive good." The third Meeting is a debate, at a large evangelical Christian church, on the how the U.S. Constitution protected slavery and whether Americans are more beholden to the Constitution or to a "higher law." (In some classes, an additional Faction, the Free Soil for White Men Faction, may form and host a fourth Meeting at Tammany Hall.)

Learning Objectives

Students who play the *Frederick Douglass, Slavery, and the Constitution, 1845* Reacting to the Past game will

- Examine the ideas and goals of the Abolitionist Movement and its key leaders, like Douglass and Garrison, as well as the beliefs of the proslavery consensus that largely dominated the country in 1845.

- Understand how inextricably linked slavery was to early American political institutions, beliefs, and practices.

- Explore contesting interpretations of Jefferson's ideas of government, the right of revolution, and slavery and race.

- Learn much about the lives of influential Americans and see how they were affected by slavery.

- Develop a deep understanding of two primary sources, the U.S. Constitution and *Narrative of the Life of Frederick Douglass*.

- See how slavery and abolitionism shaped not only the antebellum era of American history but the whole of American civilization.

In addition, as in all Reacting to the Past games, students will

- Experience both teamwork and competition with their classmates.

- Improve their skills in persuasive communication, with written and spoken work.

Required Readings

In addition to this game book, all players need their own copy of the *Narrative of the Life of Frederick Douglass, an American Slave, Written by Himself,* first published in May 1845. (We recommend the Norton Critical Edition, 2nd edition, edited by William L. Andrews and William S. McFeely, which may be bundled with this game book at a significant discount.) Finally, the instructor will provide everyone with a confidential role sheet, consisting of a handful of pages.

PROLOGUE: A MORNING WITH THE NEWSPAPERS

Astor House Hotel, July 1845, New York City

A distinguished, elderly American, Albert Gallatin (b. 1761), who was secretary of the treasury under Presidents Jefferson and Madison and a noted diplomat, is the last living American statesman from the Founding Fathers' generation. He spends the morning alone with his thoughts and the newspapers in the Astor House Hotel . . .

h, you do still find much of real interest in the many newspapers of New York City! Today, you have nothing to interrupt your reading until twelve o'clock. Nothing, that is, unless you doze off, which you can do now, when little urgent work demands your attention, as it did for most of your life.

The city provides dozens of newspapers, each propounding the viewpoint of an editor who aims to express his ideas in vivid, evocative words to shape what men think and know about the world. This competitive exchange of ideas in the country's press is the lifeblood of democracy and of mankind's ability to govern itself. This remains true, you believe, even when some of the newspapers make themselves into scandal sheets.

You look forward to reading and thinking all morning—the popular New York *Herald*, and Mr. William Cullen Bryant's always thoughtful *Evening Post*. Nowadays Horace Greeley's *New-York Tribune* has a girl, Margaret Fuller, reviewing books! The *New York Aurora*, the *Mirror*, and so many other newspapers—these make up the foundation of democracy and public opinion. You can't wait to plunge in. Lately some stories by a Walt Whitman have caught your eye. His pen is uncommonly good. The dailies of Philadelphia and Boston remain informative, and they now arrive in New York the day after publication. Railroads and steamships have transformed everything. And you don't forget about the weekly from Boston that intrigues you, the notorious abolition paper, the *Liberator*.

In this stack of papers are even some of the dailies from London, brought over within ten days by steamship. When you were younger, it'd take months and months to get the English papers. When you worked in the cabinets of Presidents Jefferson and Madison, the need for news from the European capitals was palpable, yet never filled. Indeed, it then took ages to get news even from across the United States (and the country was much smaller then).

Here at the hotel, you're a guest of John Jacob Astor. You've not read anything by the English writer Charles Dickens, another guest at the Astor House, besides his book-length essay *American Notes*, on his first and much celebrated trip to the United States in 1842. He is mostly known for his made-up stories. Fiction bores you, although it's become extremely popular. You did not meet this Dickens during your years in London—back then, he must have been a youth or mere child, but you look forward to meeting him now. Mr. Astor also expects John Quincy Adams, whom you greatly respect; he and Henry Clay aided you in negotiating the Treaty of Ghent, which ended the War of 1812. You will be glad to see the good Mr. Clay as well.

Now, that scoundrel from Tennessee James Polk seems bound to bring us into wars with Mexico and the United Kingdom, all at once. Only a fool would seek one war, and only an imbecile would risk two, as Polk does now. Yet the Electoral College has sent this fool to the White House.

You've been reading American newspapers ever since you immigrated to the United States from Switzerland in 1780. You have seen countless changes in the press and in the country too, in those sixty-five years. In the 1780s newspapers greatly increased in number and in frequency of publication and have continued growing for six decades. You recall the first daily newspapers, and now the country is brimming with them! How communication has advanced, with the advent of the steam press. The voices of democracy abound in print as never before in the history of man.

Nowadays, American politics increasingly centers on the issue of slavery. Last year, 1844, the slavery question was enough to throw the presidential election to James K. Polk of Tennessee, the most expansionist, proslavery candidate in the race. Why? Because a mere handful of votes for the Abolitionist candidate James Birney of the Liberty Party let Polk snatch New York from Henry Clay. With New York's electoral votes, Polk was elected. The empire of liberty that you and Mr. Jefferson envisioned, and which was expanded by the Louisiana Purchase, is increasingly at jeopardy due to political controversies fostered by slavery. Can the country endure this divide?

As a young man you were a member of the Pennsylvania Society for Promoting the Abolition of Slavery. In those days nobody who wanted to end slavery would make the extreme statements that William Lloyd Garrison and other Abolitionists now voice. Slavery was understood then, by all intelligent citizens, as a problem to be solved—not a sin immune to compromise, as the Abolitionists now claim it is.

Plainly, these Garrisonians do not value the nation: they openly call for the country's dissolution, since the union of the states protects and strengthens slavery. They call this "disunionism." Ending slavery, they say, must come before anything else, due to a "higher law." You disagree, but this Abolitionist doctrine is well reasoned. They are shockingly radical people, the Abolitionists. Revolutionaries. The Abolitionist press, like the *Liberator*, is provocative and bold. Nearly all Americans reject the Abolitionist goal of immediate, universal, uncompensated emancipation of the slaves, with full civic and political equality for the freed colored people.

While the Abolitionists' call for disunionism and their repudiation of the Constitution for its proslavery design are rejected by nearly all Americans, North and South, you've noticed that the Abolitionists have successfully made slavery *the* topic of discussion, everywhere. Abolitionists want to transform the world, and they never stop pressing their goals. While greatly outnumbered, their persistent moral advocacy makes them a powerful force in the democratic United States of America. They are revolutionary—and impatient.

When you first arrived on these shores, promoting manumission (the voluntary freeing of slaves) was widespread. In the 1780s and 1790s, most Americans of the Revolutionary generation supported reforms to elevate the condition of mankind. That, after all, was what the Revolution was fought for and why the nation was created: to achieve liberty and equality. Do not all men deserve liberty? A great many slave owners of that generation voluntarily freed their slaves, in the North and in the Chesapeake Bay states. You remember General Washington doing so in his will; he never defended slavery as good. The Revolutionary War–era manumissions created a class of free people of color within the slave states and in the North. But, of course, that willingness to manumit slaves never reached the lower South, the Carolinas and Georgia. Even in the Chesapeake, this willingness of some members of the planter class to support manumission had vanished by 1800. By then, however, the northern states had all enacted emancipation, gradually or suddenly, creating the "free states" of the North.

But as slavery ended in the northern states, slavery in the South grew stronger, more profitable, and more deeply rooted in that region's politics and culture. While tobacco was in decline, cotton cultivation rapidly spread, yielding tremendous profit to plantation owners and to the New York merchants who financed and marketed cotton; you're well aware the whole business rests on the backs of slaves. Cotton fast became the major product for the whole American economy. As "King Cotton" reached new territory, so did slavery; from the east coast states it moved west into Alabama and Louisiana and then up the Mississippi River Valley into Missouri and Arkansas. You've observed how criticizing slavery has become controversial and rare and accepting slavery's existence is now increasingly seen as prudent.

Years before the election of 1800 and the rise of King Cotton, Mr. Jefferson ceased making even his few hesitant, halting public objections to the institution. He had made all of his antislavery comments before you knew him. He never criticized the "peculiar institution" after 1790 and remained a slave owner all his life, though you're sure he treated well the hundreds of men, women, and children he owned. While nowadays Abolitionists would flay him with words for owning humans, Jefferson was born into Virginia's planter class, which owed its very existence to slaveholding. You deplore all judgments of men based on the condition of their birth.

The Abolitionists' claims for the rights of the colored man have logical validity, you think, if measured by the Revolutionary principles of the Declaration of Independence. All men are created equal and possess equal rights. To deny this is to deny the validity of self-government! But can this be achieved in a country built on enslaving millions of people? This is the contradiction at the center of not only Mr. Jefferson's life, you'd argue, but of the whole United States of America.

That radical colored pamphleteer David Walker drew on America's Revolutionary origins with his *Appeal to the Coloured Citizens of the World*. Walker's assertion that the colored people have an unalienable right to revolution alarmed the slaveholder class. But Walker was right, wasn't he? All men are created equal and deserve equality of rights.

This truth is terrifying in its implications; you know Mr. Jefferson was horrified by it, as he expressed these fears to you and wrote about them in his *Notes on Virginia.*

Now the Abolitionists seek to put justice first for the colored slaves, no matter the constitutional basis for the union. Will the Abolitionist viewpoint grow stronger, popular enough to set the course for a democratic nation? You very much doubt any early triumph of abolitionism: anti-colored prejudice is almost universal among white Americans, as that careful observer of the United States the Frenchman Alexis de Tocqueville has observed. John C. Calhoun claims that abolitionism is gaining control of the government. Many in the South share this absurd, paranoid view and denounce every slight criticism of the slave system as dangerous.

You believe the territorial expansion of slavery must end, disagreeing with those southern leaders who ardently champion it. Annexing Texas to the United States would be a great mistake, yet many powerful interests insist on it; doing so would start a war of territorial conquest. You knew Calhoun in Washington, and he has little love of the United States. But he is smart, strategic, and politically farsighted. He could be right about what's necessary to keep the union together: ironclad protections of the slave-holder class. You see in the papers that he is to give a speech at a banquet in his honor this week; it will held at Delmonico's, just a few blocks from the Astor House.

For all their zeal, the Abolitionists correctly insist that the American political system is based on the Constitution giving extra political power to the slaveholding class of the South. They point to this fact and deplore it. Calhoun points to the same fact and celebrates it because it allows the slaveholding class to dominate the national government.

Abolitionists term the slaveholders' political and constitutional dominance "the Slave Power." You admit what every statesman and politician knew when creating the American government and what every informed citizen still knows: that the Constitution gives the slave states extra representation in the House of Representatives and in the electoral college, through the three-fifths clause. Indeed, therefore, the slave states dominate the three branches of the federal government and have since it was created. The Constitution also obligates the free states to return runaway slaves to their owners. Further, the Constitution allowed slave states to reopen the barbaric Atlantic slave trade for twenty years. That horrid trade had effectively been shut down by the Revolutionary struggle in 1775.

Rather than resulting from conspiracy, as Abolitionists imagine, these constitutional protections for the slaveholders' power resulted from political negotiations in 1787. They were accepted by the states when they ratified the Constitution. Much was conceded to the slaveholders in 1787 as the Constitution was written, to keep South Carolina and Georgia in the new nation. Could the United States have endured, or cohered, without those two states? Of course, politics and accommodations go hand in hand. Powerful interests demand powerful accommodations. Injustices can result, and the injustice of slavery is great indeed.

Slaves are people. Everybody knows that. What's disputed is whether the colored people are inferior or equal to whites, whether Blacks are entitled to any rights and, if so, what rights? You are well aware that this kind of thinking is volatile: slaves by definition have no rights. To talk of human rights for colored people is to talk of ending slavery. That would be revolution, just as surely as 1776 was revolution.

Slaves are people. Everybody knows that. What is disputed is ... whether Blacks are entitled to any rights and, if so, what rights?

To you, it is clear that if Americans believe their great Declaration of Independence, they must agree that slaves are endowed with rights equal to any person's. To treat them as chattel is a violation of mankind's sacred right to liberty. Rousseau said that man is born free and yet everywhere he is in chains. Does not American slavery prove his charge? What else could the American Revolution mean, if not the right of self-government for all men? Yet today, you lament, most Americans do not share this belief about the Revolution's heritage. Even if they did, how could the principle be enacted into practice, without massive violence and suffering?

While Jefferson was burdened by his slaves, you are sure he took good care of them. Other slave masters, then and now, you know, ruthlessly use slaves for profit and pleasure. For Jefferson and his social class, slave labor alone made their way of life possible; and Jefferson feared that, if the Blacks were freed, they'd murderously seek revenge on the whites.

The price for pursuing ideals—like independence of the United States or freedom for all the colored slaves—can be more than merely unpleasant disagreements; it can lead to turmoil, violence, and chaos. The virtues of maintaining a well-ordered society cannot be exaggerated: starvation and violence are often the fate of ordinary people in times of upheaval. You think of the French citizens who suffered for decades after the overthrow of their monarchy. This illustrates why prudence "will dictate that Governments long established should not be changed for light and transient causes," as the Declaration says. You ask yourself, Are the evils of slavery "sufferable" or do they warrant immediate abolition? Even at risk to national survival?

How does the Declaration's wisdom about prudence and liberty apply to the demand for immediate abolition? The Abolitionists may rightly grasp the moral principles of the situation, but practicalities elude them. They have no feasible plan for ending slavery and arrogantly disdain even the need for a practical plan. Yet ending slavery could cause drastic social upheaval and be harmful for all, at least initially.

In the last dozen years, slavery has become a major, intractable political issue. Previously, slavery was regarded as a problem that required periodic negotiation and compromise—hence the Constitution itself and, later, the Missouri Compromise. Slavery, if reduced to an intractable, partisan issue, may well split the nation. Nobody wanted that in your day, but now a deep split seems to be the goal of Calhoun men and Garrisonians alike.

Back in the 1780s, as a young man you joined efforts to end slavery. You did so as a matter of conscience and as a practical reformer. Neither you nor like-minded men then imagined that all the slaves could be, or should be, *immediately* emancipated and made legal equals to white citizens. You're proud that Pennsylvania was among the first states to enact emancipation. This was a major achievement for all mankind. Before the northern states did so, no other place on earth ever *voluntarily* abolished slavery. This northern emancipation was done by law, and gradually over a period of decades. This is an accomplishment that the South should emulate.

Now, however, the Abolitionists call for *immediate, total emancipation, without compensation or expatriation.* Abolitionists even call for full equality for Black people, an unprecedented radical Revolutionary goal. Such demands are virtually unimaginable and appear unobtainable. But didn't the world think that of the Revolution of 1776?

You wonder, Are Americans now incapable of a new revolution that puts the founding ideals of the Declaration of Independence into practice for the colored people as well as the white? You still recall being startled by the ideas of the Abolitionist "Declaration of Sentiments," from a dozen years ago, proclaiming the colored people of the United States to be Americans, countrymen, and equal citizens. That declaration, like every issue of Garrison's *Liberator*, contains radical demands, dangerous to the country and for the colored people too: immediate freedom could leave them free to starve. But the principles are uncontestable, if one agrees with the country's immortal Declaration of Independence.

You worry, though. How can emancipation be achieved without horrific violence against the Blacks, as Jefferson warned in *Notes on Virginia*? Respectful, thoughtful leaders will not enact risky, unproven policies. More fundamentally, you doubt many Americans will ever embrace abolitionism and equal rights for Blacks. Promoting that goal seems to put free Blacks at risk of mob violence in the urban North. One must ask, Are the Abolitionists sincere in proclaiming their opposition to violence or do they seek a bloodbath?

In these modern times—*the 1840s!*—slavery is increasingly treated *not* as a regular political problem subject to compromise and partial solutions but as a moral issue, far above political give and take. Both extremes insist that slavery permits no concessions to the other side. Daily in your newspapers, you read about how the slave states' leaders insist that slavery is indispensable to their region, sanctioned by the Constitution, and ordained by God and thus cannot be questioned or challenged by any American. The defenders of slavery demand, and often secure, outright violent suppression of Abolitionists and the burning of their writings. Many respectable Americans advocate putting Abolitionists in prison for their political beliefs—an outrage! Calhoun demands that the free states forcefully suppress the abolition societies and the Abolitionist press. He would create an American Bastille, fill it with Abolitionists, and have soldiers fire upon citizens who dissent.

You were horrified when you learned of the mob violence that greeted the dedication of Philadelphia's grand Pennsylvania Hall in May 1838: it was burned down by an anti-Abolitionist mob the very week it opened. Placards posted throughout the city proclaimed, "A convention to effect the immediate emancipation of the slaves throughout the country is in session in the city, and it is the duty of citizens who entertain a proper respect for the Constitution of the Union and the right of property to interfere."[2] Abolitionists and reformers were beaten. Are not mob attacks on people's freedom of speech and assembly just as threatening as anything King George III did?

Won't chaos ensue if slavery is deemed too morally important for any compromise? How can reasonable men—statesman, politicians, voters—address a problem that the most interested parties define as absolutely incapable of being resolved, short of the utter surrender or destruction of their opponents? What are leaders to do if they can't split the differences between conflicting parties? Demanding capitulation by one's opponents isn't a sustainable basis for self-government. It points toward widespread chaos and maybe even civil war. In the long run, you don't see how this will aid the colored people. How can a nation be governed without compromise, without negotiation? By tyranny alone, perhaps.

Can the issue of slavery now be settled by some new great compromise? How could that be done when the opposing sides are made up of stubborn zealous advocates? Senator Calhoun argued in 1837 that for Congress merely to receive Abolitionist petitions calling for an end to slavery in the District of Columbia would, for the South, "be fatal. If we concede an inch, concession would follow concession—compromise would follow compromise." Any readiness to compromise is, he says, a willingness "to become slaves." The Calhoun men demand the forcible suppression of Abolitionists in the North, and mob violence has already suppressed many abolition advocates in the free states.

John Quincy Adams courageously opposed that line of thought and its infamous spawn, the Gag Rule of the House. Abolitionists are terribly unpopular in every state. Overwhelmingly, most people in the North want to avoid all controversies related to slavery, but they reject southern restrictions on freedom of speech. You've seen many reports of unrest: Garrison was mobbed and nearly lynched in both Boston and New York City; the Abolitionist newspaperman Elijah Lovejoy was murdered in Alton, Illinois, and his printing press destroyed; and cities across the North have suffered countless anti-Abolitionist riots. Abolitionist lecturers have been hounded and badly beaten. Schools and orphanages for colored children have been destroyed by mobs of white men. Peaceful colored men and women have been assaulted in their homes, in their churches, on the streets, and on railroad cars.[3]

For the seven long years the Gag Rule was in effect, the House of Representatives refused even to receive petitions of citizens calling for emancipation in the District of Columbia. In the North as in the South, most people are violently opposed to any hint of equality for the colored people. Fugitive slave Frederick Douglass says color prejudice in the North is more common than in the slave South. Wasn't he nearly killed in Pendleton, Indiana, by respectable men of property for the offense of seeking to speak his mind?

This anti-Abolitionist violence against peaceful colored people is tantamount to a rejection of our Revolutionary heritage: life and liberty for all, the rule of law, and self-government. Many Americans, North and the South, harbor such hatred against the colored people that they deny free Black people even the most basic rights of mankind. The powerful John C. Calhoun champions the view that Jefferson's great Declaration was flatly wrong because, Calhoun says, men are inherently unequal and "there never has yet existed a wealthy and civilized society in which one portion of the community did not, in point of fact, live on the labor of another." Government, according to Calhoun, exists to perpetuate the social domination of some people over others. Can this view be accepted without rejecting the American idea?

Clearly there can be no rapid or early solution to the problems arising from slavery that now confront the country. But you believe talk will be essential to any settlement. On the other hand, you know no series of gatherings—not the literary forum hosted by Mr. Dickens later today, or any banquet honoring a politician, or any meeting at a political hall or church—can hope to resolve the slavery problem for the entire nation. Men, however must attempt to reason with one another, mustn't they? Ideas matter! Beliefs shape behavior.

Ah, you must have dozed off. You've slept much of the morning, and barely touched today's newspapers. Soon, you lunch with John Jacob Astor and that English writer Charles Dickens. You're looking forward to seeing John Quincy Adams and Henry Clay. Mr. Dickens has invited many people to his literary forum; he wants to hear what everybody has to say about the book by that man Douglass, a runaway slave from Maryland. You read the little book last night. A colored man wrote it, eloquently. To you, it echoes themes of other American documents that speak of the right to overthrow unjust governments and of man's inalienable rights to life, liberty, and the pursuit of happiness. He embeds these ideas in a story of a slave's pain and aspirations for freedom and dignity. You hope to hear this Douglass and to size up what kind of a man he is.

Douglass's book focuses too much on arguing over Christianity for your taste, but so very many people are enthusiastic about religion these days. And evidently many slaveholders try to justify slavery as being biblically sanctioned.

Oh, your tea is cold, and the maid is calling. As you get up, your aged body trembles a bit, but you tremble ever more for the prospects facing your beloved country.

HOW TO REACT

Reacting to the Past is a series of historical role-playing games. Set in moments of heightened historical tension, the games place students in the roles of historical figures. By reading the game book and their individual role sheets, students discover their objectives, potential allies, and the forces that stand between them and victory. They must then attempt to achieve victory through formal speeches, informal debate, negotiations, and (occasionally) conspiracy. Outcomes sometimes part from actual history; a debriefing session at the end of the game sets the record straight.

The following is an outline of what you will encounter in Reacting and what you will be expected to do.

Game Setup

Your instructor will spend some time before the beginning of the game helping you understand the historical context for the game and the game's structure. (See "The Rules of the Game" on page 57 in this game book.) During the setup period, you will use several different kinds of materials:

- The game book (from which you are reading now), which includes historical information, rules and elements of the game, and essential documents.

- Your role sheet (provided by your instructor), which includes a short biography of the historical figure you will model in the game as well as that person's ideology, victory objectives, responsibilities, and resources. Your role may be an actual historical figure or a realistic composite.

Read all of this material before the game begins. And just as important, go back and reread these materials throughout the game. A second and third reading while *in role* will deepen your understanding and alter your perspective because ideas take on a different aspect when seen through the eyes of a partisan actor.

Students who have carefully read the materials and who know the rules of the game will invariably do better than those who rely on general impressions and uncertain memories.

Game Play

Once the game begins, class sessions are presided over by students. In most cases, a single student serves as a kind of presiding officer. The instructor then becomes the Gamemaster (GM) and takes a seat in the back of the room. Though he or she will not lead the class sessions, the GM may pass private notes to the players, announce important events, and remind players of the game's timetable. The GM can redirect proceedings that have gone off track.

Once at the podium (see page 59 in this game book), the student has the floor and must be heard.

Role sheets contain private, secret information, which students are expected to guard. You are advised, therefore, to exercise caution when discussing your role with others. However, keeping your own counsel, or saying nothing to anyone, is not an option. To achieve your objectives, you *must* speak with others. You will never muster the voting strength to prevail without allies. Collaboration and coalition building are at the heart of every game.

Some games feature strong alliances called *Factions*, which are tight-knit groups with fixed objectives. Games with Factions all include roles called Indeterminates, or, in this game, Independents. They operate outside of the established Factions. Not all Independents are entirely neutral; some have very strong views on certain issues, even if they don't align exactly with one of the Factions. If you are in a Faction, cultivating Independents is in your interest because they may be convinced to support your position; find out what each Independent seeks to achieve. If you are lucky enough to have drawn the role of an Independent you should be pleased; you will likely play a pivotal role in the outcome of the game.

Game Requirements

Students in Reacting use persuasive writing, public speaking, critical thinking, teamwork, negotiation, problem solving, collaboration, adapting to changing circumstances, and working under pressure to meet deadlines. Your instructor will explain the specific requirements for your class. In general, though, a Reacting game asks you to perform three distinct activities:

Reading and Writing. This standard academic work is carried on more purposefully in a Reacting course because what you read is put to immediate use, and what you write is meant to persuade others to act the way you want them to. The reading load may have slight variations from role to role; the writing requirement depends on your particular course. Papers are often policy statements, but they can also be autobiographies, battle plans, spy reports, newspapers, poems, or after-game reflections. Papers provide the foundation for the speeches delivered in class.

Public Speaking and Debate. In the course of a game, everyone is expected to deliver at least one formal speech from the podium (the length of the game and the size of the class will determine the number of speeches). Debate follows. Debate can be impromptu, raucous, and fast-paced and results in decisions voted on by the body. Gamemasters may stipulate that students must deliver their papers from memory when at the podium or may insist that students wean themselves from dependency on written notes as the game progresses.

Wherever the game imaginatively puts you, it will surely not put you in the classroom of a twenty-first-century American college. Accordingly, the colloquialisms and familiarities of today's college life are out of place. Never open your speech with a salutation like "Hi guys" when something like "Fellow citizens!" would be more appropriate.

Never be friendless when standing at the podium. Do your best to have at least one supporter back up your ideas, ask friendly questions, or otherwise come to your defense. Note passing and side conversations, while common occurrences, will likely spoil the effect of your speech; so you and your supporters should insist on order before such behavior becomes too disruptive. Ask the presiding officer to assist you, if necessary, and the Gamemaster as a last resort.

Strategizing. Communication among students is an essential feature of Reacting games. You may find yourself writing emails, texting, attending out-of-class meetings, or gathering for meals on a fairly regular basis. The purpose of frequent communication is to lay out a strategy for advancing your agenda, thwarting the agenda of your opponents, and to hatch plots to ensnare individuals troubling to your cause. When communicating with a fellow student in or out of class, always assume that he or she is speaking to you in role. If you want to talk about the "real world," make that clear.

Counterfactuals

Plenty of public meetings on various public issues were actually held in **antebellum** America. Most were gatherings of *like-minded* people, focusing on common goals or problems. The Meetings of this game, however,

Antebellum in Latin means "before the war." In American history, the term is used to designate the few decades before the Civil War, roughly 1830–61.

are composed of people with *sharply differing* viewpoints and radically divergent socioeconomic positions in American society. This counterfactual allows for an immediate, face-to-face collision of ideas.

The game's Meetings are realistic in that they *could* have happened: the people in the game all lived at the same time, and the issues they confront in the Meetings were most certainly widely discussed at the time by Americans from all walks of life, regions, and politics. All the issues of this game were analyzed, debated, and disputed—intensively—by countless people in antebellum America. Raging conflicts centered on these questions, which were taken quite seriously for an even broader range of Americans than are represented in this game. The arguments took place at length on pulpits and in sermons, in rival newspapers, across speakers' platforms, in taverns, on the floors of the Senate and the House of Representatives, and in political campaigns for state and federal offices.

Still, we need to understand that the range of issues and types of people involved in the intellectual clashes of this game were not, in actual history, often expressed in personal, face-to-face encounters such as the discussions you'll have while playing this game. The nation's foremost defenders of slavery never willingly inhabited the same pulpit, literary forum, or banquet, with outspoken Abolitionists. Sojourner Truth never had the chance to speak her truth directly to men like John Calhoun or Thomas Dew. Nor did northern whites represented by characters like the Whiskey Dealer, the Illinois Lawyer, and the Dockworker, have direct, sustained intellectual exchanges with Blacks or Abolitionists or with members of the national political and commercial elite. Likewise, few national politicians talked directly with those who saw the Constitution as a "pact with the Devil and covenant with Death." Nor were free people of color able to directly challenge men who argued that Black people had no claim on any rights anywhere in the United States.

A second counterfactual feature of this game involves women's participation in public discussions involving males and females together, what was then called a "promiscuous" audience. Many characters in the game are female, yet in 1845 in the United States, it was quite rare and still controversial for women to speak to mixed audiences of men and women. Indeed, it was controversial for women to express opinions at all on public issues; the public realm was for men alone. Female Abolitionists were the first in the United States to challenge this taboo on women's public speaking, declaring that women were not inherently disqualified from participating in the public issues of the world. They, in fact, were some of the first feminists. For the other female characters in the game, unique personal circumstances allow them to evade the gendered prohibition on women speaking in public, at least at these 1845 Meetings. But most American women, upholding women's proper place, refused to participate in meetings with women speakers.

NOTE

The now-famous July 1848 Seneca Falls women's rights convention is still three years off, but even at Seneca Falls, not all participants embraced the idea of women speaking to mixed audiences. Frederick Douglass was there, and did.

 PART 2: HISTORICAL BACKGROUND

SLAVERY AND FREEDOM IN THE UNITED STATES, FROM THE REVOLUTION TO 1846

When Albert Gallatin left his native Switzerland for the newly formed, Revolutionary United States of America in 1780, slavery in his new country was being challenged from all sides. In nearly every rebellious former colony, free Blacks were demanding recognition as citizens, joining those still enslaved in petition campaigns and court suits, often successfully, to liberate those still in bondage. These demands for freedom had a wartime legacy.

Taking advantage of the confusion of warfare, the British royal governor of Virginia, Lord Dunmore, had in 1776 promised freedom to all slaves who deserted their rebellious masters and served in the king's army. Over eight hundred slaves enlisted immediately, and historian Benjamin Quarles estimates that by the time of Gallatin's arrival close to twenty thousand Blacks were fighting in the British cause—fighting for their freedom and against American independence. The ranks of the armed and newly emancipated swelled further because difficulties in obtaining white volunteers led Revolutionary legislatures to grant freedom to as many as five thousand slaves who were fighting in their militias. In the southern countryside, at least ten thousand enslaved people had escaped to Spanish or French settlements, made their way to Indian villages, or fled to the North. Never before in "New World" history had so many African-descended people so forcefully seized the moment to secure their freedom. Jefferson's Revolutionary assertion that "all men are created equal" was generating, as historian Bernard Bailyn has termed it, an unprecedented "contagion of liberty."

As the Revolution continued the contagion spread, particularly in the New England and Mid-Atlantic regions where slavery, though commonly practiced, was never the primary driver of regional economies dominated by free laborers. Here leading patriots concluded that an excruciating contrast was becoming too obvious to justify: the juxtaposition between their own demands for liberty from royal "tyranny" and the grinding exploitation of African American slaves. Slaveholders "who every day barter away another man's liberty" would soon "care little for their own," warned pamphleteer James Otis, a conviction that other Revolutionary leaders such as John Adams, Josiah Quincy, Thomas Paine, Alexander Hamilton, and Benjamin Franklin openly embraced. Soon enough, some of these men would number among Gallatin's close associates, and all became active in movements to abolish slavery within their own states. A series of Massachusetts court decisions in the early 1780s held that slavery violated the state's constitution, abolishing slavery in the commonwealth. Over the next decade, Hamilton in New York and Franklin in Pennsylvania (along with Gallatin) championed legislation that secured gradual emancipation in both states. By 1804 every northern state had enacted such laws, thereby creating permanent distinctions between free and slave states, and perhaps more significantly, between North and South.

Black Life in the North during the Early Republic

In northern cities like Boston, New York, and Philadelphia, the same free Blacks who had joined the enslaved in petition campaigns and had fought in the patriot cause began dramatically transforming their own communities. A generation of "Black founders," as historian Richard S. Newman has called them, such as James Forten, Richard Allen, Russell Parrott, and James Easton, established independent churches, Masonic lodges, self-help societies, manual labor schools, and cultural associations. All these institutions were devoted to promoting "respectability" for free African Americans and emancipation for the enslaved. By the 1780s and 1790s Black leaders in every major northern city were building on these impressive precedents, which evoked the support of sympathetic whites.

Philadelphia's Quakers were quick to organize the first association in the emerging new nation devoted exclusively to abolition, the Society for the Relief of Negroes Unlawfully Held in Bondage. Joining them were many others who were equally zealous for moral improvement in the name of economic progress: powerful politicians, manufacturing magnates, bankers, commodity traders, and lawyers. The dynamic commercial and entrepreneurial sectors of northern society were based largely on free labor, and none of their significant leaders depended on slavery for wealth or social position, and neither did Gallatin (a supremely talented political economist who would become Jefferson's secretary of the treasury). Within the slave states, freed Blacks were too few in number to threaten white supremacy. Instead, to high-minded commercial entrepreneurs like Gallatin, emancipation would foster economic progress and social harmony by removing Blacks' resentments and motives for rebellion.

In the end, these arguments prevailed, in the North. By 1804, as already noted, every northern state had rid itself of slavery, but only gradually, grudgingly, and through processes that had deeply negative consequences for the emancipated. Racism and the economic interests of local slaveholders generated lengthy delays. After emancipation in the North, Blacks encountered not racial equality but viciously enforced segregation, economic marginalization, wholesale denials of political rights, and terrible moments of violent white racism. Once accomplished, moreover, emancipation became a convenient way for white northerners to excuse their own bigotry and deny their slavery-ridden past while smugly contrasting their virtuous Abolitionist past and "free labor" present to the behavior of the South's planter class.

For all those limitations, however, this was a remarkable historical achievement: Abolitionists, Black and white, succeeded in collaborating with powerful politicians to put slavery peacefully to an end. In the Revolutionary South, by contrast, abolitionism made no headway at all. There, masters feared increasingly for their fundamental authority as the enslaved made the Revolution their own by fleeing, fighting, and signing emancipation petitions. For planters, such behavior threatened their social dominance and economic interests as nothing else could.

Southern Society

During the century before the Revolution, slavery had deeply embedded itself in all aspects of southern life. Slaveholding settlers had made it a central article of faith that Black bondage was fundamental for order, liberty, and prosperity. At the time of the Revolution, thirty-five out of a hundred southerners were of African descent. Blacks made up 30 to 40 percent of those living in Maryland, Virginia, and North Carolina. In some areas of coastal South Carolina and Georgia Blacks outnumbered whites by as much as five to one. Natural increases in the number of settled slaves plus continuing slave importations from Africa were easily absorbed by the ever-expanding global markets for tobacco, rice, sugar, and cotton.

Every southern colony was dominated by owners of large plantations, often related by marriage, who directed the political process, controlled the economy, and defined social norms. These planters led their states in the Revolution—George Washington, Thomas Jefferson, James Madison, Patrick Henry, John Rutledge, and Richard Henry Lee begin a much longer list. Small slaveholders who owned only one or two **chattel,** non-slaveholding farmers, and white day laborers always constituted a large majority of the South's white population. For these reasons, much of the area's social stability depended on a clear ordering of unequals—proud over humble, rich over poor, male over female, and white over Black. In the Deep South—that is, in South Carolina, Georgia, lower Virginia and western North Carolina—these lesser whites felt deep affinities with elite slaveholders, depended on their patronage, and largely deferred to their social and economic power. In the upper South, particularly in Delaware, eastern Maryland, northern and eastern Virginia, the situation differed in regions where prosperous people with German, Scotch-Irish, or Quaker backgrounds made family farming and commerce, not slave-based production, their primary economic activity. But even in these locales slaveholders played an important social and economic role, and the instinct to protect their institution exerted a powerful force.

In antebellum America, **chattel** meant a slave or group of slaves. The term originated in Middle English and Medieval Latin, to describe tangible, moveable property (not real estate or buildings), such as cattle. Later chattel was widely used in the Americas to refer to property in slaves, who could be bought, sold, and moved.

For all these reasons, some southern slaveholders responded to the Revolution's antislavery overtones by attempting to humanize the institution, but few sought to abolish it. Masters, they insisted, must treat their slaves with paternal care, avoiding if possible the exercise of naked power. Barbarous punishments, such as branding and castration, were expunged from upper South slave codes. Restrictions on voluntary manumissions were loosened and significant planters, such as George Washington, made detailed provisions in their wills for the eventual emancipation of their slaves. But throughout the South, slavery retained its unchallenged supremacy, proving itself exceptionally adaptable and resilient, despite the dislocations of the Revolution. Commodity prices and borrowing costs remained favorable, and planters expanded their acreage while confirming again the plantation's undeniable centrality to the entire southern economy. The enslaved themselves inadvertently strengthened the social order further by serving as a racial counterweight against a restive white lower class that might otherwise have applied the Revolution's demands for equality in struggles against their planter class "betters." In decades to come lower-class whites would continue to express racial solidarity with elite slaveholders, thereby repressing social conflicts within the ruling race.

Thus did the Revolution ultimately endowed the planter elite with powerful reinforcement. But with power came the need to mount stronger defenses. Slaveholders now had to accustom themselves to an emerging group of free states on their northern border in which antislavery-minded Yankees, Black as well as white, went enthusiastically forward with emancipation projects. Slaveholders knew full well that the Revolution had inspired many people, their own enslaved workers foremost among them, to harbor unprecedented hostility and resentment against their particular way of life.

Putting Slaveholder Power into the Constitution: The Convention of 1787

Little wonder then, that most southern delegates approached the Constitutional Convention of 1787 determined that any new national government must solidify their power. Their resolve was fortified by the knowledge that among the Philadelphia Convention's delegates were many northern representatives identified with antislavery causes and that Abolitionist feeling in the North was growing ever stronger. During the same summer of 1787 that the Constitutional Convention met in Philadelphia, the Continental Congress in New York City enacted the Northwest Ordinance, prohibiting slavery in territories north of the Ohio River and east of the Mississippi River. This significantly extended the boundaries from which additional free states would be created. Given these circumstances, in the opinion of some historians, the Founding Fathers faced a historic opportunity to write national abolition into the new Constitution. One imagines that such would have been Albert Gallatin's hope. Yet it is unlikely that the Founders could have managed slavery's extinction as much as some may have wished to do so, since slaveholders in the South were fiercely opposed to any national government that did not enshrine the slaveholders' power.

Slaveholders constituted the most powerfully organized bloc at the Constitutional Convention: they were capable of undermining the Convention simply by walking out. To the nationalistic Founding Fathers, this was a result to be avoided at all costs. Thus they carefully avoided any attack on the sanctity of private property, human property included—arguments that would have been necessary to any plan for emancipation. By 1787, moreover, many Americans urgently sought a definition for their newly minted nation that could overcome their sharp regional differences. To be an "American," they decided, was to be not Indian and not African but instead to possess "white" skin.[4] For all these reasons the framers of the Constitution wove unassailable guarantees for the planters throughout their document, protecting the institution of slavery rather than freeing enslaved people.

The framers registered their distaste for what became known as the "peculiar institution" by avoiding the words *slave* and *slavery* in the Constitution. And in Article I, Section 9, they allowed Congress to outlaw the African slave trade after 1808. This provision is often mistaken for being antislavery, but because it permitted states to reopen the Atlantic slave trade for twenty years, it was actually proslavery: The anti-British boycotts and the Revolutionary War had basically stopped the Atlantic slave trade to North America more than a decade before the 1787 Constitutional Convention.

In the finished Constitution, slaveholding delegates most ardently seeking to perpetuate slavery got what they wanted: ironclad protections for slavery. Article IV affirmed the master's right to recover escaped slaves from the free states. Article V established a very difficult process for amending the Constitution; consequently, no antislavery northern majority could ever ban slavery in the United States (see also pages 51–53 and 106 in this game book).

But Article I, Section 2, granted the most substantial concession of all, by giving the slave states extra power over the new national government. The **three-fifths clause** provided that three-fifths of the slave population was to be counted for purposes of "direct taxes" (if such were ever passed by Congress, which it did only twice briefly), for apportioning representation in the House of Representatives, and for determining the number of electors from each state to the Electoral College (which the Constitution created in Article III). Thus the Constitution guaranteed slaveholders political power in Congress and in the election of the president that far exceeded their actual numbers. The Constitution and the government it created recognized the slave owners' authority over their chattel as the supreme law of the land. No other country in the modern world had ever so directly included a slaveholding class in its national government. The Constitution created, among other things, the first national government in the modern world so dominated by slave owners.

Article 1, Section 2 of the Constitution, known as the **three-fifths clause**, gave the slave states extra power in the new national government by counting three-fifths of the slaves ("all other Persons") to determine the number of each state's representatives in Congress and its votes in the Electoral College. This ensured that the federal government was dominated by slaveholders.

In the decades after the Constitution was ratified in 1789, politically engaged Americans were to disagree bitterly about slavery's relationship to the Constitution. Though it is clear to us in retrospect that the document sanctioned slavery, it contained many other sectional compromises and ambiguities of language that opened it to explosively conflicting interpretations. Southern secessionists, northern unionists, and quarreling factions of Abolitionists were all to find historical justifications for irreconcilable points of view about the government's power over slavery. Since the Constitution itself set no boundaries for these discussions, such disagreements would become limitless, bitter, and ultimately irreconcilable. But for the moment, with nationhood achieved under the new federal union, the antislavery impulse of the Revolution quickly dissipated. Conflict generated by slavery and African American resistance to slavery, however, most certainly did not.

As free Blacks continued building their churches, benevolent associations, and schools, they also extended political stratagems to assert their citizenship first learned during the Revolution. In major northern cities they organized their own brigades, marched in militia musters, and rallied to commemorate patriotic occasions. Their frequent petitions to Congress provoked objections from slaveholding politicians. Even more disturbing were free Blacks' increasingly successful efforts to protect the escaped slaves who were reaching their communities, which put them in open defiance of the Fugitive Slave Act of 1793.

American Slavery in the New Republic

Collaboration between freed and enslaved also expanded African Americans' political horizon beyond the new republic. In both North and South, mobile artisans, seafarers, coastal boatmen, and dockworkers, both enslaved and free, received and transmitted news from the wider world. Reports of the outbreak of revolution in 1791 in the Caribbean resonated quickly across the southern states, as tens of thousands of Blacks, free and enslaved, rose in Haiti in a successful rebellion against their French oppressors. Slaveholders fleeing that island accompanied by their (presumably) loyal slaves sought refuge in Virginia, the Carolinas, and Georgia, raising the specter of insurrection within the American South. Nervous planters responded by choking off slave importations, restricting voluntary manumissions and deporting free Blacks living in their midst.

The fears that prompted these policies were fully justified. The nineteenth century opened with two decades of unprecedented violence on the part of the enslaved, the most volatile period for Black rebellion until the Civil War. The first uprising, in 1800, involved an attempt by enslaved artisans led by Gabriel Prosser to capture Richmond, Virginia; kill its leading planters; and spread the rebellion into the countryside. Prosser's conspiracy was uncovered before it could be carried out, but evidence unearthed by terrified investigators suggested that the project had involved Black boatmen and artisans, who traveled freely around the state. Thirty summary executions later, authorities declared the insurrection ended. But as slaveholders well knew, the information networks among the enslaved exposed by this crisis remained very much in operation. The second outbreak, in Louisiana in January 1811, witnessed full-scale rebellion by as many as five hundred armed slaves and fugitive slave insurgents known as "maroons." Military officials reported that they had killed sixty-six rebels in battle and hanged another twenty-one before declaring the insurrection ended.[5] Soon after came the War of 1812, which brought new opportunity for self-emancipation. Thousands of slaves fled to the British side knowing that there freedom awaited. Others exploited the chaos of war to attempt insurrections of their own, as in Virginia in 1812 and 1813, where authorities unearthed at least two serious conspiracies. By 1814 Maryland and Virginia slaveholders had begun relocating their slaves inland to keep them away from advancing British armies.

In 1816, vigilant planters uncovered two more slave conspiracies, one in Virginia led by George Boxley, a white man, and another set for July 4 in Camden, South Carolina. These were only the most prominent of the many plots, murders, arsons, and poisonings reported by southern newspapers during this era. Finally, in 1821, in Charlestown, South Carolina, local whites ruthlessly suppressed what they believed to be an ambitious conspiracy led by free Black Denmark Vesey and involving (once again) large numbers of enslaved artisans and boatmen who oper-ated in the state's coastal areas. "The slaves in many parts of the United States have made attempt to make themselves Masters of our Country by rising in arms against us," one editorialist lamented. All the while, in cities across the North, Black Abolitionists continued welcoming and protecting escapees.

To shore up security as the turmoil mounted, slaveholders found a useful instrument in the federal government as it was designed in 1787. The Fugitive Slave Act of 1793 (reprinted on page 110 in this game book) was an essential tool, as exemplified in the case of the Territory of Florida. The United States acquired Florida in 1819 by a treaty with Spain. Over the next two decades, at the behest of planters, the U.S. Army was deployed into the territory to root out Seminole Indians, who were harboring fugitive slaves from Georgia and South Carolina. This inaugurated a series of expensive wars that dragged on well into the 1830s. Diplomats also began working assiduously to recover fugitives who had found freedom on foreign shores, particularly with the British, and federal officials devel-oped prosecutorial strategies to enforce the Fugitive Slave Act.

Territorial expansion, however, proved to be the federal government's most effective mechanism for securing planters' interests. As the century turned, waves of white settlers poured into newly opened territories, which quickly organized themselves as the new slave states of Kentucky (1793), Tennessee (1796), Louisiana (1812), Mississippi (1817), and Alabama (1819). This enormous swath of territory, all of it south of the Ohio River, was either ceded by the defeated British in 1783 or was obtained as part of the 1803 Louisiana Purchase negotiated with France by Thomas Jefferson's administration. Significantly, the ruler of France, Napoleon Bonaparte, had been motivated to sell the territory of Louisiana in North America after losing its more valuable sugar colony of Haiti, due to the successful armed uprising there. Holding Louisiana without Haiti was plainly unappealing imperial policy.

No one in Congress proposed prohibiting slavery in this vast "southwestern" territory because, although these areas had been French or British colonies, slavery had already become well established. Nevertheless, from 1793 to 1819, a mere twenty-six years, slavery's territorial space within the United States had more than doubled. Still more significant, its dominance in the nation's economy was becoming incontestably established.

As the new century opened, Eli Whitney's cotton gin created vast opportunities to adapt enslaved labor to an extraordinarily profitable commodity: short-staple cotton. The rich soils of the newly formed states promised its limitless cultivation. Equally important, planters in soil-depleted areas of Virginia, Maryland, and the Carolinas now had enormous incentives to engage in the **domestic slave trade,** by selling off their "surplus chattel" to labor-hungry slaveholders farther west. Between 1820 and 1860, as natural increases in enslaved populations kept pace with accelerating white birth rates and as the center of slave-labor production shifted from the upper South tobacco to lower South cotton, the domestic slave trade tore apart as many as two million African American families. Upon this devastation the planters and their economic allies built an economic juggernaut that, by 1840, constituted slavery as the second-largest capital asset in the entire national economy, exceeded only by investment in real estate itself. Banking, insurance, transport, manufacturing, and wholesale and retail sales of all sorts only begin a list of the goods and services from all parts of the nation that underwrote expanding production of **King Cotton.** By the 1820s slavery had in this respect breached its regional limits by making itself the irreplaceable engine of the nation's economic expansion.

The **domestic slave trade**, also called the "second Middle Passage," involved the forced migration of more than a million people, sold from the Chesapeake region to the west and southwest. It transformed African American life.[6]

The term **King Cotton** signified the dominance of cotton over the American economy and politics.

Racism North of Slavery

As slavery increasingly dominated the American economy and politics, its geographic perimeters also became increasingly well defined. Americans North and South began to believe there were natural boundaries of climate and geography outside of which slavery could not extend and that the equal balance between free and slave states would be maintained as America expanded westward. Accordingly, when Ohio (1803), Indiana (1816), and Illinois (1818) entered the Union, each directly prohibited slavery in its state constitution. Michigan followed in 1837. But while these new states prohibited slavery, each at the same time legislated stringently against free African Americans by denying them suffrage, abridging their legal rights, and limiting even their ability to legally enter or live in these states.

Many white settlers hailed from the upper South and brought their proslavery prejudices with them. Those from New England usually objected vehemently both to slavery and to the prospect of having Black neighbors. As Ohio's governor observed to his Kentucky counterpart in 1817, citizens of his state harbored not only "a universal prejudice against the principle of slavery" but also a "universal" wish to "get rid of every species of negro population." For African Americans to reside in these "free" states typically meant harsh segregation, economic marginalization, systematic harassment, and terrifying white violence.

The American Colonization Society, founded in 1816, offered a respectable outlet for some of this white bigotry, and for the feelings of those genuinely troubled by slavery and the desperate circumstances of free Blacks, by promoting the "Colonization" of American Blacks in Africa. Copying a British example, the society proposed to resettle free Blacks in the west African colony of Liberia, while encouraging "enlightened" slaveholders to implement piecemeal emancipations. Here, it was hoped, was also a way to allay misgivings that widespread manumission would saddle the nation with an intolerably large and volatile free Black population or, worse, stimulate insurrections on behalf of those still enslaved. The idea of eradicating slavery at a glacial pace by transporting unwilling Blacks to Liberia would prove impossible, financially and logistically. In addition, skittish planters suspected the scheme was a subtle attack on the master–slave relationship. Several thousand African Americans actually did emigrate in the decades before 1860, believing that white racial hatred guaranteed their unrelieved misery if they remained in the United States. But soon after the society's formation, vocal Black leaders throughout the nation rejected the **Colonization movement** as a racist plot, a position that serious Abolitionists maintained almost without exception before the Civil War. "[We] prefer to be colonized in the most remote corner of the land of our nativity, to being exiled to a foreign country," exclaimed free African Americans from Richmond, Virginia, in 1817.

The **Colonization movement** was the effort to remove former slaves from the United States, ostensibly to elevate these individuals, but most colonized Blacks were coerced into migrating to Africa.

Despite these grave weaknesses, Colonization gained influential supporters during the 1820s. Respected ministers and nationally prominent slaveholding politicians, such as Henry Clay, James Monroe, and John Marshall, held national offices in the American Colonization Society, which also conducted ambitious fund-raising and recruitment campaigns in England and in the United States. At least they were doing *something* about slavery, colonizationists sincerely insisted, by urging masters to practice charity, not brutality, and to prepare their slaves for manumission and overseas missions by teaching them sound Christian morals and practical job skills. In colonizationists' view, they were trying to improve the lot of the nation's Blacks by assisting them in beginning their lives anew in Liberia, forever free from American white supremacy.

But by appealing to sincere reformers, the American Colonization Society also yielded consequences that its founders neither predicted nor welcomed. Its publications honestly reported some of the most gruesome aspects of slavery and white supremacy. Idealistic young northerners who supported Colonization, such as William Lloyd Garrison, Gerrit Smith, and Lewis Tappan, found such information disturbing. Soon enough, each would issue militant demands for the institution's immediate abolition and condemn Colonization as a program that actually protected slavery by offering racist palliatives, not forthright solutions. After stimulating these reformers' initial misgivings, the society thus became the focus of their wholesale rebellion against it. In this respect, at the opening of the 1830s, Colonization served as the catalyst for creating a genuinely radical white Abolitionist Movement. Colonization was also attacked by David Walker, a free Black author, in his *Appeal to the Coloured Citizens of the World* (1829), a Revolutionary pamphlet that shaped African American thought for decades to come (see page 111 in this game book for an excerpt).

Though colonizationists made no direct attacks on slavery, many politicians were hardly as circumspect. As early as the 1790s New England voters were proving receptive to the charge that the policies of slave owners were directly threatening free states' interests, and southern congressmen were quick to protest measures inimical to their peculiar institution. For instance, efforts by New England entrepreneurs to develop maple sugar as an export commodity came into conflict with trade policies favored by Deep South cane sugar planters. By the early 1800s serious sectional tensions were surfacing in national party politics.

Growing Sectional Tensions

New England Federalists responded to the election of the Democratic-Republican slaveholder Thomas Jefferson in 1800 by rallying New England voters to defend their regional interests against the growing threat of "Virginia influence." Without the three-fifths clause, John Adams would have won reelection in 1800. The Constitution's three-fifths clause, Federalists warned, already gave slaveholders a hugely disproportionate advantage in determining the nation's affairs. With Jefferson's purchase of the vast Louisiana Territory, some New Englanders warned, sectional power would forever slip away from the free states in the northeast.

When Jefferson instituted a trade embargo against Great Britain in 1808, crippling New England's economy, and when his successor, Virginian James Madison, went to war in 1812, New England Federalists became fully convinced that Democratic-Republican slaveholders were set on destroying their region's commerce and political power. As one of Massachusetts politician Daniel Webster's deeply aggrieved constituents put it, "All the pleasure I have is anticipating the time when I shall march in armor on the FARTHEST GEORGIA and trample the planters under my feet." Railing against the three-fifths clause and against the immorality of slavery, New England clerics sermonized hotly and Federalist newspapers filled their pages with sectional anger. With grassroots voters mobilized against the "slave interest," representatives of five New England states convened in Hartford, Connecticut, in 1814 to promote amendments to the Constitution repealing the three-fifths clause and to consider the possibility of secession. These efforts show New England discontent with the proslavery constitutional system, but they failed to change it.

After the War of 1812, the Federalist Party collapsed and so did sectional conflict, only to be reinvigorated as a result of slavery's rapid expansion. As planters extended their system into new southwestern states and territories, their agents began infiltrating the free states, kidnapping free Blacks, and purchasing "term slaves," who were awaiting gradual emancipation. Northern state legislatures responded with anti-kidnapping laws and laws guaranteeing the eventual freeing of term slaves. Just as troubling were energetic (though unsuccessful) efforts by transplanted white southerners living in Indiana in 1814 and Illinois in 1818 to legalize slavery in these emerging states despite the Northwest Ordinance of 1787, which prohibited slavery in these territories. Meantime, dissident Democratic-Republicans in the mid-Atlantic states openly revolted after discovering that slaveholders from their own party were blocking their efforts to obtain federal government aid to rebuild their region's economy after the War of 1812. Slaveholders, they protested, had become the "chief power" within their own party, and they wondered whether slavery itself had "become dangerous to the liberty, commerce and manufactures of the free states."

While none of these early disagreements threatened to divide the union or necessarily foreshadowed civil war, their accumulating impact was nevertheless significant. Politicians were discovering early on that since slavery was inextricably involved in so much of the nation's legislative business, it was impossible to avoid disagreements on the subject during debates on fundamental issues of war, diplomacy, state making, and public policy. In the North, moreover, antislavery ideology mobilized voters.

Groups such as the New England Federalists in the early 1800s and the mid-Atlantic Jeffersonians in the 1820s rallied their constituents with direct attacks on slavery that reflected both partisan motives and serious moral objections to the peculiar institution. As we have seen, particularly disturbing to citizens of the North was the kidnapping of their free African American neighbors by agents of unscrupulous slaveholders. This raised deep fears that the power of slavery was now extending a corrupting influence directly into the free states.

> Before the Civil War, far more free people of color in the North were kidnapped and sold into slavery in the South than Black slaves successfully escaped the South to a free life in the North or in Canada.

The Missouri Compromise

It was precisely the compounding northern fear of an aggressive Slave Power that led to the political system's first flirtation with secession. Congress, over stringent northern protests, admitted Missouri to the union as a slave state in 1820. After the Missouri Territory had applied for statehood in 1819 with a constitution legalizing slavery, New England and upper Midwestern Congressmen vocally demanded that the nation's republican future, which lay in its western settlements, should not be jeopardized by any expansion of slave labor. Congress, they insisted, must explicitly

Free labor is labor performed by people who have the freedom to accept or decline work and can bargain for better compensation. Free labor was seen in the nineteenth century as the antithesis of slave labor, which had no such freedoms.

prohibit slavery's further expansion to ensure a national future shaped by the unimpeded territorial advance of **free labor.** Otherwise slavery's increasing power would prove unstoppable. "Where will it end?" queried a representative from New York State. "Your lust for acquiring is not yet satisfied. You must have Florida. Your ambition rises. You covet Cuba, and obtain it. You stretch your arms to the other islands of the Gulf of Mexico and they become yours." Southern politicians hotly responded that no territorial limitations should ever be placed on the growth of their peculiar institution and that slavery itself should be promoted across the expanding republic because it constituted a "positive good" not only for the nation's economy but also for the well-being of the enslaved themselves.

With Missouri, the issue of slavery's role in westward expansion had suddenly awakened deeply conflicting visions of the republic's future development. But at the same time, this issue also provoked an urgent desire among a majority of politicians in both sections for engineering a union-preserving compromise. To sustain the equal balance between North and South, Maine was admitted as a free state along with Missouri as a slave state, while slavery was also excluded from Louisiana Purchase lands north of 36 degrees, 30 minutes. But this settlement—the so-called Missouri Compromise, engineered in Congress largely by Henry Clay—left an ambiguous legacy. Congress had clearly legislated slavery's explicit prohibition by excluding it from some of the Louisiana Purchase territories. Was that a precedent, slaveholders worried, on which future Congresses might build still further restrictions? At the same time, Congress had also mandated an exact balance between "free" and "slave" as two new states entered the Union. Were future Congresses enjoined to replicate this pattern? Must Congress henceforth simultaneously legislate in favor of both slavery and freedom, or did it have the power to legislate in favor of either to the exclusion of the other?

In this manner, the lessons of history suggested by the settlement of the Missouri crisis opened boundless opportunities for sectional conflict as the nation continued its rapid expansion. For the moment, however, crisis had been averted, and relieved politicians began taking pains to avoid contention over slavery. The discovery of Denmark Vesey's massive slave conspiracy in Charlestown, South Carolina, the following year (1821) added further to the consensus that the less controversy about slavery the better.

The Democratic Party Created to Bolster Slavery in the South and White Supremacy Nationwide

Acting on just this assumption, powerful political operatives such as New York's Martin Van Buren worked in the late 1820s across the **Mason–Dixon Line** to create a trans-sectional political organization, the Democratic Party, which was designed to bring about less controversy over slavery in national politics. While electing slaveholder Andrew Jackson as president in 1828 the new party explicitly campaigned on a platform that upheld slavery in the South and white supremacy across the nation by catering explicitly to the prejudices of urban workers, lower-class southern whites, recent immigrants, planters, proponents of forced Indian removal, and anyone else who set a high value on maintaining his sense of "whiteness." Now there were heavy sanctions against challenging the interests of slaveholders, expulsion from the party foremost among them.

In the North, aspirants to careers in the Democratic Party had to obtain approval from slaveholding party chiefs, such as South Carolinian John C. Calhoun and Jackson himself. When anti-Jacksonian dissidents coalesced into the Whig Party in the early 1830s, they relied on similar strategies for getting votes and recruiting leaders. Neither party dared alienate proslavery interests in the South or racist supporters of slavery and white supremacy throughout the free states.

The Missouri crisis left a potent political legacy: although the Whigs and Democrats competed fiercely throughout the 1830s and 1840s, now membership in either party required suppressing all criticism of slavery. The South, of course, had a long history of heavily enforced white supremacy and a free, white social order. Thus the emergence of this interparty consensus in the slave states was hardly surprising. In the North, by contrast, rapidly compounding racial tensions were developing throughout the 1820s that drastically reshaped the political system from one that had recently fostered sectional conflict into one designed to stifle all opposition to slavery.

The **Mason–Dixon line** was drawn by two surveyors in the eighteenth century to set the border between Maryland and Pennsylvania. It gradually became not only the literal line between slave and free states but also the figurative line between freedom and slavery.

Racist Violence in the North

As life in northern cities became more complicated in the 1820s, tensions between people of differing skin colors became more volatile. Industrialization fostered a rapid transition from artisan work to wage labor, which, in turn, attracted waves of immigrants from all over the British Isles and particularly Ireland. New immigrants seeking jobs in a tightening labor market viewed their African American neighbors as unwelcome competitors. More important, they saw in them their own diminishing ability to shape their futures as independent men. Irish Catholics in particular feared personal "enslavement" to the Protestant bosses who paid their wages. Acting on these anxieties, they claimed to be white just like all other free citizens. Then they asserted their whiteness through acts of aggression against their free Black neighbors.

On the opposite end of the social spectrum, elite white lawyers, ministers, and businessmen noted these increasing frictions and convinced themselves that free African Americans constituted an ever more turbulent, dangerous people who deserved Colonization if not something worse. Free Blacks, for their part, refused to abandon their hard-fought struggles, dating from the Revolution, to claim full citizenship and build respectable communities around their schools, churches and voluntary organizations. To them, the American Colonization Society was a racist conspiracy by whites to force their deportation. David Walker's *Appeal* articulated powerfully this African American rejection of Colonization. A few years later, William Lloyd Garrison's book-length pamphlet *Thoughts on African Colonization* (1832), based largely on quotations from the Colonization Society's publications, discredited Colonization as a serious response to the moral objections to slavery. After 1832, nobody seriously proposed that Colonization would address the moral problems of enslaving people. Threats by these white elitists as well as by the white lower orders required the sternest responses.

Such racial volatility turned the 1820s and 1830s into years of mounting racial tyranny throughout the free states. Lower-class whites felt mounting impunity to abuse, vandalize, and even murder African Americans. Race riots erupted in Philadelphia, New York City, Hartford, and Boston. In Cincinnati, in 1829, armed mobs terrorized Black neighborhoods for three successive nights, leaving homes and churches in rubble, several dead, and more than six hundred traumatized people contemplating exile in southern Canada. Bigotry also overtook northern state legislatures as politicians in Ohio, Indiana, Illinois, Pennsylvania, New York, and Connecticut approved new state constitutions based on universal white manhood suffrage while methodically stripping free Blacks of their citizenship. White Americans in the North no less than in the South had now made white skin color the ultimate criterion for living "free" or "degraded" in a "democratic" republic.

EMERGENCE OF IMMEDIATE ABOLITIONISM

In this tightly suppressive environment of racialized politics, even the American Colonization Society's piecemeal approaches engendered suspicion from slaveholders. Deeply serious Abolitionists remained few, isolated, and unorganized. Quaker activists, such as newspaper editors Benjamin Lundy and Elihu Embree, worked on the fringes of the upper South, subsisted on meager readerships, and were all but ignored. So were Black New York City Abolitionists John B. Russwurm and Samuel Cornish, pioneering editors of *Freedom's Journal*, the nation's first newspaper owned and operated by African Americans (published 1827–28).

But on a much deeper level, complex forces were also at work throughout the 1820s that would lead in the next decade to the sudden emergence of an Abolitionist Movement of unparalleled scope and intensity. This movement would be an interracial one, led by idealistic white New Englanders in alliance with militant African Americans. Inspired by Christian egalitarianism and a profound sense of personal responsibility, young men and women of both races launched an unprecedented effort to convince their fellow Americans that slavery was a terrible sin, that it must be immediately eliminated with no compensation to slaveholders, and that racial prejudice was at war with Christianity. Just as the nation's political system and the social order supporting it were closing ranks against all dissent against slavery, radical activists in the North began taking up the cause of "immediate, unconditional emancipation." It is difficult to imagine a more dangerous or, if one prefers, a more perfectly timed and necessary moment for launching a deeply radical crusade against slavery.

Historians cite January 1, 1831 as the moment when immediate abolitionism entered the public consciousness. On that date, a young Bostonian, William Lloyd Garrison, launched his remarkable newspaper, the *Liberator*, with this equally remarkable promise:

> The essential beliefs of immediate Abolitionists were that slavery was a sin against God; that slavery must be abolished immediately, everywhere, with no compensation to slaveholders; and that Black people deserved absolute full equality with whites. This third belief distinguished immediate Abolitionists from other antislavery sentiments.

> I *will be* harsh as truth and as uncompromising as justice. On this subject I do not wish to think, or speak, or write with moderation No! no! Tell a man whose house is on fire to give a moderate alarm; tell him to moderately rescue his wife from the hands of the ravisher; tell the mother to gradually extricate her babe from the fire into which it has fallen;—but urge me not to moderation in a cause like the present. I am in earnest—I will not equivocate—I will not excuse—I will not retreat a single inch and I WILL BE HEARD.

The Great Awakening, Evangelicalism, and Immediate Abolitionism

Reflected in this vibrant outburst of moral outrage was a deep religious vision that had its origins in a wave of evangelical Protestant religious revivals known as "the Great Awakening," which swept across New York State and New England in the 1820s. Led by powerful ministers such as Charles Grandison Finney and Lyman Beecher, this mass religious outpouring emphasized the individual's free-will choice to embrace an instantaneous conversion experience, an inward "moral revolution" that freed a person to renounce sin and strive for personal holiness. Once "saved" the individual should bring God's truth to the unredeemed and combat the evils that sin inevitably perpetuated—drunkenness, impiety, sexual license, and the exploitation of the defenseless.

The initial white leaders of this new radical idea of immediate abolitionism included Congregationalists such as brothers Lewis and Arthur Tappan, Gerrit Smith, Theodore Dwight Weld, and Elizur Wright Jr.; Baptists such as Garrison; and radical Quakers such as Lucretia Mott, Arnold Buffum, and John Greenleaf Whittier. To their ears, these doctrines confirmed that slavery was the most God-defying sin of all and the most corrosive cause of disharmony among His people. They saw slave owning as inherently a sin and proclaimed that slave masters must immediately free their slaves, must stop sinning.

In what other system did exploitation of the defenseless occur more frequently and brazenly? Where was sexual debauchery more constant than the violations masters forced on their female slaves? What impiety could be more brazen than in the master's refusal to permit the enslaved to read Scripture? Where was brutality more evident than in the master's heavy applications of whipping and his willingness to dismember all family ties of the enslaved?

The Abolitionists' solution to all these terrible questions was the truth of immediate emancipation, pressed loudly and earnestly on the consciences of all American citizens, slaveholders and non-slaveholders alike. Calling their strategy **moral suasion** Abolitionists believed that theirs was a message of healing and reconciliation. With appeals to conscience they would inspire masters to release their slaves, thereby advancing the nation toward a peaceful moral revolution that would end racial conflict, assuage the bitter enmity between masters and the enslaved, and quell political conflict between North and South. "Our object is to save life, not to destroy it," Garrison declared in 1831. "Make the slave free . . . and every possibility [is] ended for servile as well as civil war."

> **Moral suasion** was the Abolitionist belief that if slaveholders and defenders of slavery were shown the moral truth of slavery, they would be morally converted and then quickly emancipate the slaves and promote equality of Black and white people.

But by adopting Christian pacifism and presenting themselves as peacemakers, these early immediate Abolitionists woefully misjudged the power of the forces opposing them. As we have seen, by 1831 slavery and white supremacy had secured tremendous dominion over American politics and society. Political parties were now explicitly designed to defend slavery and crush its opponents. As the country expanded deeply into the southwest and southern planters transitioned from tobacco to cotton, slavery assumed its place as the cornerstone of the nation's economy and slaveholders as dominate in national politics. The fundamental assumption that defined the political order, North and South, was that only whites could exercise citizenship and would mobilize, sometimes violently, against those claiming otherwise. Compounding the dangers inherent in this situation were three additional events—each immensely divisive, sectionally and racially—that guaranteed the wholesale rejection of immediate emancipation not just by slaveholders but by nearly all Americans, North as well as South.

The first of these three events, the Nullification Crisis in South Carolina (1828–33), revealed just how enraged slaveholders were to become in response to the Abolitionists' appeals. Even before the appearance of the *Liberator*, extremist planters in this state were mobilizing militia and threatening secession to protect slavery from perceived external threats, presumably implied in disputes with President Andrew Jackson over tariff rates. The second event brought forward militant African American pamphleteer David Walker, who in 1829 and 1830 published his landmark *Appeal to the Coloured Citizens of the World,* which eloquently excoriated whites for their bigotry and free Blacks for their apathy and called, if freedom was

> Walker's *Appeal to the Coloured Citizens of the World* was one of the most influential African American political statements of the century and a deeply argued engagement with the ideas of the Declaration of Independence.

not granted, for slaves to rise in violent revolution. The pamphlet was widely reprinted in the North and, worse from the planters' point of view, smuggled into the hands of the enslaved by free Black sailors who plied the coastal trade between Boston and points south.

Then in late 1831, in Southampton County, Virginia, the third of these events reached a full-scale crisis when enslaved insurrectionist Nat Turner led an uprising that took the lives of fifty-five whites and a far greater number of Blacks. Turner's rebellion scared the entire white South; provoked tremendous violence against Blacks, slave and free, suspected of rebellious plots; and inspired in the Virginia legislature a serious, if short-lived, debate on the institution of slavery (see page 124 in this game book). Nat Turner's revolt was shocking to whites not only because of its violence against whites but because it was carried out without a plan or advance preparation. Turner decided it was the day for revolt, and many slaves decided to join in, on the spot.

As sectional rancor and fears of Black insurrection suddenly compounded, immediate Abolitionists perceived not deep danger but confirmation that a God who hated slavery was making his anger clear. In response, they believed, the planters would repent and convert. "The whole system . . . will fall to pieces with a rapidity that will astonish," one immediatist exclaimed in 1832. Thus reassured, they began undertaking unimaginably dangerous and ambitious tasks. From 1831 through 1837 immediate Abolitionists became whirlwinds of agitation. They vigorously canvassed the free states, creating dozens of local antislavery societies, numerous newspapers, and blizzards of pamphlets and petitions. In tandem with free Black activists in northern cities, they directly confronted white supremacy by founding integrated schools, churches, and voluntary organizations where people of both sexes associated freely. "Promiscuous assemblies" was what their increasingly hostile detractors called them. By 1835, Abolitionists were flooding the U.S. Post Office with pleas addressed directly to slaveholders and home delivered to repent and emancipate. The next year they inaugurated their Great Petition Campaign by bombarding the U.S. House of Representatives with a flood of citizens' demands for federal legislation against slavery. Never before in the history of the United States had the subject of human bondage so dominated public discussion.[7]

Anti-Abolitionist Violence in the North

The impact of this cyclonic agitation vastly exceeded the immediatists' modest numbers, which were never more than a small slice of the northern population. More important, it also ended in unqualified disaster. Elected officials from President Jackson on down joined with civic leaders of every sort, ministers from nearly all denominations, and ordinary whites throughout the republic in a harrowing barrage of repression and terror. In the South, mobs ransacked post offices and burned Abolitionist mailings, while state legislatures voted cash bounties for capturing leading Abolitionists. Suspected Abolitionist sympathizers faced being tarred and feathered, whipped, and incarcerated. In elections across the nation these two parties—the Democrats and the Whigs—campaigned on platforms advocating white supremacy and the suppression of the Abolitionists.

Mayhem erupted in Boston, Philadelphia, Utica, Rochester, Pittsburgh, Syracuse, New Haven, and Cincinnati (again), as well as in innumerable smaller communities, as mobs assaulted Black communities and Abolitionist meetings. Finally, in 1837, in Alton, Illinois, Elijah Lovejoy, an embattled Abolitionist editor who rejected nonviolence, seized his rifle to confront a crowd outside his newspaper's office and was cut down in a fusillade of gunfire. His paper and press were destroyed. Garrison as usual best summarized the Abolitionists' blasted hopes for inducing the national conscience to undergo a peaceful moral revolution:

> When we first unfurled the banner of the Liberator . . . we did not anticipate that in order to protect slavery, the free states would trample under foot all law and order, and government, or brand the friends of liberty as incendiaries and outlaws. . . . It did not occur to us that almost every religious sect and every political party would side with the oppressor.

Abolitionism Splits into Three Factions

Severely bloodied, shocked, and confused but hardly defeated, immediatists quickly began debating new approaches that addressed the bald fact that moral suasion had failed. By 1840, three quarreling factions had developed conflicting responses, which irreparably split the Movement. The first—led by Garrison; the formidable orator Wendell Phillips; and the *grande dame* of Boston abolitionism, Maria Weston Chapman—argued that the nation's values had been exposed as being so irredeemably corrupted that Abolitionists must flee from established religious denominations, boycott all elections, repudiate the federal union and demand northern secession (what they called disunionism). The proslavery U.S. Constitution, they proclaimed, was "A Covenant With Death—An Agreement With Hell!"

The second Abolitionist faction, headed by businessman Lewis Tappan and minister Amos Phelps, insisted that the Movement remain true to its programs of evangelization. The third faction, led by clergyman Joshua Leavitt, mathematics professor Elizur Wright Jr., and slaveholder-turned-Abolitionist James Gillespie Birney, argued that the U.S. Constitution was actually an antislavery document that compelled Abolitionists to organize an emancipationist political party, the Liberty Party they called it, that would compete against the Whigs and Democrats. By 1840, Abolitionist unity had been permanently shattered. Significantly, while they differed greatly on strategies, these three factions all adhered to the core beliefs of immediate abolition.

Since their efforts had mobilized a proslavery constituency instead of emancipating slaves, what had the Abolitionists actually accomplished by 1840? Several answers seem clear. Just when a powerful political consensus was developing in the late 1820s to suppress all opposition to slavery, Abolitionists forced their potent vision of egalitarianism into the nation's political consciousness. White supremacists everywhere as well as in the planter class now found themselves assailed as never before by Black and white critics with radical conceptions of equality. The Abolitionists were also enlisting the unprecedented participation of women, who leveled wholesale challenges to male as well as to white supremacy. As the 1840s opened and Garrisonians advocated boycotts of the political system while their opponents within abolitionism organized the Liberty Party, it was indisputable that immediate Abolitionists had made themselves into powerful competitors in the nation's market place of ideas, infusing it with highly egalitarian visions and vocabulary. Thanks to their efforts and theirs alone, slavery and white supremacy were now subjects Americans could no longer avoid, as both were under sustained rhetorical and moral attack.

One further outcome of the moral suasion campaigns proved fraught with danger for North–South relations and for the stability of the nation's two-party political system. Throughout the 1830s, significant numbers of ordinary northerners found themselves increasingly disturbed by anti-Abolitionist violence exploding around them. While few had embraced immediatism, such Yankees increasingly worried that slaveholders and their northern allies harbored contempt for the rights to assemble, speak, and petition. They came to believe that the undermining of such freedoms was having a deeply corrupting influence on the nation's political culture. Far too many Yankee politicians, businessmen, and ministers seemed all too willing to do the white South's bidding by mobbing the Abolitionists, destroying their printing presses, enacting the Gag Rule, and treating everyone's civil liberties as what immediatist Theodore Dwight Weld termed "hollow counterfeits."

This conviction that the civil liberties of all Americans were threatened marked the appearance of a compelling ideological formulation: fear of an aggressive **Slave Power conspiracy.** Northern sentiments were sympathetic to this notion as the decade closed. Sensing this shift in public opinion, immediatists began drawing sharp distinctions between their own uncompromising egalitarian beliefs and those of people who expressed concern about losing their personal rights but who cared nothing for those of the enslaved. Many historians since have also insisted on this distinction. Such anti-southern resentments, they correctly point out, accepted the continuance of slavery and were too often accompanied by deep-seated feelings of white supremacy. *Antislavery*, they insist, must never be confused with *abolitionism*.

> The **Slave Power conspiracy** was the belief that the slaveholding class conspired to expand its control over the United States, thereby limiting the freedoms of northerners and expanding the territory of slavery into the west and the north as well.

This distinction between abolitionism and antislavery, while useful, can also be misleading when assessing the Abolitionists' political impact. For one thing, militant slaveholders never bothered making such a fine discrimination.

Moreover, immediatists understood their mission to be one of liberating the entire nation from slavery, not just the South, a view that bespoke their own deep-seated concern for the free states' civil liberties. Most important, as historian Leonard Richards has pointed out, influential new constituencies within the North began blending abolition and antislavery, while developing their own strenuous political objections to the values of the planter class.[8]

The idea of a Slave Power conspiracy found its deepest support in a broad geographic swath rooted in New Hampshire and Vermont that spread into western Massachusetts; encompassed upstate New York; and extended across the northern portions of Ohio, Indiana, and Illinois. Not coincidentally, these were precisely the regions where Abolitionists had their greatest success in their early efforts to spread their message of "moral revolution." This was because for all their ideological differences over immediatism, Abolitionists and these citizens shared a great deal in common in terms of religious outlook and social values.

Each of these areas had been initially settled by Puritan-descended Yankees who, much like the immediatists, shared deep allegiances to evangelical religion. At the same time, powerful economic forces were transforming these regions from clusters of isolated villages and family farms into hubs of cash-crop agriculture and commercial enterprise. Such rapid changes likewise worked in the immediatists' favor. Lake and river shipping, canals, and eventually railroads linked urban markets from Chicago and Cleveland through Buffalo, Rochester, Syracuse, Albany, and thence to New York City. Throughout this region newspapers, public schools, and private academies multiplied, thereby broadening citizens' political interests and heightening their involvement in controversies such as mobbings of Abolitionists, the destruction of Black neighborhoods, and the ransacking of mailbags. Like the Abolitionists, the citizens of these northern areas believed that material and moral progress was advanced by values that were the antithesis of those of the slave South: free labor, evangelical morality, family stability, upward social mobility, and republican governance. These values increasingly cohered in much of northern society, but appeared wholly absent from the South.

The planters, those exploiters of two million slaves, stood condemned in Yankees' eyes as wallowing in their deeply perverted habits, a critique they shared fully with the Abolitionists. Poorer white southerners were seen by people in the North as being repressed by a pernicious "slaveocracy," reduced to ignorant poverty. Evangelicals saw plantation owners as unleashing their primal lusts in gambling halls and race tracks, on dueling grounds, and especially against defenseless women in the slave quarters. There was a pervasive, mounting fear that twisted plantation values threatened the cherished social order of the North. Moved to immediatism after facing a local mob, upstate New Yorker Gerrit Smith expressed these fears succinctly when insisting in 1836 that northerners must oppose slavery in "self-defense." If not destroyed, he predicted, the slaveocracy would surely continue its "aggression . . . and effectually prepare the way for reducing northern laborers into a heard of slaves."

The Petition Campaign and the Gag Rule

Abolitionists channeled northern fears directly into the political process by initiating an unprecedented campaign to inundate the U.S. House of Representatives with antislavery petitions. These petitions were written to appeal to all people suspicious of the Slave Power, not just immediate Abolitionists, thus garnering a wide range of signatures. Instead of demanding outright universal abolition, the petitions demanded more restricted measures, such as ending slavery in the District of Columbia, stopping the interstate slave trade, and banning the admission of new slave states to the federal union. The very act of signing such petitions allowed unprecedentedly large numbers of previously uninvolved people a safe yet politically potent way to express their hostility to the slave South. The petitions were passed door to door by local volunteers, most of them women, which created new networks of anti-southern activism and female empowerment.

By 1836, congressmen found themselves facing over 30,000 antislavery petitions. In 1837 that number jumped to close to 100,000, and by May 1838 the American Anti-Slavery Society's Great Petition Campaign had generated an extraordinary 415,000 petitions, the majority signed by women who had now made themselves the grassroots engine of the Abolitionist Movement. Thus deluged, the House of Representatives, in 1836, responded by enacting its highly controversial Gag Rule, stipulating that antislavery petitions could not be debated and, once received, must be automatically tabled with no discussion.

The House's Gag Rule amounted to a blunt, unilateral curtailment of a citizen's constitutional right of petition. That fact spurred further sectional controversy. Enacted just when anti-Abolitionist violence was at its peak, and in operation until late 1844, this rule played an enormously influential role in stimulating North–South estrangement. Through their petitions, which now included demands to repeal the Gag Rule, ordinary citizens from the North's most heavily evangelical regions were now projecting their growing objections to slavery and the Slave Power directly into the nation's two-party system.

Whatever their affiliation, Whig or Democrat, southern politicians united in support of the Gag Rule. The most militant planters, Democratic Party followers of South Carolina's John C. Calhoun, agitated for an even more repressive measure, hoping that Abolitionists' objections would drive their section to unite around extreme defenses of "southern rights." Equally dedicated to protecting their peculiar institution, southern Whigs, led by Henry Clay, endorsed the Gag Rule as it stood, arguing that a federal union supported by an anti-Abolitionist majority in the North protected slavery better than the secession-tinged position of the states-rights southern Democrats. Whatever their party preferences, however, southern politicians agreed that any suggestion that slavery constituted an abomination must be vigorously suppressed in all such discussions, no matter where they were held: in newspapers, mailed pamphlets, incendiary broadsides, Sunday sermons, or debates on the floor of the House of Representatives. In response, increasing numbers of northern citizens joined immediate Abolitionists in insisting that the Slave Power conspiracy's Gag Rule was obliterating their rights of assembly, speech, press, and petition.

As the petitions piled up and the Gag Rule continued, sectional disruption spread through the House of Representatives. In early 1837 former President John Quincy Adams, now a Whig congressman from Massachusetts, rose to defend civil liberties by presenting antislavery petitions in defiance of the Gag Rule and by forcing antislavery subjects into debates as confrontationally as possible. Since Adams enjoyed unshakable support from his constituents, he soon became the recipient of antislavery petitions from all over the North, but by 1838 other antislavery Whig representatives joined him, notably Joshua Giddings from northeastern Ohio's Western Reserve, Seth Gates from New York's "Burnt-Over District," and William Slade from heavily abolitionized western Vermont. Their arrival marked a transformation of American politics that was replete with implications for Abolitionists, for slaveholders and the enslaved, for politicians of all persuasions, and for the generation that witnessed the coming of the Civil War.

The Rise of Antislavery Voters in the North

The accelerating counterpoint between Abolitionist agitation and proslavery suppression was now creating concentrations of northern voters who insisted their representatives express opposition to slavery, to transgressions against civil liberties, and to the conduct of the planter class. In total contravention to politicians' proslavery consensus, these voters supplied their representatives with stern mandates to address slavery questions openly and often. As the sectional crisis deepened during the 1840s and 1850s over slavery's further extension into western territories, early insurgents such as Adams and Giddings were joined by still others who relied on antislavery voters to define their political commitments. Some were insurgent Democrats, such as Senator John Parker Hale of New Hampshire, Salmon P. Chase of Ohio, and Representative David Wilmot of Pennsylvania. Others claimed Whig allegiances, such as Representative George W. Julian from Indiana, Representative Thaddeus Stevens of Pennsylvania, single-term Illinois congressman Abraham Lincoln, Senators Charles Sumner and Henry Wilson of Massachusetts, and Senator William Seward of New York.

Whatever their party allegiance, all of these politicians could justly claim to be self-made men, and in this respect their biographies corresponded to their constituents' deepest social values. Northern voters and representatives alike placed the highest premium on education, moral self-improvement, sobriety, thrift, technological innovation, and economic independence, which taken together, struck many as the antithesis of slaveholding. Their ideology, as they phrased it, celebrated "free soil, free labor and free men."[9]

As the Hartford Convention (1814) and the Missouri crisis (1819–20) remind us, open North–South conflict was hardly new. Nevertheless, the transformed setting in which pro- and antislavery politicians operated in the late 1830s ensured their impact would be far more volatile and deeply felt than heretofore. On both sides of the Mason–Dixon Line the now-entrenched two-party system of Whigs versus Democrats structured themselves on mass political awareness and widespread voter participation based on universal white manhood suffrage. By the end of the decade, the telegraph, railway, steam press, postal system, and mass-produced newspaper, not to mention the greatly increased frequency of elections on the state and local levels, turned political campaigning into something like an endlessly popular sport. Such contests, as historian Eric Foner has suggested, generated strong personal loyalties and networks of communication that knit relationships between governors and the governed more tightly than ever before. This guaranteed that conflicts over slavery generated in Washington, D.C. would rapidly radiate through the public at large and back to the politician's constituents. By a reverse application of the same process, Abolitionist or proslavery agitation initiated at the local level registered rapidly in congressional deliberations.

No one demonstrated this dynamic more dramatically than did antislavery Ohioan Joshua R. Giddings, a Whig who resigned his seat in Congress in 1842 after being all-but-unanimously censured by his fellow representatives. His offense (a spectacularly defiant one) was putting before the House resolutions that upheld the right of the enslaved to secure their freedom by slaying their oppressors while being transported in the coastal slave trade. Rushing home to his deeply abolitionized district, he stood for reelection, won by a huge majority, and returned in triumph to Washington with instructions from his constituents to reintroduce his "insurrectionary" resolutions. This he immediately did, driving slaveholders to apoplexy but incurring no further congressional penalty. Here was a legislative environment in which hot-blooded planters and antislavery zealots exercised markedly disproportionate powers, a problem to which Whigs and Democrats developed differing responses.[10]

The challenge to the Whig Party created by the rise of antislavery voters and politicians proved complex but solvable, at least through the elections of 1840. Representatives such as Giddings and Adams and other less-contentious congressmen who supported them were nevertheless fully credentialed members of that party. Whig strategists had no choice but to rely on the renegades' votes to secure legislative victories on matters apart from slavery that were vital to the party's success. Impressive Whig majorities in evangelical strongholds, where fears of the Slave Power ran deepest, increasingly supported these insurgent congressmen, and constituents in other like-minded districts increasingly pressured their reluctant representatives to take stronger stands. In this manner, by 1840, northern Whig loyalty and antislavery ideology were becoming intertwined. Whatever their private views of sectional issues, increasing numbers of northern Whig representatives found their constituents urging them to vote against renewal of the Gag Rule, to endorse the abolition of slavery in the District of Columbia, to question the 1793 Fugitive Slave Law, and to resist slavery's expansion into western territories. Other issues they supported were the Whig's economic agenda of a national bank, higher tariffs, and internal improvements.

The Whig Response

In the face of antislavery pressure, the Whigs forged a united North–South party by adopting Colonization as a featured component of their party's ideology. By so doing, conservative northern Whigs could, for the benefit of their constituents, claim to be concerned about slavery while reassuring their southern cohorts. They could denounce the evils of abolitionism and stress the importance of ridding the nation of its Black population. As anti-Abolitionist violence exploded in the North and conflict over the Gag Rule mounted in the 1830s, northern Whig editors and party leaders condemned with equal fervor "firebrand" Abolitionists, "insolent, ungovernable" Blacks, and working-class "rabble" bent on "mob rule." These indictments constituted a reassuring proslavery message from northern to southern Whigs. At the same time, party spokesmen praised the "temperate statesmanship" of national Whig leaders, who were also colonizationism's most prominent national exponents: Kentucky slaveholder Henry Clay along with Edward Everett and Daniel Webster, both from Massachusetts. In 1840 and 1844, when the national Whig Party nominated presidential candidates, it was no accident that their choices were slaveholding colonizationists William Henry Harrison and Henry Clay.

By adopting this strategy, northern Whigs found an effective way to contrast their positions on slavery and race from those of their hated competitors—the openly racist, violence-prone, stridently proslavery northern Democrats—while still maintaining the confidence of their southern allies. With Colonization confirming their allegiances to "whiteness" and slave owning, northern Whigs felt free to satisfy their antislavery constituents by roundly condemning Democrats as "tools of the Slave Power" for promoting proslavery violence and for supporting the suppression of antislavery petitions. All the while, southern Whigs well appreciated the deeper motives underlying these tactics as well as the fact that they strengthened the Whigs' overall performance against the Democrats in national elections. If, however, southern Whigs ever decided that their northern colleagues were betraying them by seriously embracing authentic antislavery values, the party's collapse would be all but foreordained.

But for the moment it was hatred of Andrew Jackson and his Democratic Party much more than a quiet intersectional agreement over slavery that ensured Whig

Party unity. As elections went forward in 1840, the nation's economy was mired in depression, responsibility for which the Whigs assigned to the Democrats' "corrupt" banking policies. Whigs also denounced the Democrats' "ruinous" tariff legislation; their "short-sighted" opposition to federal financing for roads, canals, and harbors; and their hard-currency monetary policies, which, they claimed, fostered "bankrupting" inflation. The Whigs' indictment continued with denunciations of Jacksonian policies that forcibly removed the Cherokee Indians, opposed curbs on the consumption of alcohol, and denied the religious sanctity of the Sabbath. It ended with scornful personal criticisms of Jackson as a duelist and bigamist, and of his successor, Martin Van Buren of New York, for "effeminacy" and "wanton degeneracy."

Despite the racist violence in the North and Abolitionist petitions to Congress in the proceeding decade, slavery constituted only a marginal issue among the multitude that energized voters in 1840 to join in torchlight parades, gather en masse to cheer political speechmaking, toast their candidates with hard cider, and mobilize in unprecedented numbers to vote for either Democrat Van Buren, a non-slaveholding New Yorker, or his Whig opponent, slaveholder William Henry Harrison. Just how minor a role slavery actually played is best measured by the woeful 6,697 votes garnered by the Abolitionists' newly formed third party, the Liberty Party, which nominated slaveholder-turned-Abolitionist James G. Birney on a single-issue immediatist platform.

Even the northern Whigs most critical of the planter class hesitated not a moment before supporting the slaveholding Harrison. Militant Giddings, for example, wrote to his eight-year-old son: "Say that you are for Harrison and reform and opposed to all northern men with southern principles." By "reform" he meant banking, internal improvements, and currency, not slavery. By "northern men with southern principles" he expressed opposition to slavery and its northern allies, but clearly not to Harrison, his party's nominee. Instead he was voicing his dismay at the openly proslavery Yankee Democrat Martin Van Buren. Giddings had not strayed from his convictions, but clearly, in this election, he did not reflexively align them directly against the planters in his party. He and his district were unwaveringly Whig. Whig victories defined his political calculus, and Van Buren, "enslaved by the Slave Power," not the slaveholding Harrison, was his obvious enemy. As long as he and others like him sustained this outlook, Whig unity across sectional lines could be maintained as well.

The Elections of 1840 and 1844 and the Annexation of Texas

Southern Whigs interpreted *reform* quite differently from Giddings, and this variance reveals the weaknesses underlying their party's superficial unity. Unlike the Democrats who easily coalesced around support for slavery and white supremacy, mutual bonding between Whigs North and South was far more complicated than shared endorsements of Colonization. As historian Charles G. Sellers has shown, of equal concern to many southern Whigs as banking and tariff policies were the disturbing memories of events that a minority of northern Whigs like Giddings approved—David Walker's *Appeal*, Garrison's *Liberator*, the Abolitionists' Great Postal Campaign, and the congressional petition campaign.[11] Southern Whigs also found deeply unsettling President Jackson's victory in the nullification crisis of 1828–33, which had been prompted by planter-extremists who had argued for states-rights doctrines they deemed vital for protecting slavery. More than any other shared belief, it was this hatred of Jackson and his party that, for quite different and clearly conflicting reasons, pulled the Whigs together across the Mason–Dixon Line. This fragile unity did its work well. Slavery, as noted, went all but unmentioned as the Whig Harrison defeated incumbent president Martin Van Buren in 1840. In the election's aftermath there seemed little prospect of serious sectional disturbance.

But just four years later, in 1844, all this had changed. Politics suddenly seethed with discord over slavery's role in the nation's development as the public divided over the all-too-explosive question that echoed from the Missouri crisis two decades earlier: must human bondage continue expanding as the United States pushed its boundaries inexorably westward? Again it was presidential election season, and the choice this time was between two quite substantial slaveholders, the Whig Kentuckian Henry Clay and the Tennessee Democrat James Knox Polk. And again, the irresolvable dilemmas that had so dangerously polarized North–South politics in 1819–20 were being visited on a new generation. When it came to conflict over slavery, the elections of 1840 and 1844 could not have more contrasting. Explaining why this was so requires a bit of backtracking.

In 1836, U.S. immigrants to the Mexican state of Texas, many of them slaveholders, rebelled against the duly constituted government of Mexico (which had abolished slavery) and established their own breakaway Republic of Texas. While some of these American immigrants to Texas had arrived legally under Mexican law, many came in violation of Mexican law: every American who brought slaves into Mexico had broken the law of Mexico. By the early 1840s, leaders of this enormous Lone Star Republic, which had a slave code and expanding enslaved population, began petitioning Congress for annexation and admission to the union. Should annexation take place, it could easily provoke war against Mexico, which, in turn, made possible still further territorial acquisition. Searching history for guidance from the Founding Fathers quickly proved at least as dangerously ambiguous as it had twenty years earlier.

Back in 1787, as we have seen, the Continental Congress had legislated slavery's prohibition by excluding it from the Northwest Territories, which in time would become Ohio, Indiana, Illinois, and Michigan. Was this the precedent on which Congress should now build a blanket restriction? Foes of the Slave Power certainly thought so. At the same time, later Congresses had contrived exact balances between free and slave as new states entered the United States: Kentucky against Ohio, Indiana against Tennessee, Maine against Missouri (after serious sectional contention), and so forth. Was Congress always enjoined to replicate this pattern of pairing? If so, might not "slave" Texas be paired with "free" Oregon, a British-held region also being infiltrated by American settlers and on which the government was setting its sights? Democrats in the North embraced this idea, condemning themselves again in the eyes of antislavery critics as "northern men with southern principles." So did moderate southern Whigs and Democrats, to the dismay of a minority of radical, fire-eating Deep South planters. For these fierce champions of slavery the clear answer was this: The U.S. Constitution gave planters the absolute right to transport their human property just like any other form of property, to any new territory or part of the United States, whatever its location. Anything short of this raised calls for nullification and promises of secession.

But whatever its similarities to the Missouri crisis, contention over Texas took place in a political environment far more sensitive to sectionalism than that of 1819–20. Back then there was no broad network of immediate Abolitionists, no highly visible Black militants, no sustained defiance of the Fugitive Slave Act, and no flood of antislavery mailings and petitions. Now for good or ill the Abolitionists' uncompromising language and defiant deeds had embedded themselves in the nation's political consciousness. Back then, the northern evangelical Bible Belt had yet to register its emphatic hatred of slavery. Back in 1819–20, already-sensitive planters had yet to undergo the multiple traumas of Nat Turner's insurrection, David Walker's *Appeal*, nullification's suppression, Garrison's *Liberator*, and so much more. And back then, there was no grassroots-driven mechanism of governance spanning North and South, the Second Party System, which transmitted sectional messages back and forth between highly mobilized voters and their responsive representatives. And finally, unlike the Missouri crisis, Texas's future was not to be settled by a Congress legislating on its own, but instead by the voting public who were to choose between the ardently expansionist Democrat Polk, the ambivalent Whig Clay, and the emancipationist James G. Birney, again the candidate of the Liberty Party in 1844.

One useful measure of these transformed political circumstances was the outsize impact on the election of Birney's Liberty Party, which, in 1840, had secured those paltry 6,696 votes. In 1844 balloting for Birney jumped almost tenfold, to 62,054. Though this was only 2.1 percent of the national vote (Birney garnered no southern votes), those particular ballots appeared to determine the election's outcome. Enraged Whigs charged this upstart third party with snatching the presidency away from Henry Clay and handing it to the militantly pro-slavery Democrat, the territorial expansionist James K. Polk of Tennessee.

Birney's fifteen thousand votes in New York State, Whigs argued, would have otherwise have gone for Clay had he not disappointed antislavery voters by backing away from his initial promise to oppose annexing Texas. Because of those fifteen thousand votes, Whigs alleged, Clay had fallen just five thousand short of capturing the Empire State and an Electoral College majority. Whatever this contention suggested to Abolitionists about the dangers of unintended consequences and whatever its validity, practically everyone at the time believed that Clay had fallen victim to the Liberty Party. More instructive than evaluating this assertion, however, is examining the political context that made it seem so plausible. This requires a full explanation of the crucial presidential election of 1844, a contest deeply influenced by Abolitionist agitation and unprecedented in its sectional divisiveness.

Henry Clay desired the presidency in 1844, and many Whig leaders in both sections supported him. But uniting the party behind Clay was not a foregone conclusion. After winning so convincingly in 1840, Whigs' attempts to enact their nationalist agenda were crushed when President Harrison died suddenly after a month in office, and his replacement, Virginia slaveholder John Tyler, a states-rights Whig, vetoed every piece of economic legislation passed in Congress by his own party, each a measure that Henry Clay advocated. A national bank, federally sponsored internal improvements, and drastic currency reform, Tyler explained, violated his strict construction view of the Constitution. Thus Tyler repudiated the Whig program and embraced the self-same principles of tightly limited government that planters invoked when defending slavery.

Then, in 1844, just as campaigning was getting under way, Tyler attempted and failed to force Texas annexation through the Senate. Twenty-eight out of twenty-nine Whig senators from states all over the union voted nay on Tyler's treaty of annexation with the Republic of Texas on June 7, 1844, but for clearly differing reasons. Southern Whigs feared annexation would generate intolerable sectional strife, threatening the union and therefore slavery. While northern Whigs agreed about protecting the union, many also insisted that these western lands should be reserved for freedom, not slavery. Although Whigs were openly united against Texas annexation, the potential for disagreement on the issue was obvious.

As Clay attempted to keep the party behind him, worrying about the South was hardly his only problem. The early 1840s witnessed several spectacular insurrections on the high seas, the most famous of which, the *Amistad* affair, resulted in a court struggle that lasted for years, culminating in a U.S. Supreme Court case, in which former president and current Whig congressman John Quincy Adams successfully argued for the rebels' release before the U.S. Supreme Court. If that weren't enough to document the party's sectional divisions, the response of northern Whigs to an important Supreme Court decision certainly was. In 1842 the Court ruled in *Prigg v. Pennsylvania* that Congress alone had the right to legislate the return of fugitive slaves. Whigs controlling

The ***Amistad*** was a Spanish ship, carrying fifty-three people who had been illegally seized in West Africa, taken to Cuba. In Havana they were put on a smaller boat, the *Amistad*, for the trip to another Cuban port. In 1839 the captives revolted, killed the captain, and tried to sail back to Africa. Instead, the ship drifted and they were apprehended off Long Island by the U.S. Navy and put into jail in Connecticut, creating a legal case that culminated in the U.S. Supreme Court deciding that the *Amistad* prisoners were not by international law slaves and must be freed. Most of the *Amistad* captives returned to Africa in 1842.[12]

state legislatures in Massachusetts, New Hampshire, Vermont, Rhode Island, and Pennsylvania responded with **personal liberty laws,** which denied federal authorities any state assistance in capturing escapees. Of little practical value to those fleeing slavery, these laws nevertheless bespoke the rising resentment of many northern Whigs to slaveholders' intrusions into their local affairs. Given these circumstances, it was hardly surprising that large numbers of northern voters, most specifically Whigs who dominated politics in New England, northern New York, and large parts of Ohio, Indiana, and Illinois, rejected the idea of adding slaveholding Texas to the union, but for reasons much opposed to those of their southern counterparts.

When it came to slavery, the three presidential candidates of 1844 fully embodied the parties that had nominated them: Clay, the tension-ridden Whigs, Polk the unified Democrats, and Birney, the immediate Abolitionists' uncompromising Liberty Party. Clay kept many slaves on his fine Kentucky plantation but was also a leading advocate of Colonization and openly critical of the worst practices of slaveholding. This posture made him acceptable to northern Whigs and to Whigs in the upper South. To Deep South planters, however, he was dangerously unreliable on Texas annexation and perhaps much else. Well aware of those against annexation but also knowing that he needed votes from others favoring it, Clay declared his qualified opposition to incorporating Texas. No annexation "at this time" was the way he phrased it. Clearly he was attempting to have it both ways by stating his position ambiguously.[13]

Polk, by contrast, as historian William Dusinberre has fully established, entertained no apologies for slavery. An exceptionally harsh slave master, he trafficked constantly in "his" Black human beings. His was a no-holds-barred plantation in which surveillance was close, beatings harsh and frequent, and slaves' diets barely maintained subsistence. Only one of every two children born to enslaved mothers on Polk's Tennessee plantation survived past age fifteen, a mortality rate shockingly above the norm for slave women's children on antebellum plantations. To Polk, Texas annexation made absolute sense and, for sectional balance, so did wresting free soil Oregon from the British. Democrats across the country embraced his sweeping expansionism, reaffirmed their support for slavery and white supremacy, and rallied to support his candidacy.[14]

The Liberty Party

Abolitionist James G. Birney, originally from Alabama, knew slaveholding just as well as did Clay and Polk. Unlike them, however, he hated it. A decade earlier he had inherited a substantial plantation from his father, had tried his hand at slaveholding, and had found it horrifying. By 1832 he had freed his slaves, had been driven out of the South for his outspoken abolitionism, and had moved to Cincinnati where mobs twice destroyed the printing presses he used to publish an Abolitionist newspaper.

Later in the decade he had broken with William Lloyd Garrison on boycotting elections. Birney had decided in a creative reading of the Constitution that it mandated slavery's abolition and that immediatists were morally bound to vote for the most Abolitionist of candidates. In 1840, these convictions had made him the Liberty Party's nominee and now, in 1844, he had been nominated again. This time, however, his party was far better organized, offered a platform that ensured far wider appeal, and had developed a much more sophisticated understanding of how to appeal to voters. Whether or not the Liberty Party cost Clay the election (as was widely believed at the time), it exerted an influence that far exceeded its size and directly affected the Texas annexation controversy.

Based on their 1840 experiences, Liberty men in 1844 well understood that the North's Bible Belt promised the greatest rewards for their electoral campaign. Here were districts where antislavery feelings ran the deepest and, not coincidentally, where the Whig Party dominated. To compete in these regions, the Liberty Party understood, it must take appealing positions on issues other than slavery that were of utmost interest to Whigs, specifically on banks, internal improvements, public land, and currency policy. Drawing Whig voters meant weaving Liberty Party positions on these issues into a broadly appealing antislavery ideology, a process that proved easy and wholly natural. Like all Abolitionists, Liberty men had long held the belief that southern economic "backwardness" blighted the nation's economy. And like all Abolitionists, they embraced glowing visions of a bountiful post-emancipation nation governed by universally free labor and assumed that conspiring slaveholders were naturally the root cause of the nation's economic ills. This Liberty Party viewpoint was an Abolitionist belief that was increasingly attractive to many northerners; slavery and free labor, it declared, were incompatible systems of labor.

From these premises the party built the argument that the government's economic policy since Jefferson's election had "been originated by the Slave Power" in order "to make free labor cheap without lowering the price of cotton." The axiom, endorsed by Whigs no less than by Democrats that slave and free labor could prosper "under the same policy" was, they scoffed, "just as absurd as perpetual motion." Here was the basis of the Liberty Party's multi-issue appeal. Bloated planters, they warned, fattened their treasuries on the fruits of slave labor while conspiring to stifle the North's economy by frustrating measures that Liberty men and loyal Whigs both endorsed—by choking off northern industry and agriculture with low tariffs and hostility to internal improvements, by depressing northern commerce with the destruction of the national banking system, and by destroying the dreams of northern workingmen and farmers when pursuing ruinous credit and land policies.

A subtle but unmistakable change was overtaking political abolitionism. Straightforward moral appeals on behalf of African Americans, the original version of immediate emancipation, were now being accompanied by broader fears that slaveholders' conspiracies subverted the North's political economy. The rules of political engagement for the Liberty Party now required de-emphasizing racial justice while formulating broader ideological appeals. No moral revolution was necessary to oppose the Slave Power on the basis of its threat to northern economic interests, and economic arguments required little sympathy for either the enslaved in the South or free Blacks in the North. Realizing this danger, Black Liberty Party members quickly warned, as one of them put it, that it would be a terrible error "to yield up . . . any of our vital principles for the sake of making it easier for others to unite with us." Individual Liberty Party members, to be sure, continued to believe steadfastly in Black emancipation and racial justice. So did maverick antislavery politicians such as Whig Joshua Giddings and Democrat Benjamin Tappan. The initial idealism of the original Abolitionists was never absent from this new anti-slavery politics. Yet deeply involved in this sensitivity to northern rights were also the makings of a white supremacist political antislavery in which racism and sectional animosity increasingly supported each other. Meantime, debate proceeded over Texas annexation and slavery's extension during the 1844 elections.

By demanding the annexation of Texas and the occupation of Oregon, the Democrats were responding to the strong expansionist urgings that developed in the early 1840s. Since 1819 the boundaries of the republic had remained fixed, but now demands mounted that the United States fulfill its **Manifest Destiny** by occupying the entire continent, an agenda inspired by a mix of contradictory motives: eastern desires for west coast trading outlets, the land hunger of pioneers, and fears of British encroachment from the west. To many planters, southwest expansion promised new land for the older slave states, where soil was showing signs of overcultivation and acreage was being converted to free-labor farming. Creating new slave states would also stimulate internal slave trading while enhancing the planter's power in Congress. Suspicious of precisely these slaveholding aspirations, many northerners nevertheless embraced Manifest Destiny as the best way to promote the most crucial interests of independent, free labor farmers, artisans, and mechanics as well as the health of republican institutions. Western territories should be distributed to individual freehold farmers to relieve urban poverty and combat compounding concentrations of agrarian wealth.

> **Manifest Destiny** was a term first used in 1845 to call for the annexation of Texas and later to justify the expansion of the American empire to all of North America and beyond.

Democrats made campaign promises in 1844 to acquire both Texas and Oregon in an attempt to mobilize the conflicting aspirations of slaveholders and free-labor family farmers seeking to gain a political advantage against the Whigs. Henry Clay, we recall, had tried to put the Texas controversy to rest by taking an ambiguous position on the issue. Now he was forced to worry about defections in the North as well as the South as voters everywhere pressed him to clarify his position in response to the expansionist Democrats. Already concerned that his ambiguous Texas position was costing him support among southern expansionists, he also had to worry about alienating northern Whigs who opposed slavery's extension and feared that annexation would bring hostilities with Mexico. Victory in such a war, moreover, could well lead to even larger acquisitions of territory and still further expansion of slavery. The Liberty Party's broad appeals to northern Whigs who demanded northern rights further magnified these misgivings. From every perspective, Clay's most challenging problem involved keeping the northern branch of his party in lockstep with its southern counterpart.

Northern evangelical voters, though loyally Whig, also harbored powerful antislavery convictions, as we have seen. More important, the way in which Whigs acted on their convictions only magnified Clay's dilemma. In 1840s Massachusetts, for example, Whigs openly supported the struggles of Black and white Abolitionists to overturn school segregation, segregation on public conveyances, and laws against racial intermarriage. In New York State, Ohio, and Pennsylvania Whigs opposed the 1793 Fugitive Slave Law by campaigning for personal liberty legislation and (unsuccessfully) for the repeal of restrictions on African American suffrage. And in Congress it was northern Whig representatives who most persistently put forward antislavery petitions and protested openly against the Gag Rule, the internal slave trade, slavery in the District of Columbia, and (most tellingly for Henry Clay) the westward expansion of slavery. Little wonder that those few Black males who were qualified to vote invariably supported the Whigs.

Fearing defections to an upstart Liberty Party that had adopted their issues to "steal" their voters, northern Whigs issued extravagant antislavery claims for Clay, picturing him as stridently against annexation and even eager to abolish slavery in the District of Columbia. The candidate's fellow Kentuckian, the hot-tempered Whig Abolitionist Cassius Clay, campaigned throughout the Midwest for his namesake, claiming "cousin Henry" as a principled opponent of slavery. Militant Joshua Giddings, also a loyal Whig, was commissioned by party leaders to claim Henry Clay for antislavery and to stress that an antislavery vote for Birney only helped secure the election of James K. Polk, the unapologetic servant of the Slave Power. Writing of Giddings, one party leader confided that this strategy would "give us the abolitionist vote of his [Giddings's] district and exert a good influence across the state by out trumping the [abolitionist] third party."

The ploy was sectionally risky because it was obvious to slaveholders, Whigs especially. The more the northern Whigs refashioned Clay as a powerful antislavery alternative to the Abolitionist Birney, the more emphatically they broadcast their own opposition to slaveholders' most pressing interests. In the process they began seriously to undercut the long-standing political consensus that had sustained their party across sectional lines. The 1844 election, in short, created within the Whig Party the first of the successive intraparty cleavages that finally paved the way to secession and civil war. While, of course, unable to predict this ultimate result, one of the North's most insightful Whig leaders, William Seward, clearly identified this new direction, observing that "[t]he reckless folly of the [Tyler] administration [in attempting Texas annexation] and the unprincipled adaption of it by our opponents have loosened our tongues." "Slavery," he accurately predicted, "is henceforth and forever one of the elements of political action in the country. The ground the public mind has traveled cannot be regained."

The election results in 1844 proved Seward an accurate prophet. Embarrassed by the antislavery claims of his northern supporters, Clay could only continue dissimulating on the Texas question, hoping to keep his party united behind him. Antislavery Whig voters responded with increasing disillusion over Clay's "slippery tactics." "He is as rotten as a stagnant fishpond on the subject of slavery and always has been," exclaimed U.S. Representative Seth Gates, writing from his "burned-over" evangelical district in upstate New York. And it was precisely voters such as Gates, Whigs charged in the aftermath of the elections, that had doomed Clay's prospects. Enough of the Whig base had switched from Clay to Birney to deliver New York State's thirty-six electoral votes, and the presidency, to James K. Polk and the ever-expanding Slave Power.

Whatever the merits of their complaints, with Polk's victory, Whigs foresaw the future with utmost clarity. Texas annexation was now unavoidable. Quite likely so was a war with Mexico, since annexing Texas would not only expand the republic but also provoke war with the Republic of Mexico. All this would also surely enflame the already serious sectional disputes over slavery within the United States, with consequences that nobody living in 1845 could fully anticipate.

ARITHMETIC AND THE CONSTITUTION
(OR, DON'T BE A FOOL)

The idea of amending the Constitution to ban slavery and thus settle all disputes arising from slavery—or of amending it to somehow reform slavery or to end it at a specific, future date—sometimes strikes students in the twenty-first century as an "obvious" way for Americans to have resolved sectional problems in the antebellum period. Therefore, some students playing this game might be tempted to pursue this idea. Reject that temptation! Nothing of the sort was plausible in the decades before the secession crisis of 1860–61. The idea was not seriously advocated then, and no such effort in this game can succeed either. All well-informed citizens in 1845 knew that amending the Constitution to settle the slavery issue was impossible. The slave states held a veto on the amending process. This was one of the proslavery features designed into the Constitution.

Consider the requirements for amending the Constitution, as defined in Article V: two-thirds of the members of each house of Congress must vote for a proposed amendment. Then the proposed amendment must be approved by three-quarters of the state legislatures to finally ratify it and add it to the Constitution. This high hurdle was meant to ensure that slavery would not be undermined by the free states by amending the Constitution. Only after the social revolution of the Civil War had abolished slavery with massive violence and displaced the planter class's monopoly on political power in the South, was it possible for emancipation to be written into the Constitution. Even then, it was not easy (as shown in Steven Spielberg's Hollywood film *Lincoln*). Because only the changes wrought by war allowed the Thirteenth Amendment to be enacted, that amendment is less a testament to the constitutional system's flexibility than to its inflexibility. Fewer than thirty amendments have been enacted, in over 225 years, out of literally tens of thousands of proposed amendments. The Framers of the Constitution deliberately made it exceedingly hard to amend. In 1845, it hadn't been amended in forty years, and then only to fix a careless error regarding the electoral college in the original Constitution, with the Twelfth Amendment.

In July 1845 there were twenty-seven states in the United States. (Florida had become a state on March 3, 1845, and Texas would become the twenty-eighth state on December 29, 1845.) Of those twenty-seven states, fourteen were slave states. So, twenty-eight U.S. senators of the fifty-four total senators were from slave states. How could any proposed antislavery amendment possibly win the support of two-thirds of the Senate, when more than half the senators were from slave states? And obtaining a two-thirds majority in the House would be most unlikely, since the slave states had extra representation in the House due to the three-fifths clause of the Constitution.

The third major obstacle to an antislavery amendment to the Constitution was the steepest: the Constitution requires that any amendment win approval by three-quarters of the states to be ratified. A majority of states in 1845 were slave states. Never before 1860 did the free states constitute anything close to three-quarters of all states. Hence no amendment on slavery could ever be ratified by three-quarters of the states as required by the Constitution, even if such an amendment had miraculously passed both houses of Congress.

These requirements for amending the Constitution are plainly stated in Article V. One of the Constitutional Convention's provisions protecting slavery in the new nation was the difficulty by design of amending the Constitution. The framers wrote a framework of government that had ironclad protections for the peculiar institution. Antebellum Americans knew this, whether they liked or disliked it. You need to know this too, both as a student playing this game and as an educated citizen of the world.

Imagine for a moment that legal slavery had *not* been ended by the Civil War in the 1860s and that it still existed in the United States today, in the very same fifteen states that had slavery in 1860. Imagine also that the United States now had 50 states today, just as it really does. In this scenario, let's further stipulate that all fifteen slave states want to retain slavery, and each of the thirty-five free states want a constitutional amendment to ban slavery for the whole country. What would be likely in this scenario? Clearly, the thirty-five free states would, today, lack the ability to enact a constitutional amendment banning slavery. (Thirty-five is less than three-quarters of fifty.) The proslavery provisions written in 1787 make amending the Constitution very, very difficult. Don't make your character into a fool by proposing what everybody in 1845 knew was impossible. Doing so could be fatal to your character.

Many Americans, North and South, were content with the status quo, which protected slavery where it existed. Abolitionists, Black and white, abhorred this popular tolerance of the evil of slavery, but it was sanctioned by the Constitution.

While most Abolitionists in this game support the Garrisonian critique of the Constitution as an evil instrument, the actual history of abolitionism was more fragmented, as discussed earlier. Increasingly some Abolitionists in the 1840s recoiled from Garrisonian disunionism as unreasonable to otherwise genuinely antislavery people in the North. Such Abolitionists sought an argument that embraced the union, the nation, and the Constitution by depicting the "true meaning" of the Constitution as being somehow genuinely Abolitionist. This argument, voiced by James G. Birney, Salmon P. Chase, Joshua Leavitt, and Asa Mahan, claimed that the Constitution can and must be read as a pro-abolition constitution, an antislavery document. John C. Calhoun and William Lloyd Garrison agree on little, but they agree that this position is preposterous: plainly, the Constitution protects slavery. In the 1850s, Frederick Douglass himself became a political Abolitionist.

Nobody of course can foresee how these conflicts will be shaped by events, the events in the life of the nation and, more modestly, the events that take place in the three Meetings of this game. Much depends on the choices to be made by the varied groups that will meet in New York City. As Alexander Hamilton observed, "Opinion, whether well or ill founded, is the governing principle of human affairs."

WHY JULY 1845?

July 1845 was six or seven weeks *after* the *Narrative of the Life of Frederick Douglass* was published but *before* its author sailed for the United Kingdom in August, for what became nearly two eventful years overseas. Douglass was in July 1845 a Garrisonian Abolitionist, but would not remain one always. In July 1845, by the laws of Maryland, Douglass was the legal property of Thomas Auld. Consequently, under Article IV of the Constitution, all free states were obligated to have him "delivered up" to his owner. The publication of his *Narrative,* which openly stated his name and details of his life, put Douglass at great risk of being reenslaved—a risk few other fugitives had previously flaunted.

July 1845 was *before* the Mexican–American War (which immediately made the expansion of slavery *the* major issue in national politics), but well *after* the Abolitionist Movement had arisen so suddenly in the 1830s.

July 1845 was *before* the Free Soil Party was formed and ran a ticket for president in 1848, but *after* the small Liberty Party had demonstrated that an anti-slavery party could impact presidential elections. By July 1845, the core beliefs that would make up the Free Soil movement were emerging as a subcurrent of northern politics.

July 1845 is well *after* the slave South voiced sharp objections against the harboring of fugitive slaves in the North, but *before* the passage of the Fugitive Slave Act of 1850 created a veritable crisis, pitting the proslavery federal government against the rights of the free states.

And July 1845 was *after* the rise of the proslavery ideology in the South but *before* southern politicians commonly advocated secession as a necessity for protecting slavery against the federal government. (After all, the slave states still firmly controlled the federal government in 1845.) John C. Calhoun had already, *before 1845,* articulated the theories that could, ultimately, justify southern secession if Abolitionist threats to slavery increased, but no proslavery leader advocated immediate secession in 1845.

While 1845 was *after* the worst anti-Abolitionist violence in the North, Abolitionists in July 1845 remained a small, despised minority in the North.

Furthermore, Charles Dickens had famously visited America for much of 1842, traveled widely around the United States, and had been welcomed everywhere by huge, eager crowds. Almost immediately he published a whole book on that trip, *American Notes for General Circulation*. He could have returned in July 1845, and he was very curious about how Americans viewed slavery, even though he despised it, as *American Notes* showed.

By playing this game, you can live in the historical moment of 1845, provided that you grapple with the issues of that moment and articulate your character's values and goals.

 PART 3: THE GAME

THE RULES OF THE GAME

The following ten rules of the game apply for the whole game, including all three Meetings.

1. The Powers of the Chairman

Each of the three Meetings of the game is chaired by a different character. These Chairmen will preside over a full Meeting, keeping it to schedule, like anyone presiding over any Meeting of citizens. *While each Chairman is bound by the rules of the game,* he will likely apply those rules in ways different from the other Chairmen. Each Chairman has unilateral, nearly complete power to set the procedures for the Meeting he chairs:

- Each Chairman decides on eligibility to vote for his Meeting, according to his own goals and values. That decision cannot be appealed or overturned.

- Each Chairman must announce voting eligibility before holding any vote.*

- *A Chairman cannot change or violate any of the rules of the game.*

- Chairmen should seek to run an orderly, respectable, influential Meeting. Plan ahead!

- Each Chairman naturally should use his Meeting to advance his goals. This matters much more than being fair. A Chairman need not be fair but does need to win the game.

- The Gamemaster can advise or instruct the Chairman, privately or publicly, on procedures and timetables.

- Chairmen can vote on Resolutions and, in the event of a tie, can cast a second vote to break the tie during the Meeting he chairs.

2. The Rule of Two

Two proposed Resolutions must be voted on in each Meeting of the game. No more than two votes are permitted per Meeting. The Chairman writes and proposes all Resolutions.

---

* *Voting eligibility in these Meetings does not follow state laws governing elections in 1845.* Voluntary organizations and meetings abounded in antebellum America and they set their own rules.

- Two means two, not more or less than two.

- The Chairman alone proposes Resolutions, nobody else. Resolutions cannot be amended from the floor. (Some Chairmen may listen to your ideas as to what should be in a Resolution, so talk to him, privately.)

- Proposed Resolutions must be available to the whole Meeting in writing before being voted on (in hard copies distributed to all or written on the board). Voting is by holding hands above the head; votes are counted by two people and the results announced immediately.

- No secret ballots. Absent students cannot vote. Voters may vote yes, no, or abstain. No proxy voting.

- Each Meeting ends immediately after its second vote.

- The net outcome of the six votes for the whole game largely decides which Faction wins the game.

- The Gamemaster may modify the Rule of Two for your class, if the GM sees a reason to do so (see Rule 10).

- Advice on voting and Resolutions:

  - Advance estimating of votes can be and should be done, of course, through conversations and communication.

  - A capable Chairman will not permit the use of his Meeting's sessions to discuss editing or revising a Resolution and will instead focus on debating substantive issues. Don't get bogged down!

  - A Chairman should seek to pass Resolutions that advance his goals.

  - The Chairman can listen to advice from anyone about, and negotiate over, what a Resolution should say or which should be presented, but not in a public session. He alone decides what to vote on. He may solicit draft language for Resolutions, but he is under no obligation to use anything submitted to him, even if he agreed to do so.

  - Chairmen can make deals on what his two proposed Resolutions say in order to secure votes. Brokering what a Resolution will say is okay, but again this needs to be done in private or semiprivate or during the Meeting's Social Hours. Making deals is practical and prudent, but needs to be done privately.

- Chairmen can alter the wording of a proposed Resolution any time before voting, provided the changes are clearly made and announced to all (for example, erased or rewritten on the board or screen).

- Each Resolution must be written; if it's not written, it is not a Resolution and can't be voted on.

- Resolutions that pass are public declarations of the opinion of the people at the Meeting. They have no force of law. But public declarations of voluntary bodies greatly influence Americans' opinions and behavior.

- Resolutions affect the reputations of characters in the game and reputations matter greatly to everyone in nineteenth-century America.

• Passed Resolutions, and how they are passed, largely determine who wins the game, for Factions and Independents alike.

3. The Rule of the Podium (the Right to Speak)

Everyone standing in line at the podium has the right to speak, when it is his or her turn: this is the Rule of the Podium.

• Everybody has the obligation to speak in character, multiple times.

• It is not the Chairman's job to arrange for you to speak: that's your responsibility. Prepare a speech and go to the podium and give it. Go to the podium to speak informally as well. Gather your thoughts, stand at the podium, and proclaim your truth!

• The Chairman has no power to bar you from going to the podium or to stop you from speaking, once you're at the front of the line. He may try to do so, but don't let him—know your rights under the rules.

• Coordinate the topics and timing of your speech with your Faction or other characters. Do so as well with the Chairman if he's friendly to your character and objectives, but expect him to be obstructive, if he's not.

• *You need to speak!* This right cannot be denied by the Chairman, even if he wants to deny it. Assert your right to speak—go to the podium!

• The Chairman's power to run the Meeting and to try to select speakers as he sees fit is trumped by the simple act of standing in line at the podium.

• However, the Chairman can limit speakers' time, when there are time pressures, as when there is a long line at the podium and class is about to end.

• The podium is the most powerful position in the room.

4. Questions and Answers Must Be Voiced

Speakers should expect questions from the floor, and, in fact, *must* get at least one question, which must then be addressed. During an age when oratory is greatly valued, it is a serious insult for the speaker to get no questions. It would mean that the speaker is deemed dull and his or her comments too useless to be noticed by either opponents or allies.

- Ask friendly questions of your allies and pointed, difficult ones of your opponents! The Q&A period must, like the speeches, be entirely in character.

- Generally, in all Meetings, the Chairman should encourage questions from the floor since dialogue contributes to the one goal everybody shares—to have a lively, dynamic experience with this game.

- Questions should pertain to what the speaker has said.

- Everybody in the class should plan and be ready to ask questions, in character and frequently; **doing so is a required activity**.

- Factions can plan for their own members to do an effective Q&A.

- Independent players can use questions and answers to reveal their concerns, to seek support, and to do favors for others.

- Often, asking good questions can earn "Intellectual Capital" (see page 67 in this game book).

5. No Abandonment of Character or Core Goals

Factions and all characters have core goals and essential principles that cannot be abandoned or repudiated during the game. Rather, they must be understood, acted on, pursued, and advocated for persuasively.

- Compromising on core goals or acting contrary to your character (abandonment) will lead to defeat for you and possibly for your Faction too.

- Abandonment will be judged by the Gamemaster and can result in any consequence that the GM deems fitting.

- Abandonment can result in the sudden death of a character (for instance, if Daniel Webster endorses abolitionism, he dies: such an endorsement would not be even remotely true to Webster).

- Passivity or inattention can also be construed as abandonment. If the GM issues a warning about abandonment, take heed!

- To avoid failing by abandonment, immerse yourself in your role, master his or her identity and beliefs, and pursue your character's objectives. Advocate your character's beliefs!

6. The Chairman Must Publicly Appoint a Deputy Chairman

The Chairman appoints a Deputy to act as Chairman if the Chairman is absent or late or resigns. In such cases, Deputy acts with the full powers of the Chairman.

- If both the Chairman and Deputy are absent on the same day, Factions may *ask* the Gamemaster to appoint a Faction member as Deputy; the GM will respond in a way that is best for the overall play of the game.

- The GM can appoint a new Chairman for any reason, anytime.

7. Nobody Can Say the n Word

Nobody can say the n word, the most hateful, racist word in American English. It was often used in the nineteenth century, but it cannot be used in this game. Classmates play this game and compete with one another in character, to advance their characters' intellectual goals. Students often must articulate nineteenth-century ideas quite opposed by students and all decent people today. Students can and do compete intellectually in this game while being respectful to their classmates, even while criticizing the beliefs and goals of opposing characters. Any use of the n word risks harming that respectful behavior. The word's power is entirely emotional, not intellectual. All characters in this game have strong, serious intellectual arguments to make. Make them! Don't personalize criticism of some nineteenth-century idea by making a personalized attack on a classmate; instead, discredit the *ideas* your character objects to. If you ever feel that a classmate has personalized issues of the game into hostility, please quickly speak to your instructor in private.

8. No Disruption of the Play of the Game by Comments Made Out of Character

Players must stay in character during the play of the game (including any Social Hours). Questions about the structure and rules of the game must be asked when the game is not in session. Do not break the pace of the game. Doing so usually shows a lack of preparation. Paying attention to what's going on, and being part of it, is required; breaking character disrupts this. Understand that your Gamemaster needs to pay attention to what's happening in the game, rather than holding private communications while the game is under way.

9. Everybody Must Actively Remain in the Game

You must continue to actively play the game, even if you think you've accomplished your objectives. Not doing so constitutes abandonment (see Rule 5).

10. The Gamemaster May Announce and Enforce New Rules

If the GM introduces new rules, they are binding. Not all the rules in a Reacting game can be made known in advance because some govern situations that only rarely arise. Additional rules or procedures, as outlined by the GM, cannot be disputed during class time because that will take away from the play of the game. Such questions can be discussed later. The GM's job is to increase the quality of the play of the game to enhance learning. The GM may give suggestions or direction to anyone in the game, when doing so benefits the educational purposes of the game.

> **NOTE**
>
> These rules apply for each Meeting of the game.

WHAT YOU NEED TO KNOW BEYOND THE RULES

- Reacting to the Past games mimic real life: greater effort and achievement are rewarded far more than minimal effort and meager achievement.

- Trying to do new things is wise and correlates with success. It's less risky to try to do too much than doing too little. Being bold, well prepared, and active in the game tends to predict success in life and in Reacting games.

- It's to your advantage to know the rules of the game and to figure out how best to use them for your character's objectives.

- Passive behavior is rarely a route to victory. Intense, creative concentration on the situation of the game and its possibilities is recommended and is well within your capacities. For instance, if your role allows you to undertake an Extraordinary Game Action (discussed later in this game book), note that it's an opportunity unique to your role (or to you and a few others). Such an action carries risks and requires work but also offers you a chance to excel.

- If you actively seek to advance your character's goals, if you get to know all the other characters in the game, and if you understand the rules and devise strategies to use them, you should find victory during your excursion into the United States in July 1845.

MAJOR ISSUES FOR DEBATE

The central intellectual clash, the conflict in beliefs, that drive this game (and also drove American society in the antebellum era) are the grounds on which many Americans accepted and defended slavery and others came to reject it, seeking its end. This clash was reflected in the *Narrative of Frederick Douglass*; the proslavery political theories of John C. Calhoun; and how the Constitution was upheld because of, and denounced for, its proslavery provisions.

The clash between defenders of slavery and white supremacy, on the one hand, and advocates of equality, on the other, is the central, defining conflict of all of American history. Many believe that it remains the central conflict in the United States today. This has *never* been a simple one-dimensional conflict. But exploring its history is vital for any comprehension of the country.

The game has *three Meetings* devoted to the discussion of these topics, but slavery gave rise to conflicts in many, many other areas as well. For example, was the Christian religion truly in support of or opposed to slavery? Douglass's *Narrative* addresses Christianity many times, but his viewpoint was not shared by most Americans. Religion-based arguments are relevant to the game's first Meeting, marginally relevant to the second Meeting, and peripheral to the third Meeting. So arguments you make in the first Meeting cannot simply be repeated for the next two.

In addition, these discussions are informed by contested views of Thomas Jefferson. Jefferson died in 1826, but thoughts on what he did, wrote, and believed are vital to American concepts of race and slavery and democracy. Even now, two centuries after Jefferson's death, Americans still debate what the "true" Jefferson believed, and these disputes were already taking place in the 1840s.

Each Meeting of the game has its own focus of discussion. Thus what you argue in one should not be identical to what was argued in any previous Meeting. The issues of the game are huge and complex. If you just repeat yourself, you've ducked the intricacies of the topics. Confront, don't duck!

WINNING THE GAME

This game has two types of victory: personal and factional.

Factional victory goes to the Faction that most fully advances its goals, most ably achieves its objectives, and avoids any taint of having endorsed the other side's goals. *Factional victory is largely defined by the net outcome of the game's six votes.* A Faction wins by preserving and clearly articulating its core values, relentlessly pushing its truths forward without compromise, and winning

WARNING ! *If you achieve your personal victory objectives early in the game and then cease being active, your personal victory is void. Avoid abandonment (see Rule 5 earlier in this game book).*

support from Independent characters. A draw between Factions is possible. Only one Faction can win outright.

Personal victory can be earned by individuals who are deeply engaged in their characters and who achieve the objectives specified in their role sheet or who strive mightily to do so, even if ultimately unsuccessful. *Personal victory objectives* are detailed in the individual role sheets and vary greatly between characters; they are especially important for Independent characters. If you articulate your character's viewpoint well, you are on the path to winning a personal victory.

A *double victory* is winning both a personal and a factional victory. Be aware that your personal objectives may conflict with your Faction's goals. Independents cannot of course win a Faction victory or a double victory.

Resolutions and Winning

The most important way of judging which Faction wins the game is the content of the six Resolutions brought to vote during the game and which ones pass and in what fashion. Passing Resolutions that affirm a Faction's core principles is imperative for winning the game. Likewise, defeating Resolutions attacking core beliefs is imperative. The content of Resolutions can also be vital for Independents.

In addition to assessing the passed Resolutions, the GM will consider the following:

- Which Faction's interests were advanced by the Resolutions that passed?

- Did either Faction abandon core values to secure Resolutions?

- Did a Faction neglect opportunities to affirm its core values to focus on more popular, but marginal goals?

- Did any Resolutions pass with a supermajority?

- Which Faction most ably argued for its core values in the run up to the vote?

- Did Independents provide compelling justifications for their alignment with a Faction and for their votes?

- Which Chairman most successfully wrote Resolutions that stated his own views while also incorporating the concerns of notable Independent characters—and got them passed in an impressive way?

The two Factions are usually well balanced against one another, so the competition should be tight. Victory is likely to depend on who has the best grasp of the historical materials, understands all the objectives of the Independents, and knows the game rules. Without good teamwork a Faction is likely to lose.

WHAT IS AT STAKE?

The game can be won or lost in a number of ways, but in no outcome is the slavery question ever resolved. That does not mean these discussions are unimportant. The antebellum clash of conflicting ideas about slavery and freedom had an extremely powerful role in the history of America. Fundamental issues were being disputed, and the game mimics those fundamental disputes. Is slavery legitimate, or not? Are the Constitution and its proslavery provisions binding? Are they beneficial or evil? Is the country guilty of great sin? Are Black people equal to whites? Should women have a role in the public sphere? Do Blacks have any rights at all?

Whoever advances most in this struggle for intellectual influence wins the game, just as changes in American beliefs about these issues drove the nation's politics in the 1840s and 1850s. Nothing mattered more.

INDEPENDENTS AND PERSUASION

The two Factions in the game are irreconcilable. One group wants to protect and continue slavery, while the other seeks to abolish it immediately. For one side to advance, the other side must be set back! Neither Faction, if true to its values, is ever willing to compromise on any fundamental belief or major goal. Factions achieve victory by persuading Independents to vote for Resolutions, not by capitulating to their mortal foes in the other Faction.

Generally, Independent characters have more power if they don't quickly align with a Faction. They should instead begin right away to make their objectives known and seek support for them. They can do this privately or publicly, as the student chooses.

> **TIP**
>
> Persuasion is the key to victory for both Factions and Independents.

Much of the American population in 1845 was independent on the issue of slavery. The principles of Abolitionists and proslavery ideologues alike were not compelling ideas to many. There were a number of factors that made it difficult for citizens to align with one camp or another. Many people then took positions they thought suited their own situations; others saw slavery as a fact of life and entertained no ideas of transforming their world into something radically different: a world without slavery. In this game, all roles are unique, and each student with an Independent role defines his or her own relationship to the struggle between the Factions, based on what the student sees as most promising for his or her character.

Further, Independent roles often have objectives vital to them but not related to the core goals of one or all Factions. This provides many Independents with room to compromise and make deals. The actions, votes, and statements coming from the Independents will probably in large measure decide which Faction wins the game; no Faction can win without the support of Independents.

The individual goals of most Independents are not easily aligned with either Faction's goals. Most Independents won't readily or even ever pick a side, but there are several points on which most but not all Independent characters might ally with a Faction, if a mutually agreeable understanding can be reached.

EXTRAORDINARY GAME ACTIONS

Many characters have the potential to engage in an additional kind of game play, called *Extraordinary Game Actions* (EGAs). Most EGAs can be initiated **only by players whose role sheets discuss them** (and only under certain conditions). Some EGAs are briefly listed here, but no further details can be disclosed (unless you're recruited to participate) until and if an EGA is begun.

- Recovering property (that is, an abduction)

- Raising the flag

- Invoking the New York State personal liberty law

- Sparking an anti-Abolitionist riot

- Burning the Constitution

- Retribution through violence

- Publishing a newspaper (all newspapermen and editors eligible)

- Doing science (Dr. Morton, please!)

- An excursion for two to Milledgeville, Georgia

- Proclaiming "liberty throughout the land"/ringing the Liberty Bell

- Choir performance

- Parades with a cause

Some EGAs can be initiated by any character or group of characters in the game, including many of those listed here as well as others that students imagine and create on their own. Talk to the Gamemaster privately.

OPTIONAL GAME ELEMENTS

Lottery of Bad Luck: Risk of Character Death

This feature is used in some classes but not all; this is up to your GM.

This game is set in antebellum America, when risks from illness and other sources of harm were widespread and unpredictable. People often suddenly died or became ill. The germ theory of disease—the key insight of modern medicine—did not exist in 1845. Life expectancy in the middle of the nineteenth century in the United States was under forty years. Healthcare was risky: whether doctors helped patients regain health or hastened their deaths was uncertain. The game mimics this aspect of American life in the antebellum era with a *Lottery of Bad Luck* held one or more times during the game.

The timing of the lottery is determined by the GM. Everyone's name is entered. Absent players have their names entered four or more times. The GM may opt to enter the names of characters who had not shown a grasp of the assigned readings multiple times. At each drawing, one or more names are drawn.

- If your name is drawn but you have $100 in Intellectual Capital (see the following section), you may cash it in, to minimize your illness. In this case, you become quite ill with a violently upset stomach and cannot speak with ease for some of that day's class due to vomiting. You will, however, recover fully by the next session and are otherwise okay.

- If you have $200 in Intellectual Capital, you may spend it. In this case, there is no detrimental effect.

- If you have no Intellectual Capital, your character dies painfully after vomiting black bile; but you may give a spur-of-the-moment deathbed speech. The GM will provide you with a new role.

Intellectual Capital: Its Value and Acquiring It

This feature is used in some classes but not all; this is up to your GM.

Intellectual Capital reduces the risks of dying in the Lottery of Bad Luck (see the previous section). Dying rarely helps one achieve one's objectives.

Further, players who earn Intellectual Capital have a greater capacity to defend themselves against EGAs launched by other players, and Intellectual Capital strengthens your own EGAs.

Intellectual achievements in the game produce Intellectual Capital. Do well on the pregame exam on the Douglass book and the Constitution, give good speeches, write good papers, show mastery of the readings, initiate worthy events in the game, and interrogate your classmates seriously and in a nineteenth-century way. Doing these things may yield awards of Intellectual Capital. Usually, it is awarded in private conversation or by note or email or just in the GM's records. Intellectual Capital is represented by $100 bank notes or simply by the GM's own records. Bank notes can also be used to show that your bank will honor a signed note from you.

BASIC OUTLINE OF THE GAME

The game takes place in three separate Meetings, imagined to occur during roughly one week in early July 1845, at three places, which are all within a few blocks of one another in New York City. Each Meeting will likely run for more than one meeting of the class. Each of the three game Meetings end immediately after its second vote.

MEETING I

LITERARY FORUM AT THE ASTOR HOUSE HOTEL

NOTE

The rules of the game apply during this and all Meetings.

The first Meeting is a Literary Forum to critique or present reactions to Douglass's recently published *Narrative*. The forum is chaired by Charles Dickens, the beloved English author and huge celebrity. Each character, each student in the game, needs to articulate his or her views, in the character's voice, on Douglass's book.

Written Assignment: articulate your character's view of Douglass's *Narrative*.

Before the first Meeting is over, deliver a critique of Douglass's *Narrative*, from the point of view of your role (unless your role sheet or GM says otherwise). This piece can also draw on other documents in this game book. You should explore the arguments made by Douglass and evaluate them from the viewpoint of your role. This assignment should prove that you

- Have read Douglass's *Narrative* and understand it.

- Understand and can articulate your character's goals.

- Can analyze Douglass from your character's viewpoint.

Complete this assignment by delivering a written version of your speech or a copy of your publication or broadsheet to the GM by the end of the first Meeting. And to influence your classmates' characters' actions in the game, it should also be posted, given, or "published" and distributed in the classroom in some fashion.

Social Hour

The Chairman or the GM may set aside some time for the characters to talk casually with one another. Stay in

NOTE

Female characters in need of honest work for very good wages should talk to Dickens.

character and remember much important business can be conducted in this informal Social Hour.

Resolutions

The Chairman must call for a vote on two Resolutions. The Meeting ends immediately after the second vote.

MEETING II

BANQUET HONORING CALHOUN AT DELMONICO'S

The second Meeting is a banquet in honor of South Carolina Senator John C. Calhoun, held at Delmonico's, the most exclusive restaurant in New York City, if not the whole country. The banquet is hosted by the leading men of commerce of New York City, and you can expect Samuel F. B. Morse to be the Chairman.

During the banquet Calhoun will give a speech explaining his "positive good" view of slavery. The hosts expect that guests—all members of the national elite and men of property and standing—will also want to speak, presenting views that more or less agree with the senator.

Whether the hosts like it or not, *all players manage to attend the Delmonico banquet.* (If uninvited, show up for class and crash the party; use the Rule of the Podium to claim your right to speak.)

NOTE

The rules of the game apply during this and all Meetings.

TIP

Remember the Rule of the Podium, even if the Chairman wants it forgotten.

Written Assignment: response to Calhoun's "Slavery as a Positive Good" viewpoint.

During the second Meeting your character must respond to Calhoun's views of slavery, which will be expressed in his speech at the banquet and in the following core texts (reprinted in this game book):

- "South Carolina Resolutions on Abolitionist Propaganda" (page 132)

- "Slavery as a Positive Good" (page 134)

- "Remarks Made during the Debate on His Resolutions, in Respect to the Rights of the States and Abolition of Slavery" (page 140)

- "Draft Remarks for Future Speech" (page 149)

See also

- "Review of the Debate in the Virginia Legislature of 1831 and 1832" (page 124)

Complete this assignment by delivering a written version of your speech or a copy of your publication or broadsheet to the GM by the end of the second Meeting. And to influence your classmates' characters' actions in the game, it should also be posted, given, or "published" and distributed in the classroom in some fashion.

Social Hour

The Chairman or the GM may set aside some time for the characters to talk casually with one another. Stay in character and remember much important business can be conducted in this informal Social Hour.

Extraordinary Game Actions

EGAs become possible at the beginning of the second Meeting. Be prepared! Eternal vigilance is the price of liberty, no matter who defines *liberty*.

Challenge to Debate the Constitution (to be made at Delmonico's): At some point during the second Meeting, Abolitionists *must* challenge the Status Quo Faction to a public debate on the Constitution and slavery; if they fail to do so, the Abolitionist Faction has lost the game. If the challenge is appropriately issued, no southern gentleman could decline without losing honor and thus the game. The challenge must

- Be made after Calhoun's speech but before the Meeting ends.

- Declare that Calhoun and other proslavery men must meet Abolitionists at the Broadway Tabernacle Church to debate the "sinfulness of the Constitution" or "prove yourselves to be cowards" by refusing (or similar words).

- Be forcefully spoken before the whole crowd.

- Include a quick condemnation of the Constitution's sinful complicity with slavery.

- Be "seconded" immediately after it is made by a second Abolitionist, who rises to call on the slaveholders to

WARNING ! *If the challenge isn't issued or if it is made weakly, instead of in a firm, attention-getting style, the game ends and the Abolitionists lose.*

"accept the challenge, or to concede that slavery as well as the Constitution is false to God and Man," or words to that affect.

If issued, the challenge must be immediately accepted by Calhoun and his allies. If they fail to do so, the Status Quo Faction has lost the game.

WARNING ! *If the challenge is issued, but it is not immediately and forcefully accepted by the Status Quo Faction, the game ends and the Abolitionists win.*

Resolutions

The Chairman must call for a vote on two Resolutions. The Meeting ends immediately after the second vote.

MEETING III

DEBATE AT THE BROADWAY TABERNACLE CHURCH

The third Meeting is a debate on the Constitution, hosted by the Abolitionists. The debate is held at the Broadway Tabernacle Church, which was built in 1836 on Broadway, between Worth Street and Catherine Lane. It can hold twenty-four hundred people and will be packed for this debate, largely by Abolitionists and their sympathizers. Since the Abolitionists uphold freedom of speech, no Abolitionist Chairman is likely to exclude anyone from voting. Abolitionists believe the cause of emancipation is advanced by open, unfettered discussion and cannot violate their belief in free debate without risking abandonment.

WARNING ! *Do not merely repeat contemporary platitudes about the Constitution; the Constitution itself and Americans' understandings of it have changed greatly over the generations. No platitude from today is going to be correct for 1845. You need to comprehend the Constitution of 1845! Study!*

Written Assignment: relevance of the Constitution to the slavery question.

During the third Meeting you need to express your character's views on the debate question. If you're a Faction member, give a detailed, passionate, analytical speech—or produce a broadside or written appeal—on the relevance of the Constitution to the slavery question from your character's viewpoint. If you're an *Abolitionist*, understand you are not a nationalist, so don't base your ideas on American nationalism or on the Constitution; instead, you act under a "higher law," which trumps the sinful Constitution. If you're a *Status Quo* Faction member, you must explain how the authors of the Constitution accepted slavery and gave

TIP

Cite, quote, and discuss *specific* slavery-related sections of the Constitution.

NOTE

The rules of the game apply during this and all Meetings.

it constitutional sanction and show why this is a good thing. Explain how the Constitution binds all Americans to preserve the peculiar institution. If you're an *Independent*, forge arguments that advance your objectives in the context of the Constitution.

Complete this assignment by delivering a written version of your speech or a copy of your publication or broadsheet to the GM by the end of the third Meeting. And to influence your class-mates' characters' actions in the game, it should also be posted, given, or "published" and distributed in the classroom in some fashion.

Pop Quiz on the Constitution

Sometime during this Meeting, the GM may distribute a quiz. This is an out-of-character intermission. No advance notice other than this statement will be provided. Your quiz performance may affect both your grade and power in the game. Prudent students will study the Constitution carefully and learn enough to be able to quickly describe the three major provisions of the Constitution that deal directly with slavery, explaining what each did in three cogent paragraphs. Students should also be able to explain how slavery is discussed in the Constitution even though the Constitution never used the words *slavery* or *slaves*.

> **NOTE**
>
> Martin Van Buren may successfully form a third Faction, known as the Free Soil for White Men. If this happens, a fourth Meeting—A Mass Meeting for Free Soil for White Men Party—may be held at New York's Tammany Hall. In some cases, the Free Soil Faction diminishes the Broadway Tabernacle debate or may replace it with its own Meeting. This would be a serious defeat for the Abolitionists and a great achievement for the racist, antislavery, white majority in the North.

Social Hour

The Chairman or the GM may set aside some time for the characters to talk casually with one another. Stay in character and remember much important business can be conducted in this informal Social Hour. Remember that the debate is being held in a church. In the nineteenth century, Americans would not serve or consume any food or drink in a church. Further, as the Broadway Tabernacle is a church, it is inconceivable that you or any other nineteenth-century American would drink whiskey, smoke cigars, or chew tobacco during the Broadway Tabernacle Meeting.

Extraordinary Game Actions

EGAs may occur during the debate. Players should realize that the several thousand Abolitionists in the church may affect how any EGA plays out . . . as might a mob of anti-Abolitionists outside, if such a mob gathers.

Resolutions

The Chairman must call for a vote on two Resolutions. The Meeting ends immediately after the second vote.

FORMAL GAME ASSIGNMENTS

During each of the three game Meetings, all students must deliver at least one piece of work to be graded, before that Meeting ends. Each should address the topic of the Meeting for which it is written and should advance your character's objectives as well as your character's general aim of becoming well-known, respected, and influential. All written and spoken work for the game should focus on persuading people in New York in 1845.

Every student in the game must submit at least one assignment during each of the game's three Meetings. Each and every one of these assignments needs to be in the voice of your assigned character. There are three different types of assignments:

- **A formal speech delivered from the podium.** The default length is two to three minutes, but your GM may alter this.

- **A publication aimed at influencing other players.** This could be a pamphlet, a letter to the editor of a New York newspaper, a newspaper or a newspaper story, or another form of publication. You must figure out how to disseminate your publication to other players.

- **A broadside.** This is a promotional poster that includes both images and writing and should articulate your character's beliefs in both media. Tape it to the wall of your classroom. Design it so that it is easy to read. Include intriguing visuals that will draw people to it. Make it as much as possible resemble broadsides from the antebellum era. (Photographs cannot yet be printed; engravings can.)

NOTE

The other students in the class are your primary audience and they should be your target audience. But your instructor may also have certain expectations beyond what's explained in your role sheet and this game book. If so, listen to his or her instructions!

TIP

You can also do more than three assignments! Completing additional assignments will benefit your grade and your game objectives.

INFORMAL COMMENTS

TIP

Spur-of-the-moment comments are excellent opportunities to ask questions. They may also impress Independent players who admire quick wit.

Every player should **make at least two informal comments in the course of the game**. They should respond to more formal comments made by other players. They need not be based on a written text and can last as long as you like. Informal comments can be spontaneous, whereas the formal speeches need to be planned and practiced.

 PART 4: FACTIONS AND ROLES

This section of the game book lists the available characters for the game. More are in the Appendix. Most instructors welcome requests from students for specific roles but can make no promise in advance of granting such requests. Many more characters exist for this game than will be assigned for your class, unless you're in a large class.

Roles with proper names (a first name and a last name) represent people who really lived, with the exception of David Walker Jr., the sole fictional character with a proper name. Students may wish to research their roles, but take care to avoid introducing anachronistic elements; this entire game takes place in July 1845.

Characters who are given descriptive names (for example, the True Jeffersonian and the Whiskey Dealer) instead of proper names are composite characters. They represent ideas and social types from the era, not a specific person. Students with these roles may create a plausible name for their character.

FACTIONS

There are two Factions: *Abolitionists* and the proslavery *Status Quo* Faction. Roles in the same Faction are united by common goals. Faction members should pursue their common goals with determination and coordinated teamwork.

Conflicts within Factions may be healthy; some may be unavoidable. No Faction is homogenous. A few Faction members have only weak loyalty to the Faction's core principles, and that may create a perception of betrayal. This possibility, however remote, suggests that other Faction members may seek to police their Faction to encourage loyalty and teamwork. Factions are likely to either win or lose the game, together, based on the total effort and effectiveness of the group as a whole.

> **TIP**
>
> If you're a Faction member, seek out Independents who you can assist without betraying any of your core beliefs.

> **TIP**
>
> If you're a member of a Faction, work with your Faction mates, learn your common goals, and actively work to pursue those goals.

Abolitionist Faction

The internal history of the Abolitionist Movement involved much factionalism and rivalry over tactics, strategy, and personality, despite the common goal of abolishing slavery. In this game, these intramovement differences are largely omitted to allow students to focus on the overarching objectives that united all Abolitionists: the immediate, universal emancipation of all slaves, with no compensation to slaveholders. In this game, Garrisonian Abolitionists make up most of the Abolitionist Faction, although Garrison had increasingly faced opposition, after 1840, from other Abolitionists. Garrison and his adherents were opposed to participating in the political system (since it was entangled with the Slave Power), opposed all forms of violence, and affirmed that moral suasion and truth telling were the most effective means for advancing emancipation. Garrison denounced the Constitution and the United States itself as corrupt at its very core, by the power of slaveholders; he advocated disunionism, which he imagined would be the departure of the free states from the union of slavery. Garrisonians opposed voting, as a capitulation to an oppressive system.

In 1845, Douglass was still a Garrisonian and most Abolitionists in this game are too. But other Abolitionists increasingly saw American elections as a way to raise sympathy for abolition and argued that the Constitution was correctly interpreted as antislavery. James G. Birney, Asa Mahn, and Joshua Leavitt are characters in the game who held these anti-Garrisonian views by 1845. Further, some Abolitionists, confronted with the ineffectiveness of moral arguments, came to look favorably on violence as a useful weapon for emancipation. African Americans like Henry Highland Garnet and David Walker forcefully articulated this liberating violence.

William Lloyd Garrison founded immediate abolitionism and the *Liberator* newspaper in 1831. His earliest and strongest support came from free people of color in the North. He rejects participating in elections as inherently corrupting and advocates disunionism, as do most Abolitionists you're likely to meet in July 1845. (For more on his ideas, see pages 123 and 128 in this game book.)

Frederick Douglass, the Abolitionist fugitive from Maryland, is a gifted orator and the author of *Narrative of the Life of Frederick Douglass*, published six weeks ago.

Sojourner Truth, a former slave from New York's Hudson Valley, is a traveling evangelical Christian, an illiterate preacher who can recite most Scriptures from memory. She is devoted to God, condemns sinfulness, and expects Judgment soon.

Mr. Barlett Shanklyn of Nova Scotia courageously led an escape from Virginia enslavers to a British warship during the War of 1812. He is a skilled blacksmith and a loyal subject of the British Empire, which stands for the liberty of all men.

A fugitive slave or two, who seek freedom for themselves and all mankind.

James Covey, a young Mende from West Africa, was captured by slave traders, and then liberated by the Royal Navy. He joined the Royal Navy, serving in the squadron suppressing the African slave trade. This brought him to New York, where he was recruited as a translator for the *Amistad* rebels.

Elizabeth Cady Stanton is a young mother of a growing family and a devoted Abolitionist, like her husband. She lives in Seneca Falls, New York.

Charles G. Finney, a Christian theologian and the most influential evangelical of the era; he sees the sin of slavery as an affront to God. He was the founding pastor for the Broadway Tabernacle.

Angelina Grimké, the sister of Sarah, likewise rejected her family's slaveholding values of the Carolina ruling class, joined and left the Society of Friends, became an Abolitionist, and asserted the rights of women to speak publicly. She is married to Abolitionist Theodore Weld.

The Status Quo Faction (aka the Proslavery Faction)

Most Americans of the antebellum era accepted slavery as an essential part of American society; after all, it had been so since well before the American Revolution. But the rise of immediate abolitionism after 1831 inspired many slaveholders to articulate an elaborate proslavery argument, and these proslavery ideologues (like Thomas Dew) make up a portion of the Status Quo Faction. Other variants of the proslavery ideology stressed the biblically sanctioned, ordained by God, nature of slavery; this was a common view of clergymen in the South, but Calvinist versions of this proslavery Christianity were also expressed by Yankees like Samuel Morse. Southern politicians stressed the necessity of slavery to the South's way of life, their confidence in the supremacy of the white race, and the protection for slavery provided by the framers of the Constitution. Countless northerners accepted slavery as an unavoidable fact of life, if not also a benefit to the supreme white race. Other Yankees understood that southern slavery was directly tied to their own accumulation of wealth. What unites this Faction is its very American devotion, in 1845, to slavery and all that it provides in American life. All the types of proslavery views laid out in the game book, and more, are represented through the characters in this Faction. Some members in this Faction see slavery as a positive good; others see it as an unavoidable evil. But all members of the Faction, like the national majority in 1845, accept both slavery and white supremacy and oppose all steps that might weaken either.

Senator John C. Calhoun of South Carolina, the chief proponent of the positive good view of slavery, is the leading ideologue of southern rights. His theories justify secession if slavery is endangered within the United States. (For more on his ideas, see pages 134, 140, 142, and 149 in this game book.) As a young man, he was a nationalist, but dropped that long ago.

Samuel F. B. Morse of New York City, currently devotes himself to converting his invention, the telegraph, into a grand business enterprise but is also a noted painter and deep thinker on religion and ethnicity. He sees slavery as no more inherently sinful than any other human institution and affirms the nation's Constitution.

The True Jeffersonian is a Virginia planter who upholds all the beliefs of the great Thomas Jefferson and asserts Jefferson's enduring value for all Americans. He sees slaveholding as a regrettable obligation, not a positive good. (For more on his ideas, see Thomas Jefferson's writings, page 88 in this game book.)

Senator Henry Clay of Kentucky, the Great Compromiser of American politics and a rich plantation owner, advocates for Colonization of freed slaves from America to Africa. He was nearly elected president last year, in 1844, as the Whig nominee, but was thwarted by the Liberty Party's "political Abolitionists," who got the Democrat James Polk elected.

Robert E. Lee of Virginia is an officer in the U.S. Army, currently stationed in Brooklyn, New York.

The Ambitious Georgian, a young man from the cotton plantations of Georgia, defends slavery as a force of civilization, prosperity, and progress.

Thomas R. Dew, president of the College of William and Mary, is one of the first and most articulate defenders of slavery, which needed no defense before the Abolitionist onslaught of the 1830s. (See page 124 in this game book.)

Sophia Auld, wife of Hugh Auld, is the woman who first taught Frederick Bailey to read and write, when Frederick lived in her home.

Colonel Edward Lloyd VI of the eastern shore of Maryland is the current head of the noted Lloyd family, which has owned land and hundreds of slaves for centuries in Maryland, including the farm on which Frederick was born in 1819.

Austin Woolfolk, the noted Baltimore slave trader, is the man to see when you want to buy or sell slaves in the Chesapeake Bay region or ship them to the Gulf.

James Brown heads the New York office of the international Brown Brothers firm.

Daniel Ladd, a prosperous factor from Newport, Florida, is visiting New York on business.

Independents

TIP

Faction members should seek arrangements of mutual advantage with as many individual Independents as possible.

The Factions compete with each other for credibility among and the support of the third major group: the Independent characters. Independents represent about one-third of the players; they hold the balance of power.

Unlike members of Factions, Independents are not members of a team; most do not start the game with a fixed position in favor of slavery or abolition. Instead, they have their own distinct goals. In most cases, they need to gain the aid of members of Factions and other Independents to achieve these goals.

To align with either Faction, Independents must articulate why that choice makes sense in reference to their character's values and goals. Consequently, Factions should try to pitch their ideas in ways that appeal to as many Independents as possible.

TIP

Faction members should listen carefully in order to learn differences between Independents. What's good for one Independent can be bad for another.

Charles Dickens, the greatest living writer in the world, is beloved on both sides of the Atlantic by millions of readers. On this second visit to the United States, his fame is unequaled by any other private citizen of the century. Nearly everybody who is anybody wants to associate with the beloved author.

Senator Daniel Webster of Massachusetts, one of the country's great statesmen and a great lawyer, is a Whig, a nationalist, and a defender of property rights. He upholds "Liberty and Union, Now and Forever, One and Inseparable." He says the return of all runaway slaves is the compelling duty of all Americans.

The Son of New Orleans is a young man now working as a clerk to a furnishing merchant in New York; he attended Harvard College at his New England mother's behest but grew up in New Orleans, where his father is engaged in business.

Edgar Allan Poe, a writer, was raised in Virginia but currently living in New York, whose poem "The Raven" has been widely noticed since its publication early this year. He hopes for enduring literary fame and possesses a unique style.

Neal Dow of Maine, a temperance advocate, sees the drinking of alcohol as the primary sin, the cause of all of society's problems. He scorns drinkers and pushes prohibition.

The Whiskey Dealer owns a drinking establishment (a grog shop) in the city; has ambitions of becoming a distiller; and is a hearty, warm, generous, welcoming fellow.

John Quincy Adams, member of Congress, is the former president whose public career includes, most recently, a seven-year fight against southern interests and their Gag Rule in the House of Representatives, which banned any discussion of Abolitionist petitions. He celebrates the repeal of the Gag Rule late last year with all advocates of free speech.

NOTE

Dave the Potter was a real man, obscure in 1845, but well known today as the brilliant creator of amazing pottery, prized by collectors and art museums.

The Daughter of Dave the Potter of South Carolina is a slave whose enslaved father is a little-known artist, Dave the Potter, a literate man and highly skilled artisan. She is in New York to serve her owner while that lady travels.

The Illinois Lawyer, in New York to conclude a settlement of tedious railroad litigation, is attending the three Meetings to meet famous people. He asserts the rule of law and the interests of whites in the west who object to both slavery and colored people.

L. L. Langstroth will become known as the father of American beekeeping; he invented a way to keep bees and collect their honey without killing the bees or destroying the hive. His Langstroth hive of moveable frames will soon become the basis for beekeeping worldwide. In the bees' social organization, he discerns God's model for harmony for mankind.

Walt Whitman, a former schoolteacher and current newspaperman, is confident that he will one day write poetry that will transform the literature of the world. Although a young man, he asks tough questions, probes contradictions, likes intelligent men, and soaks up the multitudes.

Martin Van Buren of New York State, the former president and longtime Democratic strategist, increasingly fears that his party is dominated by the slaveholding South. He abhors Abolitionists, but recognizes the growth of antislavery views in the North. A loyal Jacksonian, he loathes Calhoun's narrow sectionalism.

> ### NOTE
>
> Van Buren might form a third Faction, the Free Soil for White Men Faction, one that is both white supremacist and opposed to slavery's expansion.

P. T. Barnum, an entertainer, a self-promoter and an owner of "museums," aims to create the best and biggest circus ever. He loves a parade.

Washington Irving, the author of many beloved stories and the elder statesmen of American letters, knows virtually everything that is knowable and has been honored to hold diplomatic posts for the U.S. government. Known for his fiction, he also writes nonfiction filled with useful, patriotic bits of hidden make-believe.

David Wilmot, an ambitious Democratic politician from Pennsylvania, was elected to Congress last year and seeks to make a name for himself by curbing the threat to free white labor posed by slavery and its territorial expansion.

 PART 5: CORE DOCUMENTS

Passages in **bold** highlight statements especially important for this game. Documents are presented in order of their publication. Note that the last two documents were not in fact published by 1845, but they include ideas already influential by the time of the game. So advance *drafts* of these two documents have been made available to players to bring the clearest expression of these ideas into the game.

THOMAS JEFFERSON

Declaration of Independence, 1776

The Declaration of Independence was adopted by the Continental Congress, meeting in Philadelphia, in July 1776. It is perhaps the most famous of documents written during the American Revolution, though today, many of its Revolutionary principles are poorly understood in the United States. The chief author of the Declaration was Thomas Jefferson of Virginia, though not until about twenty years later was his authorship widely known. Jefferson may be the first American who embraced the Declaration's principles as abstractions but was unable to accept that the truly Revolutionary ideas of the Declaration apply, logically and morally, to all people. The Declaration famously proclaims that "all men are created equal" and possess "certain unalienable Rights," including "Life, Liberty and the pursuit of Happiness." It asserts that, if government becomes intolerantly oppressive, people have an inherent right to revolution. Nothing in the Declaration of Independence suggests that some people are unworthy of these rights; but Jefferson, a slaveholder, never recognized the rights of slaves to liberty or the pursuit of happiness and feared Virginia slaves might someday assert their right to revolt against all that oppressed them.

SOURCE: *U.S. Declaration of Independence, 1776.*

IN CONGRESS, JULY 4, 1776.

The unanimous Declaration of the thirteen united States of America,

*W*hen in the Course of human events, it becomes necessary for one people to dissolve the political bands which have connected them with another, and to assume among the powers of the earth, the separate and equal station to which the Laws of Nature and of Nature's God entitle them, a decent respect to the opinions of mankind requires that they should declare the causes which impel them to the separation.

We hold these truths to be self-evident, that all men are created equal, that they are endowed by their Creator with certain unalienable Rights, that among these are Life, Liberty and the pursuit of Happiness.——That to secure these rights, Governments are instituted among Men, deriving their just powers from the consent of the governed,——That whenever any Form of Government becomes destructive of these ends, it is the Right of the People to alter or to abolish it, and to institute new Government, laying its foundation on such principles and organizing its powers in such form, as to them shall seem most likely to effect their Safety and Happiness. Prudence, indeed, will dictate that Governments long established should not be changed for light and transient causes; and accordingly all experience hath shewn, that mankind are more disposed to suffer, while evils are sufferable, than to right themselves by abolishing the forms to which they are accustomed. But when a long train of abuses and usurpations, pursuing invariably the same Object evinces a design to reduce them under absolute Despotism, it is their right, it is their duty, to throw off such Government, and to provide new Guards for their future security.——Such has been the patient sufferance of these Colonies; and such is now the necessity which constrains them to alter their former Systems of Government. The history of the present King of Great Britain is a history of repeated injuries and usurpations, all having in direct object the establishment of an absolute Tyranny over these States. To prove this, let Facts be submitted to a candid world.

He has refused his Assent to Laws, the most wholesome and necessary for the public good.

He has forbidden his Governors to pass Laws of immediate and pressing importance, unless suspended in their operation till his Assent should be obtained; and when so suspended, he has utterly neglected to attend to them.

He has refused to pass other Laws for the accommodation of large districts of people, unless those people would relinquish the right of Representation in the Legislature, a right inestimable to them and formidable to tyrants only.

He has called together legislative bodies at places unusual, uncomfortable, and distant from the depository of their public Records, for the sole purpose of fatiguing them into compliance with his measures.

He has dissolved Representative Houses repeatedly, for opposing with manly firmness his invasions on the rights of the people.

He has refused for a long time, after such dissolutions, to cause others to be elected; whereby the Legislative powers, incapable of Annihilation, have returned to the People at large for their exercise; the State remaining in the mean time exposed to all the dangers of invasion from without, and convulsions within.

He has endeavoured to prevent the population of these States; for that purpose obstructing the Laws for Naturalization of Foreigners; refusing to pass others to encourage their migrations hither, and raising the conditions of new Appropriations of Lands.

He has obstructed the Administration of Justice, by refusing his Assent to Laws for establishing Judiciary powers.

He has made Judges dependent on his Will alone, for the tenure of their offices, and the amount and payment of their salaries.

He has erected a multitude of New Offices, and sent hither swarms of Officers to harrass our people, and eat out their substance.

He has kept among us, in times of peace, Standing Armies without the Consent of our legislatures.

He has affected to render the Military independent of and superior to the Civil power.

He has combined with others to subject us to a jurisdiction foreign to our constitution, and unacknowledged by our laws; giving his Assent to their Acts of pretended Legislation:

For Quartering large bodies of armed troops among us:

For protecting them, by a mock Trial, from punishment for any Murders which they should commit on the Inhabitants of these States:

For cutting off our Trade with all parts of the world:

For imposing Taxes on us without our Consent:

For depriving us in many cases, of the benefits of Trial by Jury:

For transporting us beyond Seas to be tried for pretended offences:

For abolishing the free System of English Laws in a neighbouring Province, establishing therein an Arbitrary government, and enlarging its Boundaries so as to render it at once an example and fit instrument for introducing the same absolute rule into these Colonies:

For taking away our Charters, abolishing our most valuable Laws, and altering fundamentally the Forms of our Governments:

For suspending our own Legislatures, and declaring themselves invested with power to legislate for us in all cases whatsoever.

He has abdicated Government here, by declaring us out of his Protection and waging War against us.

He has plundered our seas, ravaged our Coasts, burnt our towns, and destroyed the lives of our people.

He is at this time transporting large Armies of foreign Mercenaries to compleat the works of death, desolation and tyranny, already begun with circumstances of Cruelty & perfidy scarcely paralleled in the most barbarous ages, and totally unworthy the Head of a civilized nation.

He has constrained our fellow Citizens taken Captive on the high Seas to bear Arms against their Country, to become the executioners of their friends and Brethren, or to fall themselves by their Hands.

He has excited domestic insurrections amongst us, and has endeavoured to bring on the inhabitants of our frontiers, the merciless Indian Savages, whose known rule of warfare, is an undistinguished destruction of all ages, sexes and conditions.

In every stage of these Oppressions We have Petitioned for Redress in the most humble terms: Our repeated Petitions have been answered only by repeated injury. A Prince whose character is thus marked by every act which may define a Tyrant, is unfit to be the ruler of a free people.

Nor have We been wanting in attentions to our Brittish brethren. We have warned them from time to time of attempts by their legislature to extend an unwarrantable jurisdiction over us. We have reminded them of the circumstances of our emigration and settlement here. We have appealed to their native justice and magnanimity, and we have conjured them by the ties of our common kindred to disavow these usurpations, which, would inevitably interrupt our connections and correspondence. They too have been deaf to the voice of justice and of consanguinity. We must, therefore, acquiesce in the necessity, which denounces our Separation, and hold them, as we hold the rest of mankind, Enemies in War, in Peace Friends.

We, therefore, the Representatives of the united States of America, in General Congress, Assembled, appealing to the Supreme Judge of the world for the rectitude of our intentions, do, in the Name, and by Authority of the good People of these Colonies, solemnly publish and declare, That these United Colonies are, and of Right ought to be Free and Independent States; that they are Absolved from all Allegiance to the British Crown, and that all political connection between them and the State of Great Britain, is and ought to be totally dissolved; and that as Free and Independent States, they have full Power to levy War, conclude Peace, contract Alliances, establish Commerce, and to do all other Acts and Things which Independent States may of right do. And for the support of this Declaration, with a firm reliance on the protection of divine Providence, we mutually pledge to each other our Lives, our Fortunes and our sacred Honor.

THOMAS JEFFERSON

Notes on the State of Virginia, 1781

The excerpts printed here focus on Jefferson's observations on slavery, Blacks in Virginia, racial differences, and related subjects (such as Indians and agriculture). The following passages express some of the earliest and most influential American statements ever on slavery and race. They are taken up in later documents, especially in Walker's Appeal. *Jefferson wrote* Notes *as a series of answers to questions presented to him, as he explained in the prefatory comment opening the book.*

Most of Jefferson's comments in "Query XIV on the Laws of Virginia" are omitted. In the section included here, Jefferson is summarizing the recommendations of a "committee of revisors," of which he was a member, that worked during the Revolutionary War to update the laws of Virginia to fit the new republican state. The committee issued a report in 1779. Some of the committee's recommendations were enacted, but not any form of emancipation for Virginia's slaves. In the selection here Jefferson describes ideas he endorsed in 1779 but that did not become law; he also articulates some broader ideas about slavery and racial differences. Further, he describes an amendment "To emancipate all slaves born after passing the act," even though no such amendment was ever proposed. Arguably, his discussion of an emancipatory amendment, which could have been but was not proposed, was aimed more at enhancing his own stature as an enlightened thinker than it was an honest account of how his ostensibly pro-emancipation ideas got nowhere in 1779—or, for that matter, ever.

SOURCE: *Thomas Jefferson,* Notes on the State of Virginia *(Boston: Lilly and Wait, 1832).*

The following Notes were written in Virginia, in the year 1781, and somewhat corrected and enlarged in the winter of 1782, in answer to Queries proposed to the author, by a foreigner of distinction, then residing amongst us. The subjects are all treated imperfectly; some scarcely touched on. * * *

February 27, 1787.

* * *

Query VI.

A notice of the mines and other subterraneous riches; its trees, plants, fruits, &c?

* * *

* * * The same Indian women, when married to white traders, who feed them and their children plentifully and regularly, who exempt them from excessive drudgery, who keep them stationary and unexposed to accident, produce and raise as many children as the white women. Instances are known under these circumstances, of their rearing a dozen children.

An inhuman practice once prevailed in this country, of making slaves of the Indians. It is a fact well known with us, that the Indian women so enslaved produced and raised as numerous families as either the whites or blacks among whom they lived.

* * *

* * * I do not mean to deny, that there are varieties in the race of man, distinguished by their powers both of body and mind. I believe there are, as I see to be the case in the races of other animals.

* * *

Query XIV.

The administration of justice, and the description of the laws?

* * *

To emancipate all slaves born after passing the act. The bill reported by the revisors does not itself contain this proposition; but an amendment containing it was prepared, to be offered to the legislature whenever the bill should be taken up, and further directing, that they should continue with their parents to a certain age, then be brought up, at the public expense, to tillage, arts or sciences, according to their geniuses, till the females should be eighteen, and the males twenty-one years of age, when they should be colonized to such place as the circumstances of the time should render most proper, sending them out with arms, implements of household and of the handicraft arts, seeds, pairs of the useful domestic animals, &c. to declare them a free and independent people, and extend to them our alliance and protection, till they have acquired strength; and to send vessels at the same time to other parts of the world for an equal number of white inhabitants; to induce whom to migrate hither, proper encouragements were to be proposed. It will probably be asked, Why not retain and incorporate the blacks into the state, and thus save the expense of supplying by importation of white settlers, the vacancies they will leave? Deep rooted prejudices entertained by the whites; ten thousand recollections, by the blacks, of the injuries they have sustained; new provocations; the real distinctions which nature has made; and many other circumstances, will divide us into parties, and produce convulsions, which will probably never end but in the extermination of the one or the other race. —To these objections, which are political, may be added others, which are physical and moral. The first difference which strikes us is that of colour.—Whether the black of the negro resides in the reticular membrane between the skin and scarf-skin, or in the scarf-skin itself; whether it proceeds from the colour of the blood, the colour of the bile, or from that of some other secretion, the difference is fixed in nature, and is as real as if its seat and cause were better known to us. And is this difference of no importance? Is it not the foundation of a greater or less share of beauty in the two races? Are not the fine mixtures of red and white, the expressions of every passion by greater or less suffusions of colour in the one, preferable to that eternal monotony, which reigns in the countenances, that immovable veil of black which covers all the emotions of the other race? Add to these, flowing hair, a more elegant symmetry of form, their own judgment in favour of the whites, declared by their preference of them, as uniformly as is the preference of the Oranootan for the black women over those of his own species. The circumstance of superior beauty, is thought worthy attention in the propagation of our horses, dogs, and other domestic animals; why not in that of man? Besides those of colour, figure, and hair, there are other physical distinctions proving a difference of race. They have less hair on the face and body. They secrete less by the kidneys, and more by the glands of the skin, which gives them a very strong and disagreeable odour. This greater degree of transpiration renders them more tolerant of heat, and less so of cold than the whites. Perhaps too a difference of structure in the pulmonary apparatus, which a late ingenious[1] experimentalist has discovered to be the principal regulator of animal heat, may have disabled them from extricating, in the act of inspiration, so much of that fluid from the outer air, or obliged them in expiration, to part with more of it. They seem to require less sleep. A black after hard labour through the day, will be induced by the slightest amusements to sit up till midnight, or later, though knowing he must be out with the first dawn of the morning. They are at least as brave, and more adventuresome. But this may perhaps proceed from a want of forethought, which prevents their seeing a danger till it be present.—When present, they do not go through it with more coolness or steadiness than the whites.

They are more ardent after their female: but love seems with them to be more an eager desire, than a tender delicate mixture of sentiment and sensation. Their griefs are transient. Those numberless afflictions, which render it doubtful whether heaven has given life to us in mercy or in wrath, are less felt, and sooner forgotten with them. In general, their existence appears to participate more of sensation than reflection. To this must be ascribed their disposition to sleep when abstracted from their diversions, and unemployed in labour. An animal whose body is at rest, and who does not reflect, must be disposed to sleep of course. Comparing them by their faculties of memory, reason, and imagination, it appears to me that in memory they are equal to the whites; in reason much inferior, as I think one could scarcely be found capable of tracing and comprehending the investigations of Euclid; and that in imagination they are dull, tasteless, and anomalous. It would be unfair to follow them to Africa for this investigation. We will consider them here, on the same stage with the whites, and where the facts are not apocryphal on which a judgment is to be formed. It will be right to make great allowances for the difference of condition, of education, of conversation, of the sphere in which they move. Many millions of them

---

1. Crawford (Jefferson's note).

have been brought to, and born in America. Most of them indeed have been confined to tillage, to their own homes, and their own society: yet many have been so situated, that they might have availed themselves of the conversation of their masters; many have been brought up to the handicraft arts, and from that circumstance have always been associated with the whites. Some have been liberally educated, and all have lived in countries where the arts and sciences are cultivated to a considerable degree, and have had before their eyes samples of the best works from abroad. The Indians, with no advantages of this kind, will often carve figures on their pipes not destitute of design and merit. They will crayon out an animal, a plant, or a country, so as to prove the existence of a germ in their minds which only wants cultivation. They astonish you with strokes of the most sublime oratory; such as prove their reason and sentiment strong, their imagination glowing and elevated. But never yet could I find that a black had uttered a thought above the level of plain narration; never saw even an elementary trait of painting or sculpture. In music they are more generally gifted than the whites with accurate ears for tune and time, and they have been found capable of imagining a small catch.[2] Whether they will be equal to the composition of a more extensive run of melody, or of complicated harmony, is yet to be proved. Misery is often the parent of the most affecting touches in poetry.

Among the blacks is misery enough, God knows, but no poetry. Love is the peculiar œstrum of the poet. Their love is ardent, but it kindles the senses only, not the imagination. Religion indeed has produced a Phyllis Whately;[3] but it could not produce a poet. The compositions published under her name are below the dignity of criticism. The heroes of the Dunciad are to her, as Hercules to the author of that poem. Ignatius Sancho[4] has approached nearer to merit in composition; yet his letters do more honour to the heart than the head. They breathe the purest effusions of friendship and general philanthropy, and show how great a degree of the latter may be compounded with strong religious zeal. He is often happy in the turn of his compliments, and his style is easy and familiar, except when he affects a Shandean fabrication of words. But his imagination is wild and extravagant, escapes incessantly from every restraint of reason and taste, and, in the course of its vagaries, leaves a tract of thought as incoherent and eccentric,

---

2. The instrument proper to them is the Banjar, which they brought hither from Africa, and which is the original of the guitar, its chords being precisely the four lower chords of the guitar (Jefferson's note).

3. I.e.; Phillis Wheatley, African-born slave poet of Boston.

4. Born on a slave ship and raised in London, he gained fame in music, writing, and acting (c. 1729–1780). Known as the "extraordinary African," he was a symbol of Africans' humanity. The book of Sancho's writings, published after his death, was one of the first books in English by a Black author.

as is the course of a meteor through the sky. His subjects should often have led him to a process of sober reasoning: yet we find him always substituting sentiment for demonstration. Upon the whole, though we admit him to the first place among those of his own colour who have presented themselves to the public judgment, yet when we compare him with the writers of the race among whom he lived, and particularly with the epistolary class, in which he has taken his own stand, we are compelled to enrol him at the bottom of the column. This criticism supposes the letters published under his name to be genuine, and to have received amendment from no other hand; points which would not be of easy investigation. The improvement of the blacks in body and mind, in the first instance of their mixture with the whites, has been observed by every one, and proves that their inferiority is not the effect merely of their condition of life.

We know that among the Romans, about the Augustan age especially, the condition of their slaves was much more deplorable than that of the blacks on the continent of America. The two sexes were confined in separate apartments, because to raise a child cost the master more than to buy one. Cato, for a very restricted indulgence to his slaves in this particular, took from them a certain price. But in this country the slaves multiply as fast as the free inhabitants. Their situation and manners place the commerce between the two sexes almost without restraint. The same Cato, on a principle of œconomy, always sold his sick and superannuated slaves. He gives it as a standing precept to a master visiting his farm, to sell his old oxen, old wagons, old tools, old and diseased servants, and every thing else become useless. 'Vendat boves vetulos, plaustrum vetus, fermenta vetera, servum senem, servum morbosum, & si quid aliud supersit vendat.' Cato de re rustica c. 2. The American slaves cannot enumerate this among the injuries and insults they receive. It was the common practice to expose in the island Æsculapius, in the Tyber, diseased slaves, whose cure was like to become tedious. The emperor Claudius, by an edict, gave freedom to such of them as should recover, and first declared that if any person chose to kill rather than expose them, it should be deemed homicide. The exposing them is a crime of which no instance has existed with us; and were it to be followed by death, it would be punished capitally. We are told of a certain Vedius Pollio, who, in the presence of Augustus, would have given a slave as food to his fish, for having broken a glass. With the Romans, the regular method of taking the evidence of their slaves was under torture. Here it has been thought better never to resort to their evidence. When a master was murdered, all his slaves, in the same house, or within hearing, were condemned to death. Here punishment falls on the guilty only, and as precise proof is required against him as against a freeman. Yet notwithstanding these and other discouraging circumstances among the Romans, their slaves were often their rarest artists. They excelled too in science, insomuch as to be usually employed as tutors to their masters' children. Epictetus, Terence, and Phædrus, were slaves. But they were of the race of whites.

It is not their condition then, but nature, which has produced the distinction. Whether further observation will or will not verify the conjecture, that nature has been less bountiful to them in the endowments of the head, I believe that in those of the heart she will be found to have done them justice. That disposition to theft with which they have been branded, must be ascribed to their situation, and not to any depravity of the moral sense. The man, in whose favour no laws of property exist, probably feels himself less bound to respect those made in favour of others. When arguing for ourselves, we lay it down as a fundamental, that laws, to be just, must give a reciprocation of right; that, without this, they are mere arbitrary rules of conduct, founded in force, and not in conscience: and it is a problem which I give to the master to solve, whether the religious precepts against the violation of property were not framed for him as well as his slave? And whether the slave may not as justifiably take a little from one, who has taken all from him, as he may slay one who would slay him? That a change in the relations in which a man is placed should change his ideas of moral right or wrong, is neither new, nor peculiar to the colour of the blacks. Homer tells us it was so 2600 years ago.

* * *

Jove fix'd it certain, that whatever day
Makes man a slave, takes half his worth away.

But the slaves of which Homer speaks were whites. Notwithstanding these considerations which must weaken their respect for the laws of property, we find among them numerous instances of the most rigid integrity, and as many as among their better instructed masters, of benevolence, gratitude and unshaken fidelity. The opinion, that they are inferior in the faculties of reason and imagination, must be hazarded with great diffidence. To justify a general conclusion, requires many observations, even where the subject may be submitted to the anatomical knife, to optical classes; to analysis by fire, or by solvents. How much more then where it is a faculty, not a substance, we are examining; where it eludes the research of all the senses; where the conditions of its existence are various and variously combined; where the effects of those which are present or absent bid defiance to calculation; let me add too, as a circumstance of great tenderness, where our conclusion would degrade a whole race of men from the rank in the scale of beings which their Creator may perhaps have given them. To our reproach it must be said, that though for a century and a half we have had under our eyes the races of black and of red men, they have never yet been viewed by us as subjects of natural history. I advance it therefore as a suspicion only, that the blacks, whether originally a distinct race, or made distinct by time and circumstances, are inferior to the whites in the endowments both of body and mind.

It is not against experience to suppose, that different species of the same genus, or varieties of the same species, may possess different qualifications. Will not a lover of natural history then, one who views the gradations in all the races of animals with the eye of philosophy, excuse an effort to keep those in the department of man as distinct as nature has formed them? This unfortunate difference of colour, and perhaps of faculty, is a powerful obstacle to the emancipation of these people. Many of their advocates, while they wish to vindicate the liberty of human nature are anxious also to preserve its dignity and beauty. Some of these, embarrassed by the question ' What further is to be done with them?' join themselves in opposition with those who are actuated by sordid avarice only. Among the Romans emancipation required but one effort. The slave, when made free, might mix with, without staining the blood of his master. But with us a second is necessary, unknown to history. When freed, he is to be removed beyond the reach of mixture.

* * *

Query XVIII.

The *particular* customs and manners that may happen to be received in that state?

    * * * There must doubtless be an unhappy influence on the manners of our people produced by the existence of slavery among us. The whole commerce between master and slave is a perpetual exercise of the most boisterous passions, the most unremitting despotism on the one part, and degrading submissions on the other. Our children see this, and learn to imitate it; for man is an imitative animal. This quality is the germ of all education in him. From his cradle to his grave he is learning to do what he sees others do. If a parent could find no motive either in his philanthropy or his self love, for restraining the intemperance of passion towards his slave, it should always be a sufficient one that his child is present. But generally it is not sufficient. The parent storms, the child looks on, catches the lineaments of wrath, puts on the same airs in the circle of smaller slaves, gives a loose to the worst of passions, and thus nursed, educated, and daily exercised in tyranny, cannot but be stamped by it with odious peculiarities. The man must be a prodigy who can retain his manners and morals undepraved by such circumstances. And with what execration should the statesman be loaded, who permitting one half the citizens thus to trample on the rights of the other, transforms those into despots, and these into enemies, destroys the morals of the one part, and the amor patriæ of the other. For if a slave can have a country in this world, it must be any other in preference to that in which he is born to live and labour for another; in which he must lock up the faculties of his nature, contribute as far as depends on his individual endeavours to the evanishment of the human race, or entail his own miserable condition on the endless generations proceeding

from him. With the morals of the people, their industry also is destroyed. For in a warm climate, no man will labour for himself who can make another labour for him. This is so true, that of the proprietors of slaves a very small proportion indeed are ever seen to labour. And can the liberties of a nation be thought secure when we have removed their only firm basis, a conviction in the minds of the people that these liberties are of the gift of God? That they are not to be violated but with his wrath? Indeed I tremble for my country when I reflect that God is just: that his justice cannot sleep forever: that considering numbers, nature and natural means only, a revolution of the wheel of fortune, an exchange of situation is among possible events: that it may become probable by supernatural interference! The almighty has no attribute which can take side with us in such a contest.—But it is impossible to be temperate and to pursue this subject through the various considerations of policy, of morals, of history natural and civil. We must be contented to hope they will force their way into every one's mind. I think a change already perceptible, since the origin of the present revolution. The spirit of the master is abating, that of the slave rising from the dust, his condition mollifying, the way I hope preparing, under the auspices of heaven, for a total emancipation, and that this is disposed, in the order of events, to be with the consent of the masters, rather than by their extirpation.

Query XIX.

The present state of manufactures, commerce, interior and exterior trade?

* * *

* * * Those who labour in the earth are the chosen people of God, if ever he had a chosen people, whose breasts he has made his peculiar deposite for substantial and genuine virtue. It is the focus in which he keeps alive that sacred fire, which otherwise might escape from the face of the earth. Corruption of morals in the mass of cultivators is a phænomenon of which no age nor nation has furnished an example. It is the mark set on those, who not looking up to heaven, to their own soil and industry, as does the husbandman, for their subsistence, depend for it on casualties and caprice of customers. Dependence begets subservience and venality, suffocates the germ of virtue, and prepares fit tools for the designs of ambition. This, the natural progress and consequence of the arts, has sometimes perhaps been retarded by accidental circumstances: but, generally speaking, the proportion which the aggregate of the other classes of citizens bears in any state to that of its husbandmen, is the proportion of its unsound to its healthy parts, and is a good enough barometer whereby to measure its degree of corruption. While we have land to labour then, let us never wish to see our citizens occupied at a work-bench, or twirling a distaff. Carpenters, masons, smiths, are wanting in husbandry: but, for the general operations of manufacture, let our workshops remain in Europe. It is better to carry provisions and materials to workmen there, than

bring them to the provisions and materials, and with them their manners and principles. The loss by the transportation of commodities across the Atlantic will be made up in happiness and permanence of government. The mobs of great cities add just so much to the support of pure government, as sores do to the strength of the human body. It is the manners and spirit of a people which preserve a republic in vigour. A degeneracy in these is a canker which soon eats to the heart of its laws and constitution.

* * *

THE UNITED STATES CONSTITUTIONAL CONVENTION

Constitution of the United States, 1787

The Constitution was written in 1787, ratified in 1787–88, and became effective in 1789. It created the federal government and has provided, since 1789, the framework of government for the United States. The first ten amendments—the Bill of Rights—were ratified in 1791. The next two amendments were ratified in 1795 and 1804. By 1845, no amendment had been adopted for forty years, and none would be until after the Civil War. Printed here is the entire text of the Constitution as it existed from 1805 to 1865. Students should recognize that in 1845 the Bill of Rights did not restrict state governments, only federal government. (This changed gradually after World War I, when the Fourteenth Amendment was interpreted as having "incorporated" the Bill of Rights as binding on state governments—a major change in the American constitutional system.)

SOURCE: *James D. Richardson, ed.,* A Compilation of the Messages and Papers of the Presidents, *1789–1902 (Washington, DC: Bureau of National Literature and Art, 1903), vol. 1, pp. 21–38.*

We the People of the United States, in order to form a more perfect Union, establish Justice, insure domestic Tranquility, provide for the common defence, promote the general Welfare, and secure the Blessings of Liberty to ourselves and our Posterity, do ordain and establish this Constitution for the United States of America.

ARTICLE. I.

Section. 1. All legislative Powers herein granted shall be vested in a Congress of the United States, which shall consist of a Senate and House of Representatives.

[Article I,] *Section. 2.* The House of Representatives shall be composed of Members chosen every second Year by the People of the several States, and the Electors in each State shall have the Qualifications requisite for Electors of the most numerous Branch of the State Legislature.

No Person shall be a Representative who shall not have attained to the Age of twenty five Years, and been seven Years a Citizen of the United States, and who shall not, when elected, be an Inhabitant of that State in which he shall be chosen.

This is the three-fifths clause.

Representatives and direct Taxes shall be apportioned among the several States which may be included within this Union, according to their respective Numbers, which shall be determined by adding to the whole Number of free Persons, including those bound to Service for a Term of Years, and excluding Indians not taxed, three fifths of all other Persons. The actual Enumeration shall be made within three Years after the first Meeting of the Congress of the United States, and within every subsequent Term of ten Years, in such Manner as they shall by Law direct. The Number of Representatives shall not exceed one for every thirty Thousand, but each State shall have at Least one Representative; and until such enumeration shall be made, the State of New Hampshire shall be entitled to chuse three, Massachusetts eight, Rhode-Island and Providence Plantations one, Connecticut five, New York six, New Jersey four, Pennsylvania eight, Delaware one, Maryland six, Virginia ten, North Carolina five, South Carolina five, and Georgia three.

When vacancies happen in the Representation from any state, the Executive Authority thereof shall issue Writs of Election to fill such Vacancies.

The House of Representatives shall chuse their Speaker and other Officers; and shall have the sole Power of Impeachment.

Section. 3. The Senate of the United States shall be composed of two Senators from each State, chosen by the legislature thereof, for six Years; and each Senator shall have one Vote.

Immediately after they shall be assembled in Consequence of the first Election, they shall be divided as equally as may be into three Classes. The Seats of the Senators of the first Class shall be vacated at the Expiration of the second Year, of the second Class at the Expiration of the fourth Year, and of the third Class at the Expiration of the sixth Year, so that one third may be chosen every second Year; and if Vacancies happen by Resignation, or otherwise, during the Recess of the Legislature of any State, the Executive thereof may make temporary Appointments until the next Meeting of the Legislature, which shall then fill such Vacancies.

No Person shall be a Senator who shall not have attained to the Age of thirty Years, and been nine Years a Citizen of the United States, and who shall not, when elected, be an Inhabitant of that State for which he shall be chosen.

The Vice President of the United States shall be President of the Senate, but shall have no Vote, unless they be equally divided.

The Senate shall chuse their other Officers, and also a President pro tempore, in the Absence of the Vice President, or when he shall exercise the Office of President of the United States.

The Senate shall have the sole Power to try all Impeachments. When sitting for that Purpose, they shall be on Oath or Affirmation. When the President of the United States is tried, the Chief Justice shall preside: And no Person shall be convicted without the Concurrence of two thirds of the Members present.

Judgment in Cases of Impeachment shall not extend further than to removal from Office, and disqualification to hold and enjoy any Office of honor, Trust or Profit under the United States: but the Party convicted shall nevertheless be liable and subject to Indictment, Trial, Judgment and Punishment, according to Law.

Section. 4. The Times, Places and Manner of holding Elections for Senators and Representatives, shall be prescribed in each State by the Legislature thereof; but the Congress may at any time by Law make or alter such Regulations, except as to the Places of chusing Senators.

The Congress shall assemble at least once in every Year, and such Meeting shall be on the first Monday in December, unless they shall by Law appoint a different Day.

Section. 5. Each House shall be the Judge of the Elections, Returns and Qualifications of its own Members, and a Majority of each shall constitute a Quorum to do Business; but a smaller Number may adjourn from day to day, and may be authorized to compel the Attendance of absent Members, in such Manner, and under such Penalties as each House may provide.

Each House may determine the Rules of its Proceedings, punish its Members for disorderly Behaviour, and, with the Concurrence of two thirds, expel a Member.

Each House shall keep a Journal of its Proceedings, and from time to time publish the same, excepting such Parts as may in their Judgment require Secrecy; and the Yeas and Nays of the Members of either House on any question shall, at the Desire of one fifth of those Present, be entered on the Journal.

Neither House, during the Session of Congress, shall, without the Consent of the other, adjourn for more than three days, not to any other Place than that in which the two Houses shall be sitting.

Section. 6. The Senators and Representatives shall receive a Compensation for their Services, to be ascertained by Law, and paid out of the Treasury of the United States. They shall in all Cases, except Treason, Felony and Breach of the Peace, be privileged from Arrest during their Attendance at the Session of their respective Houses, and in going to and returning from the same; and for any Speech or Debate in either House, they shall not be questioned in any other Place.

No Senator or Representative shall, during the Time for which he was elected, be appointed to any civil Office under the Authority of the United States, which shall have been created, or the Emoluments whereof shall have been encreased during such time; and no Person holding any Office under the United States, shall be a Member of either House during his Continuance in Office.

Section. 7. All Bills for raising Revenue shall originate in the House of Representatives; but the Senate may propose or concur with Amendments as on other Bills.

Every Bill which shall have passed the House of Representatives and the Senate shall, before it become a Law, be presented to the President of the United States; If he approve he shall sign it, but if not he shall return it, with his Objections to that House in which it shall have originated, who shall enter the Objections at large on their Journal, and proceed to reconsider it. If after such Reconsideration two thirds of that House shall agree to pass the Bill, it shall be sent, together with the Objections, to the other House, by which it shall likewise be reconsidered, and if approved by two thirds of that House, it shall become a Law. But in all such Cases the Votes of both Houses shall be determined by Yeas and Nays, and the Names of the Persons voting for and against the Bill shall be entered on the Journal of each House respectively. If any Bill shall not be returned by the President within ten Days (Sundays excepted) after it shall have been presented to him, the Same shall be a Law, in like Manner as if he had signed it, unless the Congress by their Adjournment prevent its Return, in which Case it shall not be a Law.

Every Order, Resolution, or Vote to which the Concurrence of the Senate and House of Representatives may be necessary (except on a question of Adjournment) shall be presented to the President of the United States; and before the Same shall take Effect, shall be approved by him, or being disapproved by him, shall be repassed by two thirds of the Senate and House of Representatives, according to the Rules and Limitations prescribed in the Case of a Bill.

Section. 8. The Congress shall have Power To lay and collect Taxes, Duties, Imposts and Excises, to pay the Debts and provide for the common Defence and general Welfare of the United States; but all Duties, Imposts and Excises shall be uniform throughout the United States;

To borrow Money on the credit of the United States;

To regulate Commerce with foreign Nations, and among the several States, and with the Indian Tribes;

To establish an uniform Rule of Naturalization, and uniform Laws on the subject of Bankruptcies throughout the United States;

To coin Money, regulate the Value thereof, and of foreign Coin, and fix the Standard of Weights and Measures;

To provide for the Punishment of counterfeiting the Securities and current Coin of the United States;

To establish Post Offices and Post Roads;

To promote the Progress of Science and useful Arts, by securing for limited Times to Authors and Inventors the exclusive Right to their respective Writings and Discoveries;

To constitute Tribunals inferior to the supreme Court;

To define and punish Piracies and Felonies committed on the high Seas, and Offences against the Law of Nations;

To declare War, grant Letters of Marque and Reprisal, and make Rules concerning Captures on Land and Water;

To raise and support Armies, but no Appropriation of Money to that Use shall be for a longer Term than two Years;

To provide and maintain a Navy;

To make Rules for the Government and Regulation of the land and naval Forces;

To provide for calling forth the Militia to execute the Laws of the Union, suppress Insurrections and repel Invasions;

To provide for organizing, arming, and disciplining, the Militia, and for governing such Part of them as may be employed in the Service of the United States, reserving to the States respectively, the Appointment of the Officers, and the Authority of training the Militia according to the discipline prescribed by Congress;

To exercise exclusive Legislation in all Cases whatsoever, over such District (not exceeding ten Miles square) as may, by Cession of Particular States, and the Acceptance of Congress, become the Seat of the Government of the United States, and to exercise like Authority over all Places purchased by the Consent of the Legislature of the State in which the Same shall be, for the Erection of Forts, Magazines, Arsenals, dock-Yards, and other needful Buildings;—And

To make all Laws which shall be necessary and proper for carrying into Execution the foregoing Powers, and all other Powers vested by this Constitution in the Government of the United States, or in any Department or Officer thereof.

[Article 1,] *Section. 9.* **The Migration or Importation of such Persons as any of the States now existing shall think proper to admit, shall not be prohibited by the Congress prior** *This is the Fugitive Slave Clause of the Constitution.* **to the Year one thousand eight hundred and eight, but a Tax or duty may be imposed on such Importation, not exceeding ten dollars for each Person.**

The Privilege of the Writ of Habeas Corpus shall not be suspended, unless when in Cases of Rebellion or Invasion the public Safety may require it.

No Bill of Attainder or ex post facto Law shall be passed.

No Capitation, or other direct, Tax shall be laid, unless in Proportion to the Census or Enumeration herein before directed to be taken.

No Tax or Duty shall be laid on Articles exported from any State.

No Preference shall be given by any Regulation of Commerce or Revenue to the Ports of one State over those of another: nor shall Vessels bound to, or from, one State, be obliged to enter, clear, or pay Duties in another.

No Money shall be drawn from the Treasury, but in Consequence of Appropriations made by Law; and a regular Statement and Account of the Receipts and Expenditures of all public Money shall be published from time to time.

No Title of Nobility shall be granted by the United States: And no Person holding any Office of Profit or Trust under them, shall, without the Consent of the Congress, accept of any present, Emolument, Office, or Title, of any kind whatever, from any King, Prince, or foreign State.

Section. 10. No State shall enter into any Treaty, Alliance, or Confederation; grant Letters of Marque and Reprisal; coin Money; emit Bills of Credit; make any Thing but gold and silver Coin a Tender in Payment of Debts; pass any Bill of Attainder, ex post facto Law, or Law impairing the Obligation of Contracts, or grant any Title of Nobility.

No State shall, without the Consent of the Congress, lay any Imposts or Duties on Imports or Exports, except what may be absolutely necessary for executing its inspection Laws: and the net Produce of all Duties and Imposts, laid by any State on Imports or Exports, shall be for the Use of the Treasury of the United States; and all such Laws shall be subject to the Revision and Controul of the Congress.

Here the Constitution creates the electoral college for selecting presidents, granting each state electoral votes according to its total congressional representation. Since the Constitution's three-fifths clause of Article I counted three-fifths of the slave population in allocating the number of Representatives— thereby increasing the slave states' power in the House—the electoral college was likewise designed to ensure that the slave states had disproportionate power in presidential elections.*

No State shall, without the Consent of the Congress, lay any Duty of Tonnage, keep Troops, or Ships of War in time of Peace, enter into any Agreement or Compact with another State, or with a foreign Power, or engage in War, unless actually invaded, or in such imminent Danger as will not admit of delay.

ARTICLE. II.

Section. 1. The executive Power shall be vested in a President of the United States of America. He shall hold his Office during the term of four Years, and, together with the Vice President, chosen for the same Term, be elected, as follows:

Each State shall appoint, in such Manner as the Legislature thereof may direct, a Number of Electors, equal to the whole Number of Senators and Representatives to which the State may be entitled in the Congress: but no Senator or Representative, or Person holding an Office of Trust or Profit under the United States, shall be appointed an Elector.

The Electors shall meet in their respective States, and vote by Ballot for two Persons, of whom one at least shall not be an Inhabitant of the same State with themselves. And they shall make a List of all the Persons voted for, and of the Number of Votes for each; which List they shall sign and certify, and transmit sealed to the

---

**Akhil Reed Amar, "The Troubling Reason the Electoral College Exists," TIME Magazine, November 8, 2016.*

Seat of the Government of the United States, directed to the President of the Senate. The President of the Senate shall, in the Presence of the Senate and House of Representatives, open all the Certificates, and the Votes shall then be counted. The Person having the greatest Number of Votes shall be the President, if such Number be a Majority of the whole Number of Electors appointed; and if there be more than one who have such Majority, and have an equal Number of Votes, then the House of Representatives shall immediately chuse by Ballot one of them for President; and if no Person have a Majority, then from the five highest on the List the said House shall in like Manner chuse the President. But in chusing the President, the Votes shall be taken by States, the Representation from each State having one Vote; A quorum for this Purpose shall consist of a Member or Members from two thirds of the States, and a Majority of all the States shall be necessary to a Choice. In every Case, after the Choice of the President, the Person having the greatest Number of Votes of the Electors shall be the Vice President. But if there should remain two or more who have equal Votes, the Senate shall chuse from them by Ballot the Vice President.

The Congress may determine the Time of chusing the Electors, and the Day on which they shall give their Votes; which Day shall be the same throughout the United States.

No Person except a natural born Citizen, or a Citizen of the United States, at the time of the Adoption of this Constitution, shall be eligible to the Office of President; neither shall any Person be eligible to that Office who shall not have attained to the Age of thirty five Years, and been fourteen Years a Resident within the United States.

In Case of the Removal of the President from Office, or of his Death, Resignation, or Inability to discharge the Powers and Duties of the said Office, the Same shall devolve on the Vice President, and the Congress may by Law provide for the Case of Removal, Death, Resignation or Inability, both of the President and Vice President, declaring what Officer shall then act as President, and such Officer shall act accordingly, until the Disability be removed, or a President shall be elected.

The President shall, at stated Times, receive for his Services, a Compensation, which shall neither be encreased or diminished during the Period for which he shall have been elected, and he shall not receive within that Period any other Emolument from the United States, or any of them.

Before he enters on the Execution of his Office, he shall take the following Oath or Affirmation:—"I do solemnly swear (or affirm) that I will faithfully execute the Office of President of the United States, and will to the best of my Ability, preserve, protect and defend the Constitution of the United States."

Section. 2. The President shall be Commander in Chief of the Army and Navy of the United States, and of the Militia of the several States, when called into the actual Service of the United States; he may require the Opinion, in writing, of the principal Officer in each of the executive Departments, upon any Subject relating to the Duties of their respective Offices, and he shall have Power to grant Reprieves and Pardons for Offences against the United States, except in Cases of Impeachment.

He shall have Power, by and with the Advice and Consent of the Senate, to make Treaties, provided two thirds of the Senators present concur; and he shall nominate, and by and with the Advice and Consent of the Senate, shall appoint Ambassadors, other public Ministers and Consuls, Judges of the supreme Court, and all other Officers of the United States, whose Appointments are not herein otherwise provided for, and which shall be established by Law: but the Congress may by Law vest the Appointment of such inferior Officers, as they think proper, in the President alone, in the Courts of Law, or in the Heads of Departments.

The President shall have Power to fill up all Vacancies that may happen during the Recess of the Senate, by granting Commissions which shall expire at the End of their next Session.

Section. 3. He shall from time to time give to the Congress Information of the State of the Union, and recommend to their Consideration such Measures as he shall judge necessary and expedient; he may, on extraordinary Occasions, convene both Houses, or either of them, and in Case of Disagreement between them, with Respect to the Time of Adjournment, he may adjourn them to such Time as he shall think proper; he shall receive Ambassadors and other public Ministers; he shall take Care that the Laws be faithfully executed, and shall Commission all the Officers of the United States.

Section. 4. The President, Vice President and all civil Officers of the United States, shall be removed from Office on Impeachment for, and Conviction of, Treason, Bribery, or other high Crimes and Misdemeanors.

ARTICLE. III.

Section. 1. The judicial Power of the United States, shall be vested in one supreme Court, and in such inferior Courts as the Congress may from time to time ordain and establish. The Judges, both of the supreme and inferior Courts, shall hold their Offices during good Behavior, and shall, at stated Times, receive for their Services, a Compensation, which shall not be diminished during their Continuance in Office.

Section. 2. The judicial Power shall extend to all Cases, in Law and Equity, arising under this Constitution, the Laws of the United States, and Treaties made, or which shall be made, under their Authority;—to all Cases affecting Ambassadors, other public Ministers and Consuls;–to all Cases of admiralty and maritime Jurisdiction;—the Controversies to which the United States shall be a Party;—to Controversies between two or more States;–between a State and Citizens of another State;—between Citizens of different States;—between Citizens of the same State claiming Lands under Grants of different States, and between a State, or the Citizens thereof, and foreign States, Citizens or Subjects.

In all cases affecting Ambassadors, other public Ministers and Consuls, and those in which a State shall be Party, the supreme Court shall have original Jurisdiction. In all the other Cases before mentioned, the supreme Court shall have appellate Jurisdiction, both as to Law and Fact, with such Exceptions, and under such Regulations as the Congress shall make.

The Trial of all Crimes, except in Cases of Impeachment, shall be by Jury; and such Trial shall be held in the State where the said Crimes shall have been committed; but when not committed within any State, the Trial shall be at such Place or Places as the Congress may by Law have directed.

Section. 3. Treason against the United States, shall consist only in levying War against them, or in adhering to their Enemies, giving them Aid and Comfort. No Person shall be convicted of Treason unless on the Testimony of two Witnesses to the same overt Act, or on Confession in open Court.

The Congress shall have Power to declare the Punishment of Treason, but no Attainder of Treason shall work Corruption of Blood, or Forfeiture except during the Life of the Person attainted.

ARTICLE. IV.

Section. 1. Full Faith and Credit shall be given in each State to the public Acts, Records, and judicial Proceedings of every other State. And the Congress may by general Laws prescribe the Manner in which such Acts, Records and Proceedings shall be proved, and the Effect thereof.

Section. 2. The Citizens of each State shall be entitled to all Privileges and Immunities of Citizens in the several States.

A Person charged in any State with Treason, Felony, or other Crime, who shall flee from Justice, and be found in another State, shall on Demand of the executive Authority of the State from which he fled, be delivered up, to be removed to the State having Jurisdiction of the Crime.

No Person held to Service or Labour in one State, under the Laws thereof, escaping into another, shall, in Consequence of any Law or Regulation therein, be discharged from such Service or Labour, but shall ▮ *This is the Fugitive Slave Clause.* **be delivered up on Claim of the Party to whom such Service or Labour may be due.**

Section. 3. New States may be admitted by the Congress into this Union; but no new State shall be formed or erected within the Jurisdiction of any other State; nor any State be formed by the Junction of two or more States, or Parts of States, without the consent of the Legislatures of the States concerned as well as of the Congress.

The Congress shall have Power to dispose of and make all needful Rules and Regulations respecting the Territory or other Property belonging to the United States; and nothing in this Constitution shall be so construed as to Prejudice any Claims of the United States, or of any particular States.

Section. 4. The United States shall guarantee to every State in this Union a Republican Form of Government, and shall protect each of them against Invasion; and on Application of the Legislature, or of the Executive (when the Legislature cannot be convened) against domestic Violence.

ARTICLE. V.

The Congress, whenever two thirds of both Houses shall deem it necessary, shall propose Amendments to this Constitution, or, on the Application of the Legislatures of two thirds of the several States, shall call a Convention for proposing Amendments, which, in either Case, shall be valid to all Intents and Purposes, as Part of this Constitution, when ratified by the Legislatures of three fourths of the several States, or by Conventions in three fourths thereof, as the one or the other Mode of Ratification may be proposed by the Congress; Provided that no Amendment which may be made prior to the Year One thousand eight hundred and eight shall in any Manner affect the first and fourth Clauses in the Ninth Section of the first Article; and that no State, without its Consent, shall be deprived of its equal Suffrage in the Senate.

ARTICLE. VI.

All Debts contracted and Engagements entered into, before the Adoption of this Constitution, shall be as valid against the United States under this Constitution, as under the Confederation.

This Constitution, and the Laws of the United States which shall be made in Pursuance thereof; and all Treaties made, or which shall be made, under the Authority of the United States, shall be the supreme Law of the Land; and the Judges in every State shall be bound thereby, any Thing in the Constitution or Laws of any State to the Contrary notwithstanding.

The Senators and Representatives before mentioned, and the Members of the several State Legislatures, and all executive and judicial Officers, both of the United States and of the several States, shall be bound by Oath or Affirmation, to support this Constitution; but no religious Test shall ever be required as a Qualification to any Office or public Trust under the United States.

ARTICLE. VII.

The Ratification of the Conventions of nine States, shall be sufficient for the Establishment of this Constitution between the States so ratifying the Same.

Done in Convention by the Unanimous Consent of the States present the Seventeenth Day of September in the Year of our Lord one thousand seven hundred and Eighty seven and of the Independence of the United States of America the Twelfth. In witness thereof We have hereunto subscribed our Names.

G°. *WASHINGTON*–Presd[t]. and deputy from Virginia

NEW HAMPSHIRE
John Langdon
Nicholas Gilman

MASSACHUSETTS
Nathaniel Gorham
Rufus King

CONNECTICUT
W[m] Sam[l] Johnson
Roger Sherman

NEW YORK
Alexander Hamilton

NEW JERSEY
Wil: Livingston
David A. Brearley
W[m] Paterson
Jona: Dayton

PENNSYLVANIA
B Franklin
Thomas Mifflin
Rob[t] Morris
Geo. Clymer
Tho[s] FitzSimons
Jared Ingersoll
James Wilson
Gouv Morris

DELAWARE
Geo: Read
Gunning Bedford jun
John Dickinson
Richard Bassett
Jaco: Broom

MARYLAND
James M[c]Henry
Dan of S[t] Tho[s] Jenifer
Dan[l] Carroll

VIRGINIA
John Blair–
James Madison Jr.

NORTH CAROLINA
W[m] Blount
Rich[d] Dobbs Spaight
Hu Williamson

SOUTH CAROLINA
J. Rutledge
*Charles Cotesworth
    Pinckney*
Charles Pinckney
Pierce Butler

GEORGIA
William Few
Abr Baldwin

AMENDMENT I.[1]

Congress shall make no law respecting an establishment of religion, or prohibiting the free exercise thereof; or abridging the freedom of speech, or of the press; or

---

1. The first ten amendments (the Bill of Rights) were ratified in 1791.

the right of the people peaceably to assemble, and to petition the Government for a redress of grievances.

AMENDMENT II.

A well regulated Militia, being necessary to the security of a free State, the right of the people to keep and bear Arms, shall not be infringed.

AMENDMENT III.

No Soldier shall, in time of peace be quartered in any house, without the consent of the Owner, nor in time of war, but in a manner to be prescribed by law.

AMENDMENT IV.

The right of the people to be secure in their persons, houses, papers, and effects, against unreasonable searches and seizures, shall not be violated, and no Warrants shall issue, but upon probable cause, supported by Oath or affirmation, and particularly describing the place to be searched, and the persons or things to be seized.

AMENDMENT V.

No person shall be held to answer for a capital, or otherwise infamous crime, unless on a presentment or indictment of a Grand Jury, except in cases arising in the land or naval forces, or in the Militia, when in actual service in time of War or public danger; nor shall any person be subject for the same offence to be twice put in jeopardy of life or limb; nor shall be compelled in any criminal case to be a witness against himself, nor be deprived of life, liberty, or property, without due process of law; nor shall private property be taken for public use, without just compensation.

AMENDMENT VI.

In all criminal prosecutions, the accused shall enjoy the right to a speedy and public trial, by an impartial jury of the State and district wherein the crime shall have been committed, which district shall have been previously ascertained by law, and to be informed of the nature and cause of the accusation; to be confronted with the witnesses against him; to have compulsory process for obtaining witness in his favor, and to have the Assistance of Counsel for his defence.

AMENDMENT VII.

In Suits at common law, where the value in controversy shall exceed twenty dollars, the right of trial by jury shall be preserved, and no fact tried by a jury, shall be otherwise re-examined in any Court of the United States, than according to the rules of the common law.

AMENDMENT VIII.

Excessive bail shall not be required, nor excessive fines imposed, nor cruel and unusual punishments inflicted.

AMENDMENT IX.

The enumeration in the Constitution, of certain rights, shall not be construed to deny or disparage others retained by the people.

AMENDMENT X.

The powers not delegated to the United States by the Constitution, nor prohibited by it to the States, are reserved to the States respectively, or to the people.

AMENDMENT XI.

The Judicial power of the United States shall not be construed to extend to any suit in law or equity, commenced or prosecuted against one of the United States by Citizens of another State, or by Citizens or Subjects of any Foreign State. [Ratified in 1798]

AMENDMENT XII.

The Electors shall meet in their respective states, and vote by ballot for President and Vice-President, one of whom, at least, shall not be an inhabitant of the same state with themselves; they shall name in their ballots the person voted for as President, and in distinct ballots the person voted for as Vice-President, and they shall make distinct lists of all persons voted for as President, and of all persons voted for as Vice President, and of the number of votes for each, which lists they shall sign and certify, and transmit sealed to the seat of the government of the United States, directed to the President of the Senate;—The President of the Senate shall, in the presence of the Senate and House of Representatives, open all the certificates and the votes shall then be counted;—The person having the greatest number of votes for President, shall be the President, if such number be a majority of the whole number of Electors appointed; and if no person have such majority, then from the persons having the highest numbers not exceeding three on the list of those voted for as President, the House of Representatives shall choose immediately, by ballot, the President. But in choosing the President, the votes shall be taken by states, the representation from each state having one vote; a quorum for this purpose shall consist of a member or members from two-thirds of the states, and a majority of all the states shall be necessary to a choice. And if the House of Representatives shall not choose a President whenever the right of choice shall devolve upon them, before the fourth day of March next following, then the Vice-President shall act as President, as in the case of the death or other constitutional disability of the President.— The person having the greatest number of votes as Vice-President, shall be the Vice-President, if such number be a majority of the whole number of Electors appointed, and if no person have a majority, then from the two highest numbers on the list, the Senate shall choose the Vice-President; a quorum for the purpose shall consist of two-thirds of the whole number of Senators, and a majority of the whole number shall be necessary to a choice. But no person constitutionally ineligible to the office of President shall be eligible to that of Vice-President of the United States. [Ratified in 1804]

The Fugitive Slave Act of 1793

Less than four years after the Constitution was ratified, Congress passed a law against runaway slaves; this law was based on Article IV, Section 2 of the Constitution. Omitted here are the first two sections of this law, dealing with ordinary criminal fugitives.

SOURCE: *"An act respecting fugitives from justice, and persons escaping from the service of their masters," in* Laws of the Territory Northwest of the River Ohio *(Cincinnati, 1833).*

* * *

SEC. 3. *And be it also enacted,* That when a person held to labor in any of the United States, or in either of the Territories on the Northwest or South of the river Ohio, under the laws thereof, shall escape into any other of the said States or Territory, the person to whom such labor or service may be due, his agent or attorney, is hereby empowered to seize or arrest such fugitive from labor, and to take him or her before any Judge of the Circuit or District Courts of the United States, residing or being within the State, or before any magistrate of a county, city, or town corporate, wherein such seizure or arrest shall be made, and upon proof to the satisfaction of such Judge or magistrate, either by oral testimony or affidavit taken before and certified by a magistrate of any such State or Territory, that the person so seized or arrested, doth, under the laws of the State or Territory from which he or she fled, owe service or labor to the person claiming him or her, it shall be the duty of such Judge or magistrate to give a certificate thereof to such claimant, his agent, or attorney, which shall be sufficient warrant for removing the said fugitive from labor to the State or Territory from which he or she fled.

SEC. 4. *And be further enacted,* That any person who shall knowingly and willingly obstruct or hinder such claimant, his agent or attorney, in so seizing or arresting such fugitive from labor, or shall rescue such fugitive from such claimant, his agent or attorney, when so arrested pursuant to the authority herein given or declared; or shall harbor or conceal such person after notice that he or she was a fugitive from labor, as aforesaid, shall, for either of the said offences, forfeit and pay the sum of five hundred dollars. Which penalty may be recovered by and for the benefit of such claimant, by action of debt, in any Court proper to try the same, saving moreover to the person claiming such labor or service his right of action for or on account of the said injuries, or either of them.

Approved [signed into law by President George Washington], February 12, 1793.

DAVID WALKER

Appeal to the Coloured Citizens of the World but in Particular and Very Expressly, to Those of the United States of America, 1829

Intellectually, David Walker was much engaged with the ideas of Thomas Jefferson, especially Jefferson's claims in Notes on the State of Virginia *about Black inferiority, which were widely accepted by white Americans in the early nineteenth century (see page 88 in this game book). But Walker also found great value in the Declaration's proclaiming mankind's right of revolution, which Walker saw as a dagger pointed at the rule of slaveholders.*

The Appeal *also takes aim at Henry Clay and the Colonization movement and repeatedly slashes at the religious claims of American slaveholders. Walker's* Appeal *is one of the key works in African American letters and of the centuries-long Black freedom struggle. (The Colonization movement said Black people in the United States should be sent "back" to Africa.)*

David Walker was born around 1796, in or around Wilmington, North Carolina, the son of a free woman of color and a slave man. As the son of a free woman, he was never a slave but grew up in a slave state and observed slavery closely. In the Wilmington area, he was part of the African Methodist tradition, and its values are clear in the Appeal: *racial solidarity and uplift; Christian evangelism and the hope for redemption in a sinful world; the Lord's imperative that men actively do right and combat the devil; and a commitment to learning, Bible reading, and human equality. Much is unknown about Walker's life, but it is clear that he left Wilmington and spent some time in Charleston, South Carolina, before moving to Boston around 1825, where he worked as a used-clothes dealer, serving many Black seamen as customers. Sean Wilentz states, "In September 1829, he published the first edition of his own pamphlet and began sending copies southward. Two revised editions appeared over the next nine months" (xv). Southern officials sought to get Boston authorities to suppress Walker and his pamphlet, but much as they deplored his work, he had violated no Massachusetts law. Southern leg-*

islatures passed "new laws banning works like Walker's; and rumors had begun to circulate that southerners had put out a price of $3,000 for Walker's head (Wilentz, xix).

He died on August 3, 1830, at his home in Boston. While there was no proof of violence, Walker's sympathizers concluded that he had been murdered—the *Appeal* had predicted that his life would be targeted by slaveholders. Many African Americans regarded him as a martyr for the cause of freedom. In contrast, southern spokesmen saw Walker as the embodiment of threatened violence and social chaos; Walker was trying to inspire slave uprisings and the killing of whites. Many southern demands for northern states to suppress Abolitionist writings were made in the wake of the *Appeal* and after the founding of the *Liberator* newspaper by William Lloyd Garrison in 1831. Garrison republished much of the *Appeal* in his *Liberator*, but he disagreed with Walker on calling for slave insurrection. Walker actively sought ways of getting his pamphlet South, and copies were found among Blacks in the coastal South. Walker was blamed by some for Nat Turner's slave rebellion in Virginia, which took place a year after his death.

SOURCE: *David Walker,* Walker's Appeal, in Four Articles; Together with a Preamble, to the Coloured Citizens of the World, but in Particular, and Very Expressly, to Those of the United States of America *(Boston, 1830).*

Preamble

* * * All I ask is, for a candid and careful perusal of this the third and last edition of my Appeal, where the world may see that we, the Blacks or Coloured People, are treated more cruel by the white Christians of America, than devils themselves ever treated a set of men, women and children on this earth.

It is expected that all coloured men, women and children, of every nation, language and tongue under heaven, will try to procure a copy of this Appeal and read it, or get some one to read it to them, for it is designed more particularly for them. Let them remember, that though our cruel oppressors and murderers, may (if possible) treat us more cruel, as Pharoah did the children of Israel, yet the God of the Etheopeans, has been pleased to hear our moans in consequence of oppression; and the day of our redemption from abject wretchedness draweth near. * * *

I am fully aware, in making this appeal to my much afflicted and suffering brethren, that I shall not only be assailed by those whose greatest earthly desires are, to keep us in abject ignorance and wretchedness, and who are of the firm conviction that Heaven has designed us and our children to be slaves and *beasts of burden* to them and their children. I * * * expect to be held up to the public as an ignorant, impudent and restless disturber of the public peace, by such avaricious creatures, as well as a mover of insubordination—and perhaps put in prison or to death. * * *

* * *

* * * The fact is, the labour of slaves comes so cheap to the avaricious usurpers, and is (as they think) of such great utility to the country where it exists, that those who are actuated by sordid avarice only, overlook the evils, which will as sure as the Lord lives, follow after the good. In fact, they are so happy to keep in ignorance and degradation, and to receive the homage and the labour of the slaves, they forget that God rules in the armies of heaven and among the inhabitants of the earth, having his ears continually open to the cries, tears and groans of his oppressed people; and being a just and holy Being will at one day appear fully in behalf of the oppressed, and arrest the progress of the avaricious oppressors; * * * not unfrequently will he cause them to rise up one against another, to be split and divided, and to oppress each other, and sometimes to open hostilities with sword in hand. * * * Will he let the oppressors rest comfortably and happy always? Will he not cause the very children of the oppressors to rise up against them, and oftimes put them to death? "God works in many ways his wonders to perform."

* * *

* * * I declare, it does appear to me, as though some nations think God is asleep, or that he made the Africans for nothing else but to dig their mines and work their farms, or they cannot believe history, sacred or profane. I ask every man who has a heart, and is blessed with the privilege of believing—Is not God a God of justice to *all* his creatures? * * *

ARTICLE I. OUR WRETCHEDNESS IN CONSEQUENCE OF SLAVERY

* * *

* * * [W]e, (coloured people of these United States of America) are the *most wretched, degraded* and *abject* set of beings that *ever lived* since the world began, and that the white Americans having reduced us to the wretched state of *slavery,* treat us in that condition *more cruel* (they being an enlighted and Christian people,) than any heathen nation did any people whom it had reduced to our condition. * * *

* * *

* * * Let our enemies go on with their butcheries, and at once fill up their cup. Never make an attempt to gain our freedom or *natural right,* from under our cruel oppressors and murderers, until you see your way clear—when that hour arrives and you move, be not afraid or dismayed; for be you assured that Jesus Christ the King of heaven and of earth who is the God of justice and of armies, will surely go before you. And those enemies who have for hundreds of years stolen our *rights,* and kept us ignorant of Him and His divine worship, he will remove. * * *

* * * Mr. Jefferson's very severe remarks on us have been so extensively argued upon by men whose attainments in literature, I shall never be able to reach, that I would not have meddled with it, were it not to solicit each of my brethren, who has the spirit of a man, to buy a copy of Mr. Jefferson's "Notes on Virginia," and put it in the hand of his son. For let no one of us suppose that the refutations which have been written by our white friends are enough—they are *whites*—we are *blacks*. We, and the world wish to see the charges of Mr. Jefferson refuted by the blacks *themselves,* * * * what the whites have written respecting this subject, is other men's labours, and did not emanate from the blacks. I know well, that there are some talents and learning among the coloured people of this country, which we have not a chance to develope, in consequence of oppression; but our oppression ought not to hinder us from acquiring all we can. * * *

But let us review Mr. Jefferson's remarks respecting us some further. Comparing our miserable fathers, with the learned philosophers of Greece, he says: "Yet notwithstanding these and other discouraging circumstances among the Romans, their slaves were often their rarest artists. They excelled too, in science, insomuch as to be usually employed as tutors to their master's children; Epictetus, Terence and Phædrus, were slaves,—but they were of the race of whites. It is not their *condition* then, but *nature,* which has produced the distinction." See this, my brethren ! ! Do you believe that this assertion is swallowed by millions of the whites? Do you know that Mr. Jefferson was one of as great characters as ever lived among the whites? * * * I say, that unless we try to refute Mr. Jefferson's arguments respecting us, we will only establish them.

* * *

* * * I must observe to my brethren that at the close of the first Revolution in this country, with Great Britain, there were but thirteen States in the Union, now there are twenty-four, most of which are slave-holding States, and the whites are dragging us around in chains and in handcuffs, to their new States and Territories to work their mines and farms, to enrich them and their children—and millions of them believing firmly that we being a little darker than they, were made by our Creator to be an inheritance to them and their children for ever—the same as a parcel of *brutes*. Are we MEN ! !—I ask you, O my brethren ! are we MEN? Did our Creator make us to be slaves to dust and ashes like ourselves? Are they not dying worms as well as we? Have they not to make their appearance before the tribunal of Heaven, to answer for the deeds done in the body, as well as we? Have we any other Master but Jesus Christ alone? Is he not their Master as well as ours?—What right then, have we to obey and call any other Master, but Himself? * * *

The whites have always been an unjust, jealous, unmerciful, avaricious and blood-thirsty set of beings, always seeking after power and authority. * * *

* * * [W]hile they were heathens, they were bad enough it is true, but it is positively a fact that they were not quite so audacious as to go and take vessel loads

of men, women and children, and in cold blood, and through devilishness, throw them into the sea, and murder them in all kind of ways. While they were heathens, they were too ignorant for such barbarity. But being Christians, enlightened and sensible, they are completely prepared for such hellish cruelties. * * *

ARTICLE II. OUR WRETCHEDNESS IN CONSEQUENCE OF IGNORANCE

* * *

The whites want slaves, and want us for their slaves, but some of them will curse the day they ever saw us. As true as the sun ever shone in its meridian splendor, my colour will root some of them out of the very face of the earth. They shall have enough of making slaves of, and butchering, and murdering us in the manner which they have. * * * I should like to see the whites repent peradventure God may have mercy on them, some however, have gone so far that their cup must be filled. * * *

* * * [F]or I must truly say, that ignorance, the mother of treachery and deceit, gnaws into our very vitals. Ignorance, as it now exists among us, produces a state of things, Oh my Lord ! too horrible to present to the world. Any man who is curious to see the full force of ignorance developed among the coloured people of the United States of America, has only to go into the southern and western states * * * where, if he is not a tyrant, but has the feelings of a human being, who can feel for a fellow creature, he may see enough to make his very heart bleed ! He may see there, a son take his mother, who bore almost the pains of death to give him birth, and by the command of a tyrant, strip her as naked as she came into the world, and apply the cow-hide to her, until she falls a victim to death in the road ! He may see a husband take his dear wife, not unfrequently in a pregnant state, and perhaps far advanced, and beat her for an unmerciful wretch, until his infant falls a lifeless lump at her feet ! Can the Americans escape God Almighty? If they do, can he be to us a God of Justice? God is just, and I know it—for he has convinced me to my satisfaction— I cannot doubt him. * * * Oh Heaven ! I am full ! ! ! ! I can hardly move my pen ! ! ! and as I expect some will try to put me to death, to strike terror into others, and to obliterate from their minds the notion of freedom, so as to keep my brethren the more secure in wretchedness. * * * There have been and are at this day in Boston, New-York, Philadelphia, and Baltimore, coloured men, who are in league with tyrants, and who receive a great portion of their daily bread, of the moneys which they acquire from the blood and tears of their more miserable brethren, whom they scandalously delivered into the hands of our *natural enemies ! ! ! ! ! !*

* * *

* * * I know that the blacks, take them half enlightened and ignorant, are more humane and merciful than the most enlightened and refined European that can be found in all the earth. Let no one say that I assert this because I am preju-

diced on the side of my colour, and against the whites or Europeans. For what I write, I do it candidly, for my God and the good of both parties: Natural observations have taught me these things; there is a solemn awe in the hearts of the blacks, as it respects *murdering* men: whereas the whites, (though they are great cowards) where they have the advantage, or think that there are any prospects of getting it, they murder all before them, in order to subject men to wretchedness and degradation under them. This is the natural result of pride and avarice. * * * [W]e must remember that *humanity, kindness* and the *fear of the Lord,* does not consist in protecting *devils.* * * * Are God and Mammon in league? What has the Lord to do with a gang of desperate wretches, who go *sneaking about the country like robbers*—light upon his people wherever they can get a chance, binding them with chains and hand-cuffs, beat and murder them as they would *rattle-snakes?* Are they not the Lord's enemies? Ought they not to be destroyed? Any person who will save such wretches from destruction, is fighting against the Lord, and will receive his just recompense. * * * I do declare it, that one good black man can put to death six white men; and I give it as a fact, let twelve black men get well armed for battle, and they will kill and put to flight fifty whites.—The reason is, the blacks, once you get them started, they glory in death. The whites have had us under them for more than three centuries, murdering, and treating us like brutes; and, as Mr. Jefferson wisely said, they have never *found us out*—they do not know, indeed, that there is an unconquerable disposition in the breasts of the blacks, which, when it is fully awakened and put in motion, will be subdued, only with the destruction of the animal existence. * * * Look upon your mother, wife and children, and answer God Almighty; and believe this, that it is no more harm for you to kill a man, who is trying to kill you, than it is for you to take a drink of water when thirsty; in fact, the man who will stand still and let another murder him, is worse than an infidel. * * * How could Mr. Jefferson but say, "I advance it therefore as a suspicion only, that the blacks, whether originally a distinct race, or made distinct by time and circumstances, are *inferior* to the whites in the endowments both of body and mind?"—"It," says he, "is not against experience to suppose, that different species of the same genus, or varieties of the same species, may possess different qualifications." [Here, my brethren, listen to him.] "Will not a lover of natural history, then, one who views the gradations in all the races of *animals* with the eye of philosophy, excuse an effort to keep those in the department of MAN as *distinct* as nature has formed them?"—I hope you will try to find out the meaning of this verse—its widest sense and all its bearings: whether you do or not, remember the whites do. This very verse, brethren, having emanated from Mr. Jefferson, a much greater philosopher the world never afforded, has in truth injured us more, and has been as great a barrier to our emancipation as any thing that has ever been advanced against us. * * * He goes on further, and says: "This *unfortunate* difference of colour, and *perhaps of faculty,* is a powerful obstacle to the emancipation of these people. Many of their advocates, while they wish to vindicate the liberty of human nature are anxious also to preserve its *dignity* and *beauty.* Some of these, embarrassed by the question, 'What further is to be done with them?' join themselves in opposition with those who are actuated by sordid avarice only." Now I ask you candidly, my suffering brethren in time, who are candidates for the eternal worlds, how could Mr. Jefferson but have given the world these remarks respecting us, when we are so submissive to them, and so much servile deceit prevail among ourselves—when we so *meanly* submit to their murderous lashes, to which neither the Indians nor any other people under Heaven would submit? * * * For my own part, I am glad Mr. Jefferson has advanced his positions for your sake; for you will either have to contradict or confirm him by your own actions, and not by what our friends have said or done for us; for those things are other men's labours, and do not satisfy the Americans, who are waiting for us to prove to them ourselves, that we are MEN, before they will be willing to admit the fact; for I pledge you my sacred word of honour, that Mr. Jefferson's remarks respecting us, have sunk deep into the hearts of millions of the whites, and never will be removed this side of eternity.—For how can they, when we are confirming him every day, by our *groveling submissions* and *treachery?*

I aver, that when I look over these United States of America, and the world, and see the ignorant deceptions and consequent wretchedness of my brethren, I am brought oftimes solemnly to a stand, and in the midst of my reflections I exclaim to my God, "Lord didst thou make us to be slaves to our brethren, the whites?" But when I reflect that God is just, and that millions of my wretched brethren would meet death with glory—yea, more, would plunge into the very mouths of cannons and be torn into particles as minute as the atoms which compose the elements of the earth, in preference to a mean submission to the lash of tyrants, I am with streaming eyes, compelled to shrink back into nothingness before my Maker, and exclaim again, thy will be done, O Lord God Almighty.

* * *

* * * [F]or colored people to acquire learning in this country, makes tyrants quake and tremble on their sandy foundation. * * *

* * *

* * * It is a notorious fact, that the major part of the white Americans, have, ever since we have been among them, tried to keep us ignorant, and make us believe that God made us and our children to be slaves to them and theirs. *Oh ! my God, have mercy on Christian Americans ! ! !*

ARTICLE III. OUR WRETCHEDNESS IN CONSEQUENCE OF THE PREACHERS OF THE RELIGION OF JESUS CHRIST

Religion, my brethren, is a substance of deep consideration among all nations of the earth. The Pagans have a kind, as well as the Mahometans, the Jews and the Christians. But pure and undefiled religion, such as was preached by Jesus Christ and his apostles, is hard to be found in all the earth. God, through his instrument, Moses, handed a dispensation of his Divine will, to the children of Israel after they had left Egypt for the land of Canaan or of Promise, who through hypocrisy, oppression and unbelief, departed from the faith.—He then, by his apostles, handed a dispensation of his, together with the will of Jesus Christ, to the Europeans in Europe, who, in open violation of which, have made *merchandise* of us, and it does appear as though they take this very dispensation to aid them in their *infernal* depredations upon us. Indeed, the way in which religion was and is conducted by the Europeans and their descendants, one might believe it was a plan fabricated by themselves and the *devils* to oppress us. But hark ! My master has taught me better than to believe it—he has taught me that his gospel as it was preached by himself and his apostles remains the same, notwithstanding Europe has tried to mingle blood and oppression with it.

* * *

* * * But Christian Americans, not only hinder their fellow creatures, the Africans, but thousands of them *will absolutely beat a coloured person nearly to death, if they catch him on his knees, supplicating the throne of grace.* This barbarous cruelty was by all the heathen nations of antiquity, and is by the Pagans, Jews and Mahometans of the present day, left entirely to Christian Americans to inflict on the Africans and their descendants, that their cup which is nearly full may be completed. I have known tyrants or usurpers of human liberty in different parts of this country to take their fellow creatures, the coloured people, and beat them until they would scarcely leave life in them; what for? Why they say "The black devils had the audacity to be found *making prayers and supplications to the God who made them ! ! ! !*" Yes, I have known small collections of coloured people to have convened together, for no other purpose than to worship God Almighty, in spirit and in truth, to the best of their knowledge; when tyrants, calling themselves *patrols,* would also convene and wait almost in breathless silence for the poor coloured people to commence singing and praying to the Lord our God, as soon as they had commenced, the wretches would burst in upon them and drag them out and commence beating them as they would rattle-snakes—many of whom, they would beat so unmercifully, that they would hardly be able to crawl for weeks and sometimes for months. Yet the American minister send out missionaries to convert the heathen, while they keep us and our children sunk at their feet in the most abject ignorance and wretchedness that ever a people was afflicted with since the world began. Will the Lord suffer this people to proceed much longer? * * * Have not the Americans the Bible in their hands? Do they believe it? Surely they do not. See how they treat us in open violation of the Bible ! ! * * * Our divine Lord and Master said, "all things whatsoever ye would that men should do unto you, do ye even so unto them." But an American minister, with the Bible in his hand, holds us and our children in the most abject slavery and wretchedness. Now I ask them, would they like for us to hold them and their children in abject slavery and wretchedness? * * * I have known pretended preachers of the gospel of my Master, who not only held us as their natural inher-

itance, but treated us with as much rigor as any Infidel or Deist in the world— just as though they were intent only on taking our blood and groans to glorify the Lord Jesus Christ. * * * What the American preachers can think of us, I aver this day before my God, I have never been able to define. They have newspapers and monthly periodicals, which they receive in continual succession, but on the pages of which, you will scarcely ever find a paragraph respecting slavery, which is ten thousand times more injurious to this country than all the other evils put together; and which will be the final overthrow of its government, unless something is very speedily done; for their cup is nearly full.—Perhaps they will laugh at or make light of this; but I tell you Americans ! that unless you speedily alter your course, *you* and your *Country are gone ! ! ! ! ! !* For God Almighty will tear up the very face of the earth ! ! ! Will not that very remarkable passage of Scripture be fulfilled on Christian Americans? Hear it Americans ! ! "He that is unjust, let him be unjust still:—and he which is filthy, let him be filthy still: and he that is righteous, let him be righteous still: and he that is holy, let him be holy still." I hope that the Americans may hear, but I am afraid that they have done us so much injury, and are so firm in the belief that our Creator made us to be an inheritance to them for ever, that their hearts will be hardened, so that their destruction may be sure. * * *

* * *

* * * Will the Lord suffer this people to go on much longer, taking his holy name in vain? Will he not stop them, PREACHERS and all? O Americans ! Americans ! ! I call God—I call angels—I call men, to witness, that your DESTRUCTION *is at hand,* and will be speedily consummated unless you REPENT.

ARTICLE IV. OUR WRETCHEDNESS IN CONSEQUENCE OF THE COLONIZING PLAN

* * *

At a meeting which was convened in the District of Columbia, for the express purpose of agitating the subject of colonizing us in some part of the world, Mr. Clay was called to the chair, * * * says he—"That class of the mixt population of our country [coloured people] was peculiarly situated; they neither enjoyed the immunities of freemen, nor were they subjected to the incapacities of slaves, but partook, in some degree, of the qualities of both. From their condition, and the unconquerable prejudices resulting from their colour, they never could amalgamate with the free whites of this country. It was desirable, therefore, as it respected them, and the residue of the population of the country, to drain them off. Various schemes of colonization had been thought of, and a part of our continent, it was supposed by some, might furnish a suitable establishment for them. But, for his part, Mr. C. said, he had a decided preference for some part of the Coast of Africa. There ample provision might be made for the colony itself, and it might be rendered instrumental to the introduction into that extensive quarter of the globe, of the arts, civilization, and Christianity."[1] * * * Are Mr. Clay and the rest of the Americans, innocent of the blood and groans of our fathers and us, their children?—Every individual may plead innocence, if he pleases, but God will, before long, separate the innocent from the guilty, unless something is speedily done—which I suppose will hardly be, so that their destruction may be sure. * * * But to return to Mr. Clay. * * * He says, "It was proper and necessary distinctly to state, that he understood it constituted no part of the object of this meeting, to touch or agitate in the slightest degree, a delicate question, connected with another portion of the coloured population of our country. It was not proposed to deliberate upon or consider at all, any question of emancipation, or that which was connected with the abolition of slavery. It was upon that condition alone, he was sure, that many gentlemen from the South and the West, whom he saw present, had attended, or could be expected to co-operate. It was upon that condition only, that he himself had attended."—That is to say, to fix a plan to get those of the coloured people, who are said to be free, away from among those of our brethren whom they unjustly hold in bondage, so that they may be enabled to keep them the more secure in ignorance and wretchedness, to support them and their children, and consequently they would have the more obedient slaves. For if the free are allowed to stay among the slaves, they will have intercourse together, and, of course, the free will learn the slaves *bad habits,* by teaching them that they are MEN, as well as other people, and certainly *ought* and *must* be FREE.

* * *

* * * Do you believe that Mr. Henry Clay, late Secretary of State, and now in Kentucky, is a friend to the blacks, further, than his personal interest extends? Is it not his greatest object and glory upon earth, to sink us into miseries and wretchedness by making slaves of us, to work his plantation to enrich him and his family? * * * This same Mr. Clay, wants to know, what he has done, to merit the disapprobation of the American people. In a public speech delivered by him, he asked: * * * "Did I bring obliquy upon the nation, or the people whom I represented?—did I ever lose any opportunity to advance the fame, honor and prosperity of this State and the Union?" How astonishing it is, for a man who knows so much about God and his ways, as Mr. Clay, to ask such frivolous questions? Does he believe that a man of his talents and standing in the midst of a people, will get along unnoticed by the penetrating and all seeing eye of God, who is continually taking cognizance of the hearts of men? Is not God against him, for advocating the murderous cause of slavery? * * *

* * *

* * * What our brethren could have been thinking about, who have left their native land and home and gone away to Africa, I am unable to say. This country is

---

1. The quotes from Henry Clay and an account of the Colonization meeting are from the newspaper *The National Intelligencer,* December 24, 1816, as noted in the Hill and Wang edition.

as much ours as it is the whites, whether they will admit it now or not, they will see and believe it by and by. ＊ ＊ ＊

＊ ＊ ＊ The Americans say, that we are ungrateful—but I ask them for heaven's sake, what should we be grateful to them for—for murdering our fathers and mothers?—Or do they wish us to return thanks to them for chaining and handcuffing us, branding us, cramming fire down our throats, or for keeping us in slavery, and beating us nearly or quite to death to make us work in ignorance and miseries, to support them and their families. They certainly think that we are a gang of fools. Those among them, who have volunteered their services for our redemption, though we are unable to compensate them for their labours, we nevertheless thank them from the bottom of our hearts, and have our eyes steadfastly fixed upon them, and their labours of love for God and man.—But do slave-holders think that we thank them for keeping us in miseries, and taking our lives by the inches?

＊ ＊ ＊

＊ ＊ ＊ We can help ourselves; for, if we lay aside abject servility, and be determined to act like men, and not brutes—the murderers among the whites would be afraid to show their cruel heads. But O, my God !—in sorrow I must say it, that my colour, all over the world, have a mean, servile spirit. They yield in a moment to the whites, let them be right or wrong—the reason they are able to keep their feet on our throats. Oh ! my coloured brethren, all over the world, when shall we arise from this death-like apathy?—And be men ! ! ＊ ＊ ＊

＊ ＊ ＊

＊ ＊ ＊ Now we have to determine whose advice we will take respecting this all important matter, whether we will adhere to Mr. Clay and his slave holding party, who have always been our oppressors and murderers, and who are for colonizing us, more through apprehension than humanity, or to this godly man who has done so much for our benefit. ＊ ＊ ＊ Let no man of us budge one step, and let slave-holders come to beat us from our country. America is more our country, than it is the whites—we have enriched it with our *blood and tears*. ＊ ＊ ＊ [A]nd will they drive us from our property and homes, which we have earned with our *blood?* They must look sharp or this very thing will bring swift destruction upon them. The Americans have got so fat on our blood and groans, that they have almost forgotten the God of armies. ＊ ＊ ＊

ADDITION.—I will give here a very imperfect list of the cruelties inflicted on us by the enlightened Christians of America.—First, no trifling portion of them will beat us nearly to death, if they find us on our knees praying to God,—They hinder us from going to hear the word of God—they keep us sunk in ignorance, and will not let us learn to read the word of God, nor write—If they find us with a book of any description in our hand, they will beat us nearly to death—they are so afraid we will learn to read, and enlighten our dark and benighted minds—They will not suffer us to meet together to worship the God who made us—they brand us with hot iron—they cram bolts of fire down our throats—they cut us as they do horses, bulls, or hogs—they crop our ears and sometimes cut off bits of our tongues—they chain and hand-cuff us, and while in that miserable and wretched condition, beat us with cow-hides and clubs—they keep us half naked and starve us sometimes nearly to death under their infernal whips or lashes (which some of them shall have enough of yet)—They put on us fifty-sixes and chains, and make us work in that cruel situation, and in sickness, under lashes to support them and their families. * * * [A]nd to crown the whole of this catalogue of cruelties, they tell us that we the (blacks) are an inferior race of beings ! incapable of self government ! !—We would be injurious to society and ourselves, if tyrants should loose their unjust hold on us ! ! ! That if we were free we would not work, but would live on plunder or theft ! ! ! ! that we are the meanest and laziest set of beings in the world ! ! ! ! ! That they are obliged to keep us in bondage to do us good ! ! ! ! ! !—That we are satisfied to rest in slavery to them and their children ! ! ! ! ! !—That we ought not to be set free in America, but ought to be sent away to Africa ! ! ! ! ! ! ! !—That if we were set free in America, we would involve the country in a civil war, which assertion is altogether at variance with our feeling or design, for we ask them for nothing but the rights of man, viz. for them to set us free, and treat us like men, and there will be no danger, for we will love and respect them, and protect our country—but cannot conscientiously do these things until they treat us like men.

* * *

* * * Some of the advocates of this cunningly devised plot of Satan represent us to be the greatest set of cut-throats in the world, as though God wants us to take his work out of his hand before he is ready. Does not vengeance belong to the Lord? Is he not able to repay the Americans for their cruelties, with which they have afflicted Africa's sons and daughters, without our interference, unless we are ordered? * * * I speak Americans for your good. We must and shall be free I say, in spite of you. You may do your best to keep us in wretchedness and misery, to enrich you and your children, but God will deliver us from under you. And wo, wo, will be to you if we have to obtain our freedom by fighting. Throw away your fears and prejudices then, and enlighten us and treat us like men, and we will like you more than we do now hate you, and tell us now no more about colonization, for America is as much our country, as it is yours.—Treat us like men, and there is no danger but we will all live in peace and happiness together. For we are not like you, hard hearted, unmerciful, and unforgiving. What a happy country this will be, if the whites will listen. * * *

* * *

* * * I also ask the attention of the world of mankind to the declaration of these very American people, of the United States.

A declaration made July 4, 1776.

It says, "When in the course of human events, it becomes necessary for one people to dissolve the political bands which have connected them with another, and to assume among the Powers of the earth, the separate and equal station to which the laws of nature and of nature's God entitle them. A decent respect for the opinions of mankind requires, that they should declare the causes which impel them to the separation.— We hold these truths to be self evident—that all men are created equal, that they are endowed by their Creator with certain unalienable rights: that among these, are life, liberty, and the pursuit of happiness that, to secure these rights, governments are instituted among men, deriving their just powers from the consent of the governed; that when ever any form of government becomes destructive of these ends, it is the right of the people to alter or to abolish it, and to institute a new government laying its foundation on such principles, and organizing its powers in such form, as to them shall seem most likely to effect their safety and happiness. Prudence, indeed, will dictate, that governments long established should not be changed for light and transient causes; and accordingly all experience hath shewn, that mankind are more disposed to suffer, while evils are sufferable, than to right themselves by abolishing the forms to which they are accustomed. But when a long train of abuses and usurpations, pursuing invariably the same object, evinces a design to reduce them under absolute despotism, it is their right it is their duty to throw off such government, and to provide new guards for their future security." See your Declaration Americans ! ! ! Do you understand your own language? Hear your language, proclaimed to the world, July 4th, 1776— "We hold these truths to be self evident—that ALL MEN ARE CREATED EQUAL ! ! that they *are endowed by their Creator with certain unalienable rights;* that among these are life, *liberty,* and the pursuit of happiness ! !" * * *

* * *

WILLIAM LLOYD GARRISON

The Liberator, January 1, 1831

The following selection is from the very first issue of the Abolitionist newspaper The Liberator, *founded by Garrison. It created a sensation with its demand for immediate abolition. The quotation in the last line is from Proverbs 29:25. Three prefatory paragraphs and a concluding poem are omitted here.*

SOURCE: *William Lloyd Garrison,* The Liberator *(Boston: William Lloyd Garrison and Isaac Knapp, Publishers, 1831), vol. 1, no. 1.*

* * *

TO THE PUBLIC.

* * *

*A*ssenting to the 'self-evident truth' maintained in the American Declaration of Independence, 'that all men are created equal, and endowed by their Creator with certain inalienable rights—among which are life, liberty and the pursuit of happiness,' I shall strenuously contend for the immediate enfranchisement of our slave population. In Park-street Church, on the Fourth of July, 1829, in an address on slavery, I unreflectingly assented to the popular but pernicious doctrine of *gradual* abolition. I seize this opportunity to make a full and unequivocal recantation, and thus publicly to ask pardon of my God, of my country, and of my brethren the poor slaves, for having uttered a sentiment so full of timidity, injustice and absurdity. A similar recantation, from my pen, was published in the Genius of Universal Emancipation at Baltimore, in September, 1829. My conscience is now satisfied.

I am aware, that many object to the severity of my language; but is there not cause for severity? I *will be* as harsh as truth, and as uncompromising as justice. On this subject, I do not wish to think, or speak, or write, with moderation. No! no! Tell a man whose house is on fire, to give a moderate alarm; tell him to moderately rescue his wife from the hands of the ravisher; tell the mother to gradually extricate her babe from the fire into which it has fallen;—but urge me not to use moderation in a cause like the present. I am in earnest—I will not equivocate—I will not excuse—I will not retreat a single inch—AND I WILL BE HEARD. The apathy of the people is enough to make every statue leap from its pedestal, and to hasten the resurrection of the dead.

It is pretended, that I am retarding the cause of emancipation by the coarseness of my invective, and the precipitancy of my measures. *The charge is not true.* On this question my influence,—humble as it is,—is felt at this moment to a considerable extent, and shall be felt in coming years—not perniciously, but beneficially—not as a curse, but as a blessing; and posterity will bear testimony that I was right. I desire to thank God, that he enables me to disregard 'the fear of man which bringeth a snare,' and to speak his truth in its simplicity and power. * * *

THOMAS R. DEW

Review of the Debate in the Virginia Legislature of 1831 and 1832

Also known as "An Essay in Favor of Slavery" and first published as a pamphlet in 1832.

SOURCE: *Thomas R. Dew,* Review of the Debate in the Virginia Legislature of 1831 and 1832 *(Richmond: T. W. White, 1832).*

*J*t is said slavery is wrong, in the *abstract* at least, and contrary to the spirit of Christianity. To this we answer—that any question must be determined by its circumstances, and if, as really is the case, we cannot get rid of slavery without producing a greater injury to both the masters and slaves, there is no rule of conscience or revealed law of God which *can* condemn us. The physician will not order the spreading cancer to be extirpated although it will eventually cause the death of his patient, because he would thereby hasten the fatal issue.

So, if slavery had commenced even contrary to the laws of God and man, and the sin of its introduction rested upon our heads, and it was even carrying forward the nation by slow degrees to final ruin—yet if it were *certain* that an attempt to remove it would only hasten and heighten the final catastrophe—then we would only be found to attempt the extirpation but we would stand guilty of a high offense in the sight of both God and man if we should rashly made the effort. But the original sin of introduction rest[s] not on our heads, and we shall soon see that all those dreadful calamities which the false prophets of our day are pointing to will never, in all probability, occur.

With regard to the assertion that slavery is against the spirit of Christianity, we are ready to admit the general assertion, but deny most positively that there is anything in the Old or New Testament which would go to show that slavery, when once introduced, ought at all events to be abrogated, or that the master commits any offense in holding slaves. The children of Israel themselves were slaveholders wand were not condemned for it. All the patriarchs themselves were slaveholders; Abraham had more than three hundred, Isaac had a "great store" of them; and even the patient and meek Job himself had *"a very great household."* When the children of Israel conquered the land of Canaan, they made one whole tribe "hewers of wood and drawers of water," and they were at that very time under the special guidance of Jehovah; they were permitted expressly to purchase slaves of the heathen and keep them as an inheritance for their posterity; and even the children of Israel might be enslaved for six years.

When we turn to the New Testament, we find not one single passage at all calculated to disturb the conscience of an honest slaveholder. No one can read it without seeing and admiring that the meek and humble Saviour of the world in no instance meddled with the established institutions of mankind; he came to save a fallen work, and not to excite the black passions of man and array them in deadly hostility against each other. From no one did he turn away; his plan was offered alike to all—to the monarch and the subject, the rich and the poor, the master and the slave. He was born in the Roman world, a world in which the most galling slavery existed, a thousand times more cruel than the slavery in our own country; and yet he nowhere encourages insurrection, he nowhere fosters discontent; but exhorts *always* to implicit obedience and fidelity.

What a rebuke does the practice of the Redeemer of mankind imply upon the conduct of some of his nominal disciples of the day, who seek to destroy the contentment of the slave, to rouse their most deadly passions, to break up the deep foundations of society, and to lead on to a night of darkness and confusion! "Let every man," (says Paul) "abide in the same calling wherein he is called. Art thou called *being* a servant? Care not for it; but if thou mayest be made free, use *it* rather" (I *Corinth. vii.* 20,21). * * * Servants are even commanded in Scripture to be faithful and obedient to unkind masters. "Servants," (says Peter) "be subject to your masters with all fear; not only to the good and gentle but to the forward. For what glory is it if when ye shall be buffeted for your faults ye take it patiently; but if when ye do will and suffer for it, yet take it patiently, this is acceptable with God" (I *Peter ii.* 18,20). These and many other passages in the New Testament most convincingly prove that slavery in the Roman world was nowhere charged as a fault or crime upon the holder, and everywhere is the most implicit obedience enjoined. We beg leave * * * to address a few remarks to those who have conscientious scruples about the holding of slaves, and therefore consider themselves under an obligation to break all the ties of friendship and kindred— dissolve all the associations of happier days to flee to a land where this evil does not exist. We cannot condemn the conscientious actions of mankind, but we must be permitted to say that if the assumption even of these pious gentlemen be correct, we do consider their conduct as very unphilosophical; and we will go further still: we look upon it as even immoral upon their own principles.

Let us admit that slavery is an evil; and what then? Why, it has been entailed upon us, and throw the slave, in consequence, unto those hands of those who have no scruples of conscience—those who will not perhaps treat him so kindly? No! This is not philosophy, it is not morality; * * * Look to the slaveholding population of our country and you everywhere find them characterized by noble and elevated sentiments, by humane and virtuous feelings. We do not find among them that cold, contracted, calculating *selfishness,* which withers and repels everything around it, and lessens or destroys all the multiplied enjoyments of social intercourse. Go into our national councils and ask for the most generous, the most disinterested, the most conscientious, and the least unjust and oppressive in their principles, and see whether the slaveholder will be passed by in the selection. * * *

Is it not a fact known to every man in the South that the most cruel masters are those who have been unaccustomed to slavery. It is well known that Northern gentleman who marry Southern heiresses are much severer masters than Southern gentlemen. * * * There may be many cruel masters, and there are unkind and cruel fathers too; but both the one and the other make all those around them shudder with horror. We are disposed to think that their example in society tends rather to strengthen than weaken the principle of benevolence and humanity.

Every one acquainted with Southern slaves knows that the slave rejoices in the elevation and prosperity of his master; and the heart of no one is more gladdened at the successful debut of the young master or miss on the great theater of the world than that of either the young slave who has grown up with them and shared in all their sports, and even partaken of all their delicacies, or the aged one who has looked on and watched them from birth to manhood, with the kindest and most affectionate solicitude, and has ever met from them all the kind treatment and generous sympathies of feeling, tender hearts. * * *

We have often heard slaveholders affirm that they would sooner rely upon their slaves' fidelity and attachment in the hour of danger and severe trial than on any other equal number of individuals; and we all know that the son or daughter who has been long absent from the parental roof, on returning to the scenes of infancy, never fails to be greeted with the kindest welcome and the most sincere and heartfelt congratulations from those slaves among whom he has been reared to manhood. * * *

A merrier being does not exist on the face of the globe than the Negro slave of the United States. * * *

Why, then, since the slave if happy, and happiness is the great object of all animated creation, should we endeavor to disturb his contentment by infusing into his mind a vain and indefinite desire for liberty—a something which he cannot comprehend, and which must inevitably dry up the very sources of his happiness.

The fact is that all of us, * * * are too prone to judge of the happiness of others by ourselves—we make *self* the standard and endeavor to draw down everyone to its dimensions—not recollecting that the benevolence of the Omnipotent has made the mind of man pliant and susceptible of happiness in almost every situation and employment. We might rather die than be the obscure slave that waits at our back—our education and our habits generate an ambition that makes us aspire at something loftier, and disposes us to look upon the slaves as unsusceptible of happiness in his humble sphere, when he may indeed be much happier than we are, and have his ambition too; but his ambition is to excel all this other slaves in the performance of his servile duties, to please and to gratify his master, and to command the praise of all who witness his exertions.

It has been contended that slavery is unfavorable to a republican spirit; but the whole history of the world proves that this is far from being the case. In the ancient republics of Greece and Rome, where the spirit of liberty glowed with the most intensity, the slaves were more numerous than the freemen. Aristotle and the great men of antiquity believed slavery necessary to keep alive the spirit of freedom. In Sparta the freeman were even forbidden to perform the offices of slaves, lest [they] might lose the spirit of independence. In modern times, too, liberty has always been more ardently desired by slaveholding communities.

* * * The menial and low offices being all performed by the blacks, there is at once taken away the greatest cause of distinction and separation of the ranks of society. The man to the north will not shake hands familiarly with his servant, and converse and laugh and dine with him, no matter how honest and respectable

he may be. But go to the south, and you will find that no white man feels such inferiority of rank as to be unworthy of association with those around him. Color alone here is the badge of distinction, the true mark of aristocracy, and all who are white are equal in spite of the variety of occupation. * * * And it is this spirit of equality which is both the generator and preserver of the genuine spirit of liberty.

WILLIAM LLOYD GARRISON

Declaration of Sentiments of the American Anti-Slavery Society, 1833

Written by Garrison, adopted at the founding convention of the American Anti-Slavery Society, and published in 1833, this Declaration assumes that Blacks in the United States are Americans, which Jefferson had denied. The Declaration of Sentiments also affirmed adherence to pacifism (thus rejecting the ideas of liberating violence, put forth by David Walker and others) and endorsed the dissolution of the Union—disunionism—as a step to weaken the slaveholders, whom the Abolitionists saw as reliant on the power and protection of the United States.

SOURCE: The text here is taken from *Selections from the Writings of William Lloyd Garrison* (Boston: R. F. Wallcut, 1852), pp. 67–71.

DECLARATION OF SENTIMENTS OF THE AMERICAN ANTI-SLAVERY CONVENTION.

*T*he Convention assembled in the city of Philadelphia, to organize a National Anti-Slavery Society, promptly seize the opportunity to promulgate the following Declaration of Sentiments, as cherished by them in relation to the enslavement of one-sixth portion of the American people.

More than fifty-seven years have elapsed, since a band of patriots convened in this place, to devise measures for the deliverance of this country from a foreign yoke. The corner-stone upon which they founded the Temple of Freedom was broadly this—'that all men are created equal; that they are endowed by their Creator with certain inalienable rights; that among these are life, LIBERTY, and the pursuit of happiness.' At the sound of their trumpet-call, three millions of people rose up as from the sleep of death, and rushed to the strife of blood; deeming it more glorious to die instantly as freemen, than desirable to live one hour as slaves. They were few in number—poor in resources; but the honest conviction that Truth, Justice and Right were on their side, made them invincible.

We have met together for the achievement of an enterprise, without which that of our fathers is incomplete; and which, for its magnitude, solemnity, and probable results upon the destiny of the world, as far transcends theirs as moral truth does physical force.

In purity of motive, in earnestness of zeal, in decision of purpose, in intrepidity of action, in steadfastness of faith, in sincerity of spirit, we would not be inferior to them.

Their principles led them to wage war against their oppressors, and to spill human blood like water, in order to be free. Ours forbid the doing of evil that good may come, and lead us to reject, and to entreat the oppressed to reject, the use of all carnal weapons for deliverance from bondage; relying solely upon those which are spiritual, and mighty through God to the pulling down of strong holds.

Their measures were physical resistance—the marshalling in arms—the hostile array—the mortal encounter. Ours shall be such only as the opposition of moral purity to moral corruption—the destruction of error by the potency of truth—the overthrow of prejudice by the power of love—and the abolition of slavery by the spirit of repentance.

Their grievances, great as they were, were trifling in comparison with the wrongs and sufferings of those for whom we plead. Our fathers were never slaves—never bought and sold like cattle—never shut out from the light of knowledge and religion—never subjected to the lash of brutal taskmasters.

But those, for whose emancipation we are striving—constituting at the present time at least one-sixth part of our countrymen—are recognized by law, and treated by their fellow-beings, as marketable commodities, as goods and chattels, as brute beasts; are plundered daily of the fruits of their toil without redress; really enjoy no constitutional nor legal protection from licentious and murderous outrages upon their persons; and are ruthlessly torn asunder—the tender babe from the arms of its frantic mother—the heart-broken wife from her weeping husband—at the caprice or pleasure of irresponsible tyrants. For the crime of having a dark complexion, they suffer the pangs of hunger, the infliction of stripes, the ignominy of brutal servitude. They are kept in heathenish darkness by laws expressly enacted to make their instruction a criminal offence.

These are the prominent circumstances in the condition of more than two millions of our people, the proof of which may be found in thousands of indisputable facts, and in the laws of the slaveholding States.

Hence we maintain—that, in view of the civil and religious privileges of this nation, the guilt of its oppression is unequalled by any other on the face of the earth; and, therefore, that it is bound to repent instantly, to undo the heavy burdens, and to let the oppressed go free.

We further maintain—that no man has a right to enslave or imbrute his brother—to hold or acknowledge him, for one moment, as a piece of merchandize—to keep back his hire by fraud—or to brutalize his mind, by denying him the means of intellectual, social and moral improvement.

The right to enjoy liberty is inalienable. To invade it is to usurp the prerogative of Jehovah. Every man has a right to his own body—to the products of his own labor—to the protection of law—and to the common advantages of society. It is piracy to buy or steal a native African, and subject him to servitude. Surely, the sin is as great to enslave an American as an African.

Therefore we believe and affirm—that there is no difference, in principle, between the African slave trade and American slavery:

That every American citizen, who detains a human being in involuntary bondage as his property, is, according to Scripture, (Ex. xxi. 16,) a man-stealer:

That the slaves ought instantly to be set free, and brought under the protection of law:

That if they had lived from the time of Pharaoh down to the present period, and had been entailed through successive generations, their right to be free could never have been alienated, but their claims would have constantly risen in solemnity:

That all those laws which are now in force, admitting the right of slavery, are therefore, before God, utterly null and void; being an audacious usurpation of the Divine prerogative, a daring infringement on the law of nature, a base overthrow of the very foundations of the social compact, a complete extinction of all the relations, endearments and obligations of mankind, and a presumptuous transgression of all the holy commandments; and that therefore they ought instantly to be abrogated.

We further believe and affirm—that all persons of color, who possess the qualifications which are demanded of others, ought to be admitted forthwith to the enjoyment of the same privileges, and the exercise of the same prerogatives, as others; and that the paths of preferment, of wealth, and of intelligence, should be opened as widely to them as to persons of a white complexion.

We maintain that no compensation should be given to the planters emancipating their slaves:

Because it would be a surrender of the great fundamental principle, that man cannot hold property in man:

Because slavery is a crime, and therefore is not an article to be sold:

Because the holders of slaves are not the just proprietors of what they claim; freeing the slave is not depriving them of property, but restoring it to its rightful owner; it is not wronging the master, but righting the slave—restoring him to himself:

Because immediate and general emancipation would only destroy nominal, not real property; it would not amputate a limb or break a bone of the slaves, but by infusing motives into their breasts, would make them doubly valuable to the masters as free laborers; and

Because, if compensation is to be given at all, it should be given to the outraged and guiltless slaves, and not to those who have plundered and abused them.

We regard as delusive, cruel and dangerous, any scheme of expatriation which pretends to aid, either directly or indirectly, in the emancipation of the slaves, or to be a substitute for the immediate and total abolition of slavery.

We fully and unanimously recognise the sovereignty of each State, to legislate exclusively on the subject of the slavery which is tolerated within its limits; we concede that Congress, under the present national compact, has no right to interfere with any of the slave States, in relation to this momentous subject:

But we maintain that Congress has a right, and is solemnly bound, to suppress the domestic slave trade between the several States, and to abolish slavery in those portions of our territory which the Constitution has placed under its exclusive jurisdiction.

We also maintain that there are, at the present time, the highest obligations resting upon the people of the free States to remove slavery by moral and political action, as prescribed in the Constitution of the United States. They are now living under a pledge of their tremendous physical force, to fasten the galling fetters of tyranny upon the limbs of millions in the Southern States; they are liable to be called at any moment to suppress a general insurrection of the slaves; they authorize the slave owner to vote for three-fifths of his slaves as property, and thus enable him to perpetuate his oppression; they support a standing army at the South for its protection; and they seize the slave, who has escaped into their territories, and send him back to be tortured by an enraged master or a brutal driver. This relation to slavery is criminal, and full of danger: IT MUST BE BROKEN UP.[1]

These are our views and principles—these our designs and measures. With entire confidence in the overruling justice of God, we plant ourselves upon the Declaration of our Independence and the truths of Divine Revelation, as upon the Everlasting Rock.

We shall organize Anti-Slavery Societies, if possible, in every city, town and village in our land.

We shall send forth agents to lift up the voice of remonstrance, of warning, of entreaty, and of rebuke.

We shall circulate, unsparingly and extensively, anti-slavery tracts and periodicals.

We shall enlist the pulpit and the press in the cause of the suffering and the dumb.

---

1. In this passage, the Declaration of Sentiments expresses the Garrisonian Abolitionist call for a breaking up of the Union of States, on the grounds that the union makes all citizens of the United States complicit in defending slavery and obeying a government controlled by the slaveholding class. Moral people, went the argument, cannot remain within immoral institutions, like the United States, but must answer to a "higher law," set by God.

We shall aim at a purification of the churches from all participation in the guilt of slavery.

We shall encourage the labor of freemen rather than that of slaves, by giving a preference to their productions: and

We shall spare no exertions nor means to bring the whole nation to speedy repentance.

Our trust for victory is solely in God. We may be personally defeated, but our principles never ! Truth, Justice, Reason, Humanity, must and will gloriously triumph. Already a host is coming up to the help of the Lord against the mighty, and the prospect before us is full of encouragement.

Submitting this Declaration to the candid examination of the people of this country, and of the friends of liberty throughout the world, we hereby affix our signatures to it; pledging ourselves that, under the guidance and by the help of Almighty God, we will do all that in us lies, consistently with this Declaration of our principles, to overthrow the most execrable system of slavery that has ever been witnessed upon earth; to deliver our land from its deadliest curse; to wipe out the foulest stain which rests upon our national escutcheon; and to secure to the colored population of the United States, all the rights and privileges which belong to them as men, and as Americans—come what may to our persons, our interests, or our reputation—whether we live to witness the triumph of Liberty, Justice and Humanity, or perish untimely as martyrs in this great, benevolent, and holy cause.

Done at Philadelphia, December 6th, A. D. 1833.

LEGISLATURE OF SOUTH CAROLINA

South Carolina Resolutions on Abolitionist Propaganda, December 16, 1835

Passed by the State legislature and sent to other states

Enslavers and southern leaders responded to the rise of immediate abolitionism with outrage that such dangerous views were being openly and freely advocated in parts of the United States. The legislature of South Carolina, heavily influenced by John C. Calhoun and his allies, passed a series of resolutions that, among other things, called the northern states to suppress the Abolitionists and their publications. The resolutions argued that since the United States was formed on an agreement that protected slavery, all antislavery criticism from people in the states was an attack on the very basis of the union.

SOURCE: Resolutions of the General Assembly of the State of South Carolina, December 1835 *(Printed by Charles W. Miller, State Printer).*

* * *

1. *Resolved,* That the formation of the Abolition Societies, and the Acts and doings of certain Fanatics, calling themselves Abolitionists, in the non-slave holding States of this confederacy, are in direct violation of the obligations of the compact of union, dissocial, and incendiary in the extreme.
2. *Resolved,* That no State having a just regard for her own peace and security, can acquiesce in a state of things by which such conspiracies are engendered within the limits of a friendly State, united to her by the bonds of a common league of political Association, without either surrendering or compromitting her most essential rights.
3. *Resolved,* That the Legislature of South Carolina, having every confidence in the justice and friendship of the non-slave holding States, announces to her co-states her confident expectation, and she earnestly requests that the governments of these States will promptly and effectually suppress all those associations within their respective limits, purporting to be Abolition Societies, and that they will make it highly penal to print, publish and distribute newspapers, pamphlets, tracts, and pictorial representations, calculated and having an obvious tendency to excite the slaves of the Southern States to insurrection and revolt.
4. *Resolved,* That, regarding the Domestic Slavery of the Southern States as a subject exclusively within the control of each of the said States, we shall consider every interference, by any other State or the General Government, as a direct and unlawful interference, to be resisted at once, and under every possible circumstance.
5. *Resolved,* In order that a salutary negative may be put on the mischievous, and unfounded assumption of some of the Abolitionists—the non-slaveholding States are requested to disclaim by legislative declaration, all right, either on the part of themselves or the government of the United States, to interfere in any manner with domestic slavery, either in the States, or in the territories where it exists.
6. *Resolved,* That we should consider the abolition of slavery in the District of Columbia, as a violation of the rights of the citizens of that District, derived from the implied conditions on which that Territory was ceded to the General Government, and as an usurpation to be at once resisted as nothing more

than the commencement of a scheme of much more extensive and flagrant injustice.

7. *Resolved,* That the Legislature of South Carolina, regards with decided approbation, the measures of security adopted by the Post Office Department of the United States in relation to the transmission of Incendiary Tracts. But if this highly essential and protective policy, be counteracted by Congress, and the United States Mail becomes a vehicle for the transmission of the mischievous documents, with which it was recently freighted, we, in this contingency, expect that the Chief Magistrate of our State, will forthwith call the Legislature together, that timely measures may be taken to prevent its traversing our Territory.

* * *

JOHN C. CALHOUN

Slavery as a Positive Good, February 6, 1837

Calhoun delivered this speech in the U.S. Senate, in response to Abolitionist petitions calling for an immediate abolition of slavery in the District of Columbia.

SOURCE: *John C. Calhoun, "Speech on the Reception of Abolition Petitions, delivered in the Senate, February 6th, 1837," in* Speeches of John C. Calhoun, Delivered in the House of Representatives, and in the Senate of the United States, *ed. Richard K. Crallé (New York: D. Appleton and Company, 1853).*

The peculiar institution of the South—that, on the maintenance of which the very existence of the slaveholding States depends, is pronounced to be sinful and odious, in the sight of God and man; and this with a systematic design of rendering us hateful in the eyes of the world—with a view to a general crusade against us and our institutions. This, too, in the legislative halls of the Union; created by these confederated States, for the better protection of their peace, their safety, and their respective institution;—and yet, we, the representatives of twelve of these sovereign States against whom this deadly war is waged, are expected to sit here in silence, hearing ourselves and our constituents day after day denounced, without uttering a word; for if we but open our lips, the charge of agitation is resounded on all sides, and we are held up as seeking to aggravate the evil which we resist. Every reflecting mind must see in all this a state of things deeply and dangerously diseased.

I do not belong to the school which holds that aggression is to be met by concession. Mine is the opposite creed, which teaches that encroachments must be met at the beginning, and that those who act on the opposite principle are prepared to become slaves. In this case, in particular, I hold concession or compromise to be fatal. If we concede an inch, concession would follow concession—compromise would follow compromise, until our ranks would be so broken that effectual resistance would be impossible. We must meet the enemy on the frontier, with a fixed determination of maintaining our position at every hazard. Consent to receive these insulting petitions, and the next demand will be that they be referred to a committee in order that they may be deliberated and acted upon. At the last session we were modestly asked to receive them, simply to lay them on the table, without any view to ulterior action. I then told the Senator from Pennsylvania (Mr. Buchanan), who so strongly urged that course in the Senate, that it was a position that could not be maintained; as the argument in favor of acting on the petitions if we were bound to receive, could not be resisted. I then said, that the next step would be to refer the petition to a committee, and I already see indications that such is now the intention. If we yield, that will be followed by another, and we will thus proceed, step by step, to the final consummation of the object of these petitions. We are now told that the most effectual mode of arresting the progress of abolition is, to reason it down; and with this view it is urged that the petitions ought to be referred to a committee. That is the very ground which was taken at the last session in the other House, but instead of arresting its progress it has since advanced more rapidly than ever. The most unquestionable right may be rendered doubtful, if one admitted to be a subject of controversy, and that would be the case in the present instance. The subject is beyond the jurisdiction of Congress—they have no right to touch it in any shape or form, or to make it the subject of deliberation or discussion.

In opposition to this view it is urged that Congress is bound by the constitution [specifically the First Amendment] to receive petitions in every case and on every subject, whether within its constitutional competency or not. I hold the doctrine to be absurd, and do solemnly believe, that it would be as easy to prove that it has the right to abolish slavery, as that it is bound to receive petitions for that purpose. The very existence of the rule that requires a question to be put on the reception of petitions, is conclusive to show that there is no such obligation. It has been a standing rule from the commencement of the Government, and clearly shows the sense of those who formed the constitution on this point. The question on the reception would be absurd, if, as is contended, we are bound to receive; but I do not intend to argue the question; I discussed it fully at the last session, and the arguments then advanced neither have been nor can be answered.

As widely as this incendiary spirit has spread, it has not yet infected this body, or the great mass of the intelligent and business portion of the North; but unless it be speedily stopped, it will spread and work upwards till it brings the two great sections of the Union into deadly conflict. This is not a new impression with me. Several years since, in a discussion with one of the Senators from Massachusetts (Mr. Webster), before this fell spirit had showed itself, I then predicted that the doctrine of the proclamation and the Force Bill, that this Government had a right, in the last resort, to determine the extent of its own powers, and enforce its decision at the point of the bayonet, which was so warmly maintained by that Senator, would at no distant day arouse the dormant spirit of abolitionism. I told him that the doctrine was tantamount to the assumption of unlimited power on the part of the Government, and that such would be the impression on the public mind in a large portion of the Union. The consequence would be inevitable. A large portion of the Northern States believe slavery to be a sin, and would consider it as an obligation of conscience to abolish it if they should feel themselves in any degree responsible for its continuance,—and that this doctrine would necessarily lead to the belief of such responsibility. I then predicted that would commence as it has with this fanatical portion of society, that they would begin their operations on the ignorant, the weak, the young, and the thoughtless,—and gradually extend upwards till they would become strong enough to obtain political control, when he and others holding the highest stations in society, would, however reluctant, be compelled to yield to their doctrines, or be driven into obscurity. But four years have since elapsed, and all this is already in a course of regular fulfillment.

Standing at the point of time at which we have now arrived, it will not be more difficult to trace the course of future events now than it was then. They who imagine that the spirit now abroad in the North, will die away of itself without a shock or convulsion, have formed a very inadequate conception of its real character; it will continue to rise and spread, unless prompt and efficient measures to stay its progress be adopted. Already it has taken possession of the pulpit, of the schools, and, to a considerable extent, of the press; those great instruments by which the mind of the rising generation will be formed.

However sound the great body of the non-slaveholding States are at present, in the course of a few years they will be succeeded by those who will have been taught to hate the people and institutions of nearly one-half of this Union, with a hatred more deadly than one hostile nation ever entertained towards another. It is easy to see the end. By the necessary course of events, if left to themselves, we must become, finally, two people. It is impossible under the deadly hatred which must spring up between the two great sections, if the present causes are permitted to operate unchecked, that we should continue under the same political system. The conflicting elements would burst the Union asunder, powerful as are the links which hold it together. **Abolition and the Union cannot co-exist**. As the friend of the Union I openly proclaim it,—and the sooner it is known the better. The former may now be controlled, but in a short time it will be beyond the power a man to arrest the course of events. We of the South will not, cannot surrender our institutions. Too maintain the existing relations between the two races, inhabiting that section of the Union, is indispensable to the peace and happiness of both. It cannot be subverted without drenching the county in blood, and extirpating one or the other of the races. Be it good or bad, it has grown up with our society and institutions, and is so interwoven with them, that to destroy it would be to destroy us as a people. But let me not be understood as admitting, even by implication, that the existing relations between the two races in the slaveholding States is an evil:—far otherwise; I hold it to be a good, as it has thus far proved itself to be to both, and will continue to probe so if not disturbed by the fell spirit of abolition. I appeal to facts. Never before has the black race of Central Africa, from the dawn of history to the present day, attained a condition so civilized and so improved, not only physically, but morally and intellectually. It came among us in a low, degraded, and savage condition, and in the course of a few generations it has grown up under the fostering care of our institutions, reviled as they have been, to its present comparatively civilized condition. This, with the rapid increase of numbers, is conclusive proof of the general happiness of the race, in spite of all the exaggerated tales to the contrary.

In the mean time, the white or European race has not degenerated. It has kept pace with its brethren in other sections of the Union where slavery does not exist. It is odious to make comparison; but I appeal to all sides whether the South is not equal in virtue, intelligence, patriotism, courage, disinterestedness, and all the high qualities which adorn our nature. I ask whether we have not contributed our full share of talents and political wisdom in forming and sustaining this political fabric; and whether we have not constantly inclined most strongly to the side of liberty, and been the first to see and first to resist the encroachments of power. In one thing only are we inferior—the arts of gain; we acknowledge that we are less wealthy than the Northern section of this Union, but I trace this mainly to the fiscal action of this Government, which has extracted much from, and spent little among us. Had it been the reverse—if the exaction had been from the other section, and the expenditure with us, this point of superiority would not be against us now, as it was not at the formation of this Government.

But I take higher ground. I hold that in the present state of civilization, where two races of different origin, and distinguished by color, and other physical differences, as well as intellectual, are brought together, the relation now existing in the slaveholding States between the two, is, instead of an evil, **a good—a positive good**. I feel myself called upon to speak freely upon the subject where the honor and interests of those I represent are involved. I hold then, that there never has yet existed a wealthy and civilized society in which one portion of the community did not, in point of fact, live on the labor of the other. Broad and general as is this assertion, it is fully borne out by history. This is not the proper occasion, but if it were, it would not be difficult to trace the various devices by which the wealth of all civilized communities has been so unequally divided, and to show by what means so small a share has been allotted to those by whose labor it was produced, and so large a share given to the nonproducing classes. The devices are almost innumerable, from the brute force and gross superstition of ancient times, to the subtle and artful fiscal contrivances of modern. I might well challenge a comparison between them and the more direct, simple, and patriarchal mode by which the labor of the African race is, among us, commanded by the European. I may say with truth, that in few countries so much is left to the share of the laborer, and so little exacted from him; or where there is more kind attention paid to him in sickness or infirmities of age. Compare his condition with the tenants of the poor houses in the more civilized portions of Europe—look at the sick, and the old and infirm slave, on one hand, in the midst of his family and friends, under the kind superintending care of his master and mistress, and compare it with the forlorn and wretched condition of the pauper in the poor house. But I will not dwell on this aspect of the question; I turn to the political; and here I fearlessly assert that the existing relation between the two races in the South, against which these blind fanatics are waging war, forms the most solid and durable foundation on which to rear free and stable political institutions. It is useless to disguise the fact. There is and always has been in an advanced stage of wealth and civilization, a conflict between labor and capital. The condition of society in the South exempts us from the disorders and dangers resulting from this conflict; and which explains why it is that the political condition of the slaveholding States has been so much more stable and quiet than of the North. The advantages of the former, in this respect, will become more and more manifest if left undisturbed by interference from without, as the country advances in wealth and numbers. We have, in fact, but just entered that condition of society where the strength and durability of our political institutions are to be tested; and I venture nothing in predicting that the experience of the next generation will fully test how vastly more favorable our condition of society is to that of other sections for free and stable institutions, provided we are not disturbed by the interference of others, or shall have sufficient intelligence and spirit to resist promptly and successfully such interference. It rests with ourselves to meet and repel them. I look not for aid to this Government, or to the other States; not but there are kind feelings towards us on the part of the great body of the nonslaveholding States; but as kind as their feelings may be, we may rest assured that no political party in those States will risk their ascendency for our safety. If we do not defend ourselves none will defend us; if we yield we will be more and more pressed as we recede; and if we submit we will be trampled under foot. Be assured that emancipation itself would not satisfy these fanatics:—that gained, the next step would be to raise the negroes to a social and political equality with the whites; and that being effected, we would soon find the present condition of the two races reversed. They and their northern allies would be the masters, and we the slaves; the condition of the white race in the British West India Islands, bad as it is, would be happiness to ours. There the mother country is interested in sustaining the supremacy of the European race. It is true that the authority of the former master is destroyed, but the African will there still be a slave, not to individuals but to the community,—forced to labor, not by the authority of the overseer, but by the bayonet of the soldiery and the rod of the civil magistrate.

Surrounded as the slaveholding States are with such imminent perils, I rejoice to think that our means of defense are ample, if we shall prove to have the intelligence and spirit to see and apply them before it is too late. All we want is concert, to lay aside all party differences, and unite with zeal and energy in repelling approaching dangers. Let there be concert of action, and we shall find ample means of security without resorting to secession, or disunion. I speak with full knowledge and a thorough examination of the subject, and for one, see my way clearly. One thing alarms me—the eager pursuit of gain which overspreads the land, and which absorbs every faculty of the mind and every feeling of the heart. Of all passions avarice is the most blind and compromising—the last to see and the first to yield to danger. I dare not hope that any thing I can say will arouse the South to a due sense of danger; I fear it is beyond the power of mortal voice to awaken it in time from the fatal security into which it has fallen.

TWO ILLINOIS LEGISLATORS

Protest in the Illinois Legislature on Slavery, March 3, 1837

This was written by Representatives Dan Stone and Abraham Lincoln, who represented Sangamon County in rural Illinois. It articulated their disagreement with several resolutions recently passed by both houses of the Illinois legislature. These resolutions denounced the growing Abolitionist organizations in the North and declared that slavery was protected by the Constitution. Abolitionism was very unpopular, in Illinois generally and especially in Sangamon County, so these politicians stood to gain no political advantage from objecting to the legislature's proslavery and anti-Abolitionist stand. Still, Stone and Lincoln deplored abolitionism. They asserted that slavery was based on "injustice and bad policy," but it was protected by the Constitution. Furthermore, they said that "promulgation of abolition doctrines" somehow made the "evils" of slavery worse. This statement is the first public objection to slavery made by Abraham Lincoln, then an obscure, ambitious man, not yet thirty years old. He remained firmly opposed to abolition for the next twenty-five years, while strongly in favor of restricting slavery's territorial expansion.

SOURCE: *Abraham Lincoln, "March 3, 1837.—Protest in the Illinois Legislature on the Subject of Slavery," in* Abraham Lincoln Complete Works: Comprising His Speeches, Letters, State Papers, and Miscellaneous Writings, *ed. John G. Nicolay and John Hay (New York: The Century Co., 1894), vol. 1.*

esolutions upon the subject of domestic slavery having passed both branches of the General Assembly at its present session, the undersigned hereby protest against the passage of the same.

They believe that the institution of slavery is founded on both injustice and bad policy; but that the promulgation of abolition doctrines tends rather to increase than to abate its evils.

They believe that the Congress of the United States has no power, under the constitution, to interfere with the institution of slavery in the different States.

They believe that the Congress of the United States has the power, under the constitution, to abolish slavery in the District of Columbia; but that that power ought not to be exercised unless at the request of the people of said District.

The difference between these opinions and those contained in the said resolutions, is their reason for entering this protest.

DAN STONE,

A. LINCOLN,

Representatives from the county of Sangamon.

JOHN C. CALHOUN

Remarks Made during the Debate on His Resolutions, in Respect to the Rights of the States and the Abolition of Slavery—December 27, 1837, *et seq.*

The two documents that follow are closely related. The first is a set of resolutions Calhoun introduced in the U.S. Senate on December 27, 1837. The second is a speech on the same subject that Calhoun delivered to the Senate on January 10, 1838.

SOURCE: *John C. Calhoun, "Remarks Made during the Debate on his Resolutions, in respect to the Rights of the States and the Abolition of Slavery,—December 27th, 1837, et seq.," in* Speeches of John C. Calhoun, Delivered in the House of Representatives, and in the Senate of the United States, *ed. Richard K. Crallé (New York: D. Appleton and Company, 1853).*

1. *Resolved,* That in the adoption of the Federal Constitution, the States adopting the same, acted severally, as free, independent and sovereign States; and that each, for itself, by its own voluntary act, entered into the Union with the view to its increased security against all dangers, *domestic,* as well as foreign,—and the more perfect and secure enjoyment of its advantages, natural, political and social.

2. *Resolved,* That, in delegating a portion of their powers to be exercised by the Federal Government, the States retained, severally, the exclusive and sole right over their own domestic institutions and police,—and are alone responsible for them; and that any intermeddling of any one or more States, or a combination of their citizens, with the domestic institutions and police of the others, on any ground, or under any pretext whatever, political, moral or religious,—with a view to their alteration or subversion, is an assumption of superiority, not warranted by the constitution;—insulting to the States interfered with,—tending to endanger their domestic peace and tranquillity; subversive of the objects for which the constitution was formed; and, by necessary consequence, tending to weaken and destroy the Union itself.

3. *Resolved,* That this Government was instituted and adopted by the several States of this Union as a common agent, in order to carry into effect the powers which they had delegated by the constitution for their mutual security and prosperity; and that, in fulfilment of their high and sacred trust, this Government is bound so to exercise its powers, as to give, as far as may be practicable, increased stability and security to the domestic institutions of the States that compose the Union; and that it is the solemn duty of the Government to resist all attempts by one portion of the Union to use it as an instrument to attack the domestic institutions of another, or to weaken or destroy such institutions, instead of strengthening and upholding them, as it is in duty bound to do.

4. *Resolved,* That domestic slavery, as it exists in the Southern and Western States of this Union, composes an important part of their domestic institutions, inherited from their ancestors, and existing at the adoption of the constitution, by which it is recognized as constituting an essential element in the distribution of its powers among the States; and that no change of opinion or feeling, on the part of the other States of the Union in relation to it, can justify them or their citizens in open and systematic attacks thereon, with a view to its overthrow; and that all such attacks are in manifest violation of the mutual and solemn pledge to protect and defend each other, given by the States respectively, on entering into the constitutional compact which formed the Union,—and, as such, is a manifest breach of faith, and a violation of the most solemn obligations, moral and religious.

5. *Resolved,* That the intermeddling of any State or States, or their citizens, to abolish slavery in this District, or in any of the territories, on the ground, or under the pretext, that it is immoral or sinful—or the passage of any act or measure of Congress with that view, would be a direct and dangerous attack on the institutions of all the slaveholding States.

6. *Resolved,* That the Union of these States rests on an equality of rights and advantages among its members; and that, whatever destroys that equality, tends to destroy the Union itself; and that it is the solemn duty of all, and more especially of this body, which represents the States in their corporate capacity, to resist all attempts to discriminate between the States in extending the benefits of the Government to the several portions of the Union; and to refuse to extend to the Southern and Western States any advantage which would tend to strengthen, or render them more secure;—or to increase their limits or population, by the annexation of new territory or States, on the assumption, or under the pretext that the institution of slavery, as it exists among them, is immoral or sinful, or otherwise obnoxious, would be contrary to that equality of rights and advantages which the constitution was intended to secure alike to all the members of the Union; and would, in effect, disfranchise the slaveholding States, by withholding from them the advantages, while it subjected them to the burdens of the Government.

JOHN C. CALHOUN

Speech on His Recent Resolutions to the U.S. Senate, January 10, 1838

* * *

He saw, said Mr. C., in the question before us the fate of the South. It was a higher than the mere naked question of master and slave. It involved a great political institution, essential to the peace and existence of one-half of this Union. A mysterious Providence had brought together two races, from different portions of the globe, and placed them together in nearly equal numbers in the Southern portion of this Union. They were there inseparably united beyond the possibility of separation. Experience had shown that the existing relation between them secured the peace and happiness of both. Each had improved; the inferior greatly; so much so, that it had attained a degree of civilization never before attained by the black race in any age or country. Under no other relation could they coexist together. To destroy it was to involve a whole region in slaughter, carnage, and desolation; and, come what will, we must defend and preserve it.

This agitation has produced one happy effect, at least—it has compelled us of the South to look into the nature and character of this great institution, and to correct many false impressions that even we had entertained in relation to it. Many in the South once believed that it was a moral and political evil. That folly and delusion are gone. We see it now in its true light, and regard it as the most safe and stable basis for free institutions in the world. It is impossible with us that the conflict can take place between labor and capital, which makes it so difficult to establish and maintain free institutions in all wealthy and highly civilized nations where such institutions as ours do not exist. The Southern States are an aggregate, in fact, of communities, not of individuals. Every plantation is a little community, with the master at its head, who concentrates in himself the united interests of capital and labor, of which he is the common representative. These small communites aggregated make the State in all, whose action, labor, and capital is equally represented and perfectly harmonized. Hence the harmony, the union, and stability of that section, which is rarely disturbed, except through the action of this Government. The blessing of this state of things extends beyond the limits of the South. It makes that section the balance of the system; the great conservative power, which prevents other portions, less fortunately constituted, from rushing into conflict. In this tendency to conflict in the North, between labor and capital, which is constantly on the increase, the weight of the South has and will ever be found on the conservative side; against the aggression of one or the other side, whichever may tend to disturb the equilibrium of our political system. This is our natural position, the salutary influence of which has thus far preserved, and will long continue to preserve our free institutions, if we should be left undisturbed. Such are the institutions which these deluded madmen are stirring heaven and earth to destroy, and which we are called on to defend by the highest and most solemn obligations that can be imposed on us as men and patriots.

ABRAHAM LINCOLN

"The Perpetuation of Our Political Institutions," an address before the Young Men's Lyceum of Springfield, Illinois, January 1838

On January 27, 1838, an obscure state legislator and young lawyer gave the following speech at the Young Men's Lyceum in Springfield. It was soon published in a newspaper, the Sangamon Journal, *in a nearby Illinois county. In later years, many saw this speech to be of major importance, but it was little noticed in 1838. Still, it did articulate a sweeping defense of the rule of law as the cornerstone of*

American civilization and identified mob violence as a threat to self-government, while rejecting both abolitionism and the demands of slavery expansionists.

SOURCE: *Abraham Lincoln, "January 27, 1837.—Address before the Young Men's Lyceum of Springfield, Illinois.," in* Abraham Lincoln Complete Works: Comprising His Speeches, Letters, State Papers, and Miscellaneous Writings, *ed. John G. Nicolay and John Hay (New York: The Century Co., 1894), vol. 1.*

In the great journal of things happening under the sun, we, the American people, find our account running under date of the nineteenth century of the Christian era. We find ourselves in the peaceful possession of the fairest portion of the earth as regards extent of territory, fertility of soil, and salubrity of climate. We find ourselves under the government of a system of political institutions conducing more essentially to the ends of civil and religious liberty than any of which the history of former times tells us. We, when mounting the stage of existence, found ourselves the legal inheritors of these fundamental blessings. We toiled not in the acquirement or establishment of them; they are a legacy bequeathed us by a once hardy, brave, and patriotic, but now lamented and departed, race of ancestors. Theirs was the task (and nobly they performed it) to possess themselves, and through themselves us, of this goodly land, and to uprear upon its hills and its valleys a political edifice of liberty and equal rights; 'tis ours only to transmit these—the former unprofaned by the foot of an invader, the latter undecayed by the lapse of time and untorn by usurpation—to the latest generation that fate shall permit the world to know. This task of gratitude to our fathers, justice to ourselves, duty to posterity, and love for our species in general, all imperatively require us faithfully to perform.

How then shall we perform it? At what point shall we expect the approach of danger? By what means shall we fortify against it? Shall we expect some transatlantic military giant to step the ocean and crush us at a blow? Never! All the armies of Europe, Asia, and Africa combined, with all the treasure of the earth (our own excepted) in their military chest, with a Bonaparte for a commander, could not by force take a drink from the Ohio or make a track on the Blue Ridge in a trial of a thousand years.

At what point then is the approach of danger to be expected? I answer, If it ever reach us it must spring up amongst us; it cannot come from abroad. If destruction be our lot we must ourselves be its author and finisher. As a nation of freemen we must live through all time, or die by suicide.

I hope I am over wary; but if I am not, there is even now something of ill omen amongst us. I mean the increasing disregard for law which pervades the country— the growing disposition to substitute the wild and furious passions in lieu of the sober judgment of courts, and the worse than savage mobs for the executive ministers of justice. This disposition is awfully fearful in any community; and that it now exists in ours, though grating to our feelings to admit, it would be a violation of truth and an insult to our intelligence to deny. Accounts of outrages committed by mobs form the every-day news of the times. They have pervaded the country from New England to Louisiana; they are neither peculiar to the eternal snows of the former nor the burning suns of the latter; they are not the creature of climate, neither are they confined to the slaveholding or the non-slaveholding States. Alike they spring up among the pleasure-hunting masters of Southern slaves, and the order-loving citizens of the land of steady habits. Whatever then their cause may be, it is common to the whole country.

It would be tedious as well as useless to recount the horrors of all of them. Those happening in the State of Mississippi and at St. Louis are perhaps the most dangerous in example and revolting to humanity. In the Mississippi case they first commenced by hanging the regular gamblers—a set of men certainly not following for a livelihood a very useful or very honest occupation, but one which, so far from being forbidden by the laws, was actually licensed by an act of the legislature passed but a single year before. Next, negroes suspected of conspiring to raise an insurrection were caught up and hanged in all parts of the State; then, white men supposed to be leagued with the negroes; and finally, strangers from neighboring States, going thither on business, were in many instances subjected to the same fate. Thus went on this process of hanging, from gamblers to negroes, from negroes to white citizens, and from these to strangers, till dead men were seen literally dangling from the boughs of trees upon every roadside, and in numbers almost sufficient to rival the native Spanish moss of the country as a drapery of the forest.

Turn then to that horror-striking scene at St. Louis. A single victim only was sacrificed there. This story is very short, and is perhaps the most highly tragic of anything of its length that has ever been witnessed in real life. A mulatto man by the name of McIntosh was seized in the street, dragged to the suburbs of the city, chained to a tree, and actually burned to death; and all within a single hour from the time he had been a freeman attending to his own business and at peace with the world.

Such are the effects of mob law, and such are the scenes becoming more and more frequent in this land so lately famed for love of law and order, and the stories of which have even now grown too familiar to attract anything more than an idle remark.

But you are perhaps ready to ask, "What has this to do with the perpetuation of our political institutions?" I answer, "It has much to do with it." Its direct consequences are, comparatively speaking, but a small evil, and much of its danger consists in the proneness of our minds to regard its direct as its only consequences. Abstractly considered, the hanging of the gamblers at Vicksburg was of but little consequence. They constitute a portion of population that is worse than useless in any community; and their death, if no pernicious example be set by it, is never matter of reasonable regret with any one. If they were annually swept from the stage of existence by the plague or smallpox, honest men would perhaps be much profited by the operation. Similar too is the correct reasoning in regard to the burning of the negro at St. Louis. He had forfeited his life by the perpetration of an outrageous murder upon one of the most worthy and respectable citizens of the city, and had he not died as he did, he must have died by the sentence of the law in a very short time afterward. As to him alone, it was as well the way it was as it could otherwise have been. But the example in either case was fearful. When men take it in their heads to-day to hang gamblers or burn murderers, they should recollect that in the confusion usually attending such transactions they will be as likely to hang or burn some one who is neither a gambler nor a murderer as one who is, and that, acting upon the example they set, the mob of to-morrow may, and probably will, hang or burn some of them by the very same mistake. And not only so; the innocent, those who have ever set their faces against violations of law in every shape, alike with the guilty fall victims to the ravages of mob law; and thus it goes on, step by step, till all the walls erected for the defense of the persons and property of individuals are trodden down and disregarded. But all this, even, is not the full extent of the evil. By such examples, by instances of the perpetrators of such acts going unpunished, the lawless in spirit are encouraged to become lawless in practice; and having been used to no restraint but dread of punishment, they thus become absolutely unrestrained. Having ever regarded government as their deadliest bane, they make a jubilee of the suspension of its operations, and pray for nothing so much as its total annihilation. While, on the other hand, good men, men who love tranquillity, who desire to abide by the laws and enjoy their benefits, who would gladly spill their blood in the defense of their country, seeing their property destroyed, their families insulted, and their lives endangered, their persons injured, and seeing nothing in prospect that forebodes a change for the better, become tired of and disgusted with a government that offers them no protection, and are not much averse to a change in which they imagine they have nothing to lose. Thus, then, by the operation of this mobocratic spirit which all must admit is now abroad in the land, the strongest bulwark of any government, and particularly of those constituted like ours, may effectually be broken down and destroyed—I mean the attachment of the people. Whenever this effect shall be produced among us; whenever the vicious portion of population shall be permitted to gather in bands of hundreds and thousands, and burn churches, ravage and rob provision-stores, throw printing-presses into rivers, shoot editors, and hang and burn obnoxious persons at pleasure and with impunity, depend on it, this government cannot last. By such things the feelings of the best citizens will become more or less alienated from it, and thus it will be left without friends, or with too few, and those few too weak to make their friendship effectual. At such a time, and under such circumstances, men of sufficient talent and ambition will not be wanting to seize the opportunity, strike the blow, and overturn that fair fabric which for the last half century has been the fondest hope of the lovers of freedom throughout the world.

I know the American people are much attached to their government; I know they would suffer much for its sake; I know they would endure evils long and patiently before they would ever think of exchanging it for another,—yet, notwithstanding all this, if the laws be continually despised and disregarded, if their rights to be secure in their persons and property are held by no better tenure than the caprice of a mob, the alienation of their affections from the government is the natural consequence; and to that, sooner or later, it must come.

Here, then, is one point at which danger may be expected.

The question recurs, "How shall we fortify against it?" The answer is simple. Let every American, every lover of liberty, every well-wisher to his posterity swear by the blood of the Revolution never to violate in the least particular the laws of the country, and never to tolerate their violation by others. As the patriots of seventy-six did to the support of the Declaration of Independence, so to the support of the Constitution and laws let every American pledge his life, his property, and his sacred honor—let every man remember that to violate the law is to trample on the blood of his father, and to tear the charter of his own and his children's liberty. Let reverence for the laws be breathed by every American mother to the lisping babe that prattles on her lap; let it be taught in schools, in seminaries, and in colleges; let it be written in primers, spelling-books, and in almanacs; let it be preached from the pulpit, proclaimed in legislative halls, and enforced in courts of justice. And, in short, let it become the political religion of the nation; and let the old and the young, the rich and the poor, the grave and the gay of all sexes and tongues and colors and conditions, sacrifice unceasingly upon its altars.

While ever a state of feeling such as this shall universally or even very generally prevail throughout the nation, vain will be every effort, and fruitless every attempt, to subvert our national freedom.

When I so pressingly urge a strict observance of all the laws, let me not be understood as saying there are no bad laws, or that grievances may not arise for the redress of which no legal provisions have been made. I mean to say no such thing. But I do mean to say that although bad laws, if they exist, should be repealed as soon as possible, still, while they continue in force, for the sake of example they should be religiously observed. So also in unprovided cases. If such arise, let proper legal provisions be made for them with the least possible delay, but till then let them, if not too intolerable, be borne with.

There is no grievance that is a fit object of redress by mob law. In any case that may arise, as, for instance, the promulgation of abolitionism, one of two positions is necessarily true—that is, the thing is right within itself, and therefore deserves the protection of all law and all good citizens, or it is wrong, and therefore proper to be prohibited by legal enactments; and in neither case is the interposition of mob law either necessary, justifiable, or excusable.

But it may be asked, "Why suppose danger to our political institutions? Have we not preserved them for more than fifty years? And why may we not for fifty times as long?"

We hope there is no sufficient reason. We hope all danger may be overcome; but to conclude that no danger may ever arise would itself be extremely dangerous. There are now, and will hereafter be, many causes, dangerous in their tendency, which have not existed heretofore, and which are not too insignificant to merit attention. That our government should have been maintained in its original form, from its establishment until now, is not much to be wondered at. It had many props to support it through that period, which now are decayed and crumbled away. Through that period it was felt by all to be an undecided experiment; now it is understood to be a successful one. Then, all that sought celebrity and fame and distinction expected to find them in the success of that experiment. Their all was staked upon it; their destiny was inseparably linked with it. Their ambition aspired to display before an admiring world a practical demonstration of the truth of a proposition which had hitherto been considered at best no better than problematical—namely, the capability of a people to govern themselves. If they succeeded they were to be immortalized; their names were to be transferred to counties, and cities, and rivers, and mountains; and to be revered and sung, toasted through all time. If they failed, they were to be called knaves, and fools, and fanatics for a fleeting hour; then to sink and be forgotten. They succeeded. The experiment is successful, and thousands have won their deathless names in making it so. But the game is caught; and I believe it is true that with the catching end the pleasures of the chase. This field of glory is harvested, and the crop is already appropriated. But new reapers will arise, and they too will seek a field. It is to deny what the history of the world tells us is true, to suppose that men of ambition and talents will not continue to spring up amongst us. And when they do, they will as naturally seek the gratification of their ruling passion as others have done before them. The question then is, Can that gratification be found in supporting and maintaining an edifice that has been erected by others? Most certainly it cannot. Many great and good men, sufficiently qualified for any task they should undertake, may ever be found whose ambition would aspire to nothing beyond a seat in Congress, a gubernatorial or a presidential chair; but such belong not to the family of the lion, or the tribe of the eagle. What! think you these places would satisfy an Alexander, a Cæsar, or a Napoleon? Never! Towering genius disdains a beaten path. It seeks regions hitherto unexplored. It sees no distinction in adding story to story upon the monuments of fame erected to the memory of others. It denies that it is glory enough to serve under any chief. It scorns to tread in the footsteps of any predecessor, however illustrious. It thirsts and burns for distinction; and if possible, it will have it, whether at the expense of emancipating slaves or enslaving freemen. Is it unreasonable, then, to expect that some man possessed of the loftiest genius, coupled with ambition sufficient to push it to its utmost stretch, will at some time spring up among us? And when such a one does, it will require the people to be united with each other, attached to the government and laws, and generally intelligent, to successfully frustrate his designs.

Distinction will be his paramount object, and although he would as willingly, perhaps more so, acquire it by doing good as harm, yet, that opportunity being past, and nothing left to be done in the way of building up, he would set boldly to the task of pulling down.

Here then is a probable case, highly dangerous, and such a one as could not have well existed heretofore.

Another reason which once was, but which, to the same extent, is now no more, has done much in maintaining our institutions thus far. I mean the powerful influence which the interesting scenes of the Revolution had upon the passions of the people as distinguished from their judgment. By this influence, the jealousy, envy, and avarice incident to our nature, and so common to a state of peace, prosperity, and conscious strength, were for the time in a great measure smothered and rendered inactive, while the deep-rooted principles of hate, and the powerful motive of revenge, instead of being turned against each other, were directed exclusively against the British nation. And thus, from the force of circumstances, the basest principles of our nature were either made to lie dormant, or to become the active agents in the advancement of the noblest of causes—that of establishing and maintaining civil and religious liberty.

But this state of feeling must fade, is fading, has faded, with the circumstances that produced it.

I do not mean to say that the scenes of the Revolution are now or ever will be entirely forgotten, but that, like everything else, they must fade upon the memory of the world, and grow more and more dim by the lapse of time. In history, we hope, they will be read of, and recounted, so long as the Bible shall be read; but even granting that they will, their influence cannot be what it heretofore has been. Even then they cannot be so universally known nor so vividly felt as they were by the generation just gone to rest. At the close of that struggle, nearly every adult male had been a participator in some of its scenes. The consequence was that of those scenes, in the form of a husband, a father, a son, or a brother, a living history was to be found in every family—a history bearing the indubitable testimonies of its own authenticity, in the limbs mangled, in the scars of wounds received, in the midst of the very scenes related—a history, too, that could be read and understood alike by all, the wise and the ignorant, the learned and the unlearned. But those histories are gone. They can be read no more forever. They were a fortress of strength; but what invading foeman could never do, the silent artillery of time has done—the leveling of its walls. They are gone. They were a forest of giant oaks; but the all-restless hurricane has swept over them, and left only here and there a lonely trunk, despoiled of its verdure, shorn of its foliage, unshading and unshaded, to murmur in a few more gentle breezes, and to combat with its mutilated limbs a few more ruder storms, then to sink and be no more.

They were pillars of the temple of liberty; and now that they have crumbled away that temple must fall unless we, their descendants, supply their places with other pillars, hewn from the solid quarry of sober reason. Passion has helped us, but can do so no more. It will in future be our enemy. Reason—cold, calculating, unimpassioned reason—must furnish all the materials for our future support and defense. Let those materials be molded into general intelligence, sound morality, and, in particular, a reverence for the Constitution and laws; and that we improved to the last, that we remained free to the last, that we revered his name to the last, that during his long sleep we permitted no hostile foot to pass over or desecrate his resting-place, shall be that which to learn the last trump shall awaken our Washington.

Upon these let the proud fabric of freedom rest, as the rock of its basis; and as truly as has been said of the only greater institution, "the gates of hell shall not prevail against it."

JOHN C. CALHOUN

Draft Remarks for Future Speech, 1848

Because this game takes place in July 1845, the following paragraphs (in reality written in 1848) should be treated as draft notes prepared by Calhoun for a speech to be given on an as-yet undetermined topic sometime in the future. For purposes of the game, these draft remarks have been circulated in the summer of 1845.

SOURCE: *John C. Calhoun, "Speech on the Oregon Bill, delivered in the Senate, June 27th, 1848,"* in Speeches of John C. Calhoun, Delivered in the House of Representatives, and in the Senate of the United States, *ed. Richard K. Crallé (New York: D. Appleton and Company, 1853).*

* * *

* * * [A] proposition which originated in a hypothetical truism, but which, as now expressed and now understood, is the most false and dangerous of all political error. The proposition to which I allude, has become an axiom in the minds of a vast many on both sides of the Atlantic, and is repeated daily from tongue to tongue, as an established and incontrovertible truth; it is, that "all men are born free and equal." I am not afraid to attack error, however deeply it may be entrenched, or however widely extended, whenever it becomes my duty to do so, as I believe it to be on this subject and occasion.

Taking the proposition literally, (it is in that sense it is understood,) there is not a word of truth in it. It begins with "all men are born," which is utterly untrue. Men are not born. Infants are born. They grow to be men. And concludes with asserting that they are born "free and equal," which is not less false. They are not born free. While infants they are incapable of freedom, being destitute alike of the capacity of thinking and acting, without which there can be no freedom. Besides, they are necessarily born subject to their parents, and remain so among all people, savage and civilized, until the development of their intellect and physical capacity enable them to take care of themselves. They grow to all the freedom, of which the condition in which they were born permits, by growing to be men. Nor is it less false that they are born "equal." They are not so in any sense in which it can be regarded; and thus, as I have asserted, there is not a word of truth in the whole proposition, as expressed and generally understood.

If we trace it back, we shall find the proposition differently expressed in the declaration of independence. That asserts that "all men are created equal." The form of expression, though less dangerous, is not less erroneous. All men are not created. According to the Bible, only two, a man and a woman, ever were, and of these one was pronounced subordinate to the other. All others have come into the world by being born, and in no sense, as I have shown, either free or equal. But this form of expression being less striking and popular, has given away to the present, and under the authority of a document put forth on so great an occasion, and leading to such important consequences, has spread far and wide, and fixed itself deeply in the public mind. It was inserted in our declaration of independence without any necessity. It made no necessary part of our justification in separating from the parent country, and declaring ourselves independent. Breach of our chartered privileges, and lawless encroachment on our acknowleged and well established rights by the parent country, were the real causes, and of themselves sufficient, without resorting to any other, to justify the step. Nor had it any weight in constructing the governments which were substituted in the place of the colonial. They were formed of the old materials and on practical and well established principles, borrowed for the most part from our own experience and that of the country from which we sprang.

If the proposition be traced still further back, it will be found to have been adopted from certain writers on government who had attained much celebrity in the early settlement of these States, and with whose writings all the prominent actors in our Revolution were familiar. Among these, Locke and Sydney were prominent. But they expressed it very differently. According to their expression, "all men in the state of nature were free and equal." * * *

* * *

TREASURY DEPARTMENT, REGISTER'S OFFICE

Summary Statement of the Value of the Exports of the Growth, Produce, and Manufacture of the United States, during the Year July 1, 1848–June 30, 1849

THE SEA.			
Fisheries—			
Dried fish, or cod fisheries		$419,092	
Pickled fish, or river fisheries, (herring, shad, salmon, mackerel)		93,085	
Whale and other fish oil		965,597	
Spermaceti oil		572,763	
Whalebone		337,714	
Spermaceti candles		159,403	
			$2,547,654
THE FOREST.			
Skins and furs		656,228	
Ginseng		182,966	
Product of wood—			
Staves, shingles, boards, hewn timber	$1,776,749		
Other lumber	60,344		
Masts and spars	87,720		
Oak bark and other dye	95,392		
All manufactures of wood	1,697,828		
Naval stores, tar, pitch, rosin, and turpentine	845,164		
Ashes, pot and pearl	515,603		
		5,078,800	
			5,917,994
AGRICULTURE.			
Product of animals—			
Beef, tallow, hides, horned cattle	2,058,958		
Butter and cheese	1,654,157		
Pork, (pickled,) bacon, lard, live hogs	9,245,885		
Horses and mules	96,982		
Sheep	16,305		
Wool	81,015		
		13,153,302	
Vegetable food—			
Wheat	1,756,848		
Flour	11,280,582		
Indian corn	7,966,369		
Indian meal	1,169,625		
Rye meal	218,248		
Rye, oats, and other small grain and pulse	139,793		
Biscuit or ship bread	364,318		
Potatoes	83,313		
Apples	93,904		
Rice	2,569,362		
		25,642,362	
			38,795,664
Tobacco			5,804,207
Cotton			66,396,967
Hemp			8,458
All other agricultural products—			
Flaxseed		4	
Hops		29,123	
Brown sugar		24,906	
Indigo		49	
			54,082
MANUFACTURES.			
Soap and tallow candles		627,280	
Leather boots and shoes		151,774	
Household furniture		237,342	
Coaches and other carriages		95,923	

Hats		$64,967	
Saddlery		37,276	
Wax		121,720	
Spirits from grain		67,129	
Beer, ale, porter, and cider		51,320	
Snuff and tobacco		613,044	
Linseed oil and spirits of turpentine		148,056	
Cordage		41,636	
Iron—pig, bar, and nails		149,358	
Castings		60,175	
All manufactures of		886,639	
Spirits from molasses		288,452	
Sugar, refined		129,001	
Chocolate		1,941	
Gunpowder		131,297	
Copper and brass		66,203	
Medicinal drugs		220,894	
			$4,191,427
Cotton piece goods—			
Printed and colored	$466,574		
White	3,955,117		
Nankeen	3,203		
Twist, yarn, and thread	92,555		
All manufactures of	415,680		
		4,933,129	
Flax and hemp—			
Cloth and thread		1,009	
Bags, and all manufactures of		4,549	
Wearing apparel		75,945	
Combs and buttons		38,136	
Brushes		2,924	
Billiard tables		701	
Umbrellas and parasols		5,800	
Leather and morocco skins (not sold per pound)		9,427	
Fire-engines and apparatus		458	
Printing presses and type		28,031	
Musical instruments		23,713	
Books and maps		94,427	
Paper and stationery		86,827	
Paints and varnish		55,145	
Vinegar		14,036	
Earthen and stone ware		10,632	
Manufactures of glass		101,419	
tin		13,143	
pewter and lead		13,196	
marble and stone		20,282	
gold and silver, and gold leaf		4,502	
Gold and silver coin		956,874	
Artificial flowers and jewelry		8,557	
Molasses		7,442	
Trunks		5,099	
Bricks and lime		8,671	
Salt		82,972	
			6,607,046
Coal			40,396
Lead			30,198
Ice			95,027
Articles not enumerated—			
Manufactured		1,408,278	
Other articles		769,557	
			2,177,835
			132,666,955

SAMUEL A. CARTWRIGHT

Diseases and Physical Peculiarities of the Negro Race, 1851

Because this game takes place in July 1845, the following document (in reality published in 1851) should be considered as an unpublished, preliminary manuscript. De Bow's Review, where Cartwright will publish this work, will be founded next year, 1846; informed southerners await the journal's inaugural issue. In his day, Cartwright was considered a leading southern medical authority, though modern readers see him as a masochist racist fraud.

SOURCE: *Samuel A. Cartwright, "Diseases and Peculiarities of the Negro Race,"* in De Bow's Review of the Southern and Western States *Vol. XI.*, ed. J. D. B. De Bow *(New Orleans: Office, 22 Exchange Place, 1851).*

DRAPETOMANIA, OR THE DISEASE CAUSING NEGROES TO RUN AWAY.

*D*rapetomania is from δραπέτης, a runaway slave, and μανία, *mad or crazy.* It is unknown to our medical authorities, although its diagnostic symptom, the absconding from service, is as well known to our planters and overseers, as it was to the ancient Greeks, who expressed, by the single word δραπέτης, the fact of the absconding, and the relation that the fugitive held to the person he fled from. I have added to the word meaning runaway slave, another Greek term, to express the disease of the mind causing him to abscond. In noticing a disease not heretofore classed among the long list of maladies that man is subject to, it was necessary to have a new term to express it. The cause in the most of cases, that induces the negro to run away from service, is as much a disease of the mind as any other species of mental alienation, and much more curable, as a general rule. With the advantages of proper medical advice, strictly followed, this troublesome practice that many negroes have of running away, can be almost entirely prevented, although the slaves be located on the borders of a free state, within a stone's throw of the abolitionists. I was born in Virginia, east of the Blue Ridge, where negroes were numerous, and studied medicine some years in Maryland, a slave state, separated from Pennsylvania, a free state, by Mason & Dixon's line—a mere air line, without wall or guard. I long ago observed that some persons considered as very good, and others as very bad masters, often lost their negroes by their absconding from service; while the slaves of another class of persons, remarkable for order and good discipline, but not praised or blamed as either good or bad masters, never ran away, although no guard or forcible means were used to prevent them. The same management which prevented them from walking over a mere nominal, unguarded line, will prevent them from running away anywhere.

To ascertain the true method of governing negroes, so as to cure and prevent the disease under consideration, we must go back to the Pentateuch, and learn the true meaning of the untranslated term that represents the negro race. In the name there given to that race, is locked up the true art of governing negroes in such a manner that they cannot run away. The correct translation of that term declares the Creator's will in regard to the negro; it declares him to be the submissive knee-bender. In the anatomical conformation of his knees, we see *"genu flexit"* written in his physical structure, being more flexed or bent, than any other kind of man. If the white man attempts to oppose the Deity's will, by trying to make the negro anything else than *"the submissive knee-bender,"* (which the Almighty declared he should be,) by trying to raise him to a level with himself, or by putting himself on an equality with the negro; or if he abuses the power which God has given him over his fellow-man, by being cruel to him, or punishing him in anger, or by neglecting to protect him from the wanton abuses of his fellow-servants and all others, or by denying him the usual comforts and necessaries of life, the negro will run away; but if he keeps him in the position that we learn from the Scriptures he was intended to occupy, that is, the position of submission; and if his master or overseer be kind and gracious in his bearing towards him, without condescension, and at the same time ministers to his physical wants, and protects him from abuses, the negro is spell-bound, and cannot run away. *"He shall serve Japheth*; he shall be his servant of servants,"* on the conditions above mentioned—conditions that are clearly implied, though not directly expressed. According to my experience, the "genu flexit"—the awe and reverence, must be exacted from them, or they will despise their masters, become rude and ungovernable, and run away. On Mason and Dixon's line, two classes of persons were apt to lose their negroes: those who made themselves too familiar with them, treating them as equals, and making little or no distinction in regard to color; and, on the other hand, those who treated them cruelly, denied them the common necessaries of life, neglected to protect them against the abuses of others, or frightened them by a blustering manner of approach, when about to punish them for misdemeanors. Before negroes run away, unless they are frightened or panic-struck, they become sulky and dissatisfied. The cause of this sulkiness and dissatisfaction should be inquired into and removed, or they are apt to run away or fall into the negro consumption. When sulky and dissatisfied without cause, the experience of those on the line and elsewhere, was decidedly in favor of whipping them out of it, as a preventive measure against absconding, or other bad conduct. It was called whipping the devil out of them.

If treated kindly, well fed and clothed, with fuel enough to keep a small fire burning all night—separated into families, each family having its own house— not permitted to run about at night to visit their neighbors, to receive visits or to use intoxicating liquors, and not overworked or exposed too much to the weather, they are very easily governed—more so than any other people in the world. When all this is done, if any one or more of them, at any time, are inclined to raise their heads to a level with their master or overseer, humanity and their own good require that they should be punished until they fall into that submissive state which it was intended for them to occupy in all after-time, when their progenitor received the name of Canaan or "submissive knee-bender." They have only to be kept in that state and treated like children, with care, kindness, attention and humanity, to prevent and cure them from running away.

DYSÆSTHESIA ÆTHIOPICA, OR HEBETUDE OF MIND AND OBTUSE SENSIBILITY OF BODY—A DISEASE PECULIAR TO NEGROES—CALLED BY OVERSEERS, "RASCALITY."

Dysæsthesia Æthiopica is a disease peculiar to negroes, affecting both mind and body in a manner as well expressed by dysæsthesia, the name I have given it, as could be by a single term. There is both mind and sensibility, but both seem to be difficult to reach by impressions from without. There is a partial insensibility of the skin, and so great a hebetude of the intellectual faculties, as to be like a person half asleep, that is with difficulty aroused and kept awake. It differs from every other species of mental disease, as it is accompanied with physical signs or lesions of the body discoverable to the medical observer, which are always present and sufficient to account for the symptoms. It is much more prevalent among free negroes living in clusters by themselves, than among slaves on our plantations, and attacks only such slaves as live like free negroes in regard to diet, drinks, exercise, etc. It is not my purpose to treat of the complaint as it prevails among free negroes, nearly all of whom are more or less afflicted with it, that have not got some white person to direct and to take care of them. To narrate its symptoms and effects among them would be to write a history of the ruins and dilapidation of Hayti, and every spot of earth they have ever had uncontrolled possession over for any length of time. I propose only to describe its symptoms among slaves.

From the careless movements of the individuals affected with the complaint, they are apt to do much mischief, which appears as if intentional, but is mostly owing to the stupidity of mind and insensibility of the nerves induced by the disease. Thus, they break, waste and destroy everything they handle,—abuse horses and cattle,—tear, burn or rend their own clothing, and, paying no attention to the rights of property, steal others, to replace what they have destroyed. They wander about at night, and keep in a half nodding sleep during the day. They slight their work,—cut up corn, cane, cotton or tobacco when hoeing it, as if for pure mischief. They raise disturbances with their overseers and fellow-servants without cause or motive, and seem to be insensible to pain when subjected to punishment. The fact of the existence of such a complaint, making man like an automaton or senseless machine, having the above or similar symptoms, can be clearly established by the most direct and positive testimony. That it should have escaped the attention of the medical profession, can only be accounted for because its attention has not been sufficiently directed to the maladies of the negro race. Otherwise a complaint of so common an occurrence on badly-governed plantations, and so universal among free negroes, or those who are not governed at all,—a disease radicated in physical lesions and having its peculiar and well marked symptoms and its curative indications, would not have escaped the notice of the profession. The northern physicians and people have noticed the symptoms, but not the disease from which they spring. They ignorantly attribute the symptoms to the debasing influence of slavery on the mind, without considering that those who have never been in slavery, or their fathers before them, are the most afflicted, and the latest from the slave-holding South the least. The disease is the natural offspring of negro liberty—the liberty to be idle, to wallow in filth, and to indulge in improper food and drinks.

In treating of the anatomy and physiology of the negro, I showed that his respiratory system was under the same physiological laws as that of an infant child of the white race: that a warm atmosphere, loaded with carbonic acid and aqueous vapor, was the most congenial to his lungs during sleep, as it is to the infant; that, to insure the respiration of such an atmosphere, he invariably, as if moved by instinct, shrouds his head and face in a blanket or some other covering when disposing himself to sleep; that in sleeping by the fire in cold weather he turns his head to it, instead of his feet, evidently to inhale warm air; that when not in active exercise, he always hovers over a fire in comparatively warm weather, as if he took a positive pleasure in inhaling hot air and smoke when his body is quiescent. The natural effect of this practice, it was shown, caused imperfect atmospherization or vitalization of the blood in the lungs, as occurs in infancy, and a hebetude or torpor of intellect—from blood not sufficiently vitalized being distributed to the brain; also a slothfulness, torpor and disinclination to exercise from the same cause—the want of blood sufficiently vitalized in the circulating system.

When left to himself, the negro indulges in his natural disposition to idleness and sloth, and does not take exercise enough to expand his lungs and to vitalize his blood, but dozes out a miserable existence in the midst of filth and uncleanliness, being too indolent, and having too little energy of mind to provide for himself proper food and comfortable lodging and clothing. The consequence is, that the blood becomes so highly carbonized and deprived of oxygen, that it not only becomes unfit to stimulate the brain to energy, but unfit to stimulate the nerves of sensation distributed to the body. A torpor and insensibility pervades the system; the sentient nerves distributed to the skin lose their feeling in so great a degree, that he often burns his skin by the fire he hovers over without knowing it, and frequently has large holes in his clothes, and the shoes on his feet burnt to a crisp, without having been conscious of when it was done. This is the disease called dysæsthesia—a Greek term expressing the dull or obtuse sensation that always attends the complaint. When aroused from his sloth by the stimulus of hunger, he takes anything he can lay his hands on, and tramples on the rights, as well as on the property of others, with perfect indifference as to consequences. When driven to labor by the compulsive power of the white man, he performs the task assigned to him in a headlong, careless manner, treading down with his feet or cutting with his hoe the plants he is put to cultivate—breaking the tools he works with, and spoiling everything he touches that can be injured by careless handling.—Hence the overseers call it "rascality," supposing that the mischief is intentionally done. But there is no premeditated mischief in the case,—the mind is too torpid to meditate mischief, or even to be aroused by any angry passions to deeds of daring. Dysæsthesia, or hebetude of sensation of both mind and body, prevails to so great an extent, that when the unfortunate individual is subjected to punishment, he neither feels pain of any consequence, nor shows any unusual resentment, more than by a stupid sulkiness. In some cases, anæsthesiæ would be a more suitable name for it, as there appears to be an almost total loss of feeling. The term "rascality" given to this disease by overseers, is founded on an erroneous hypothesis, and leads to an incorrect empirical treatment, which seldom or never cures it.

The complaint is easily curable, if treated on sound physiological principles. The skin is dry, thick and harsh to the touch, and the liver inactive. The liver, skin and kidneys should be stimulated to activity and be made to assist in decarbonizing the blood. The best means to stimulate the skin is, first, to have the patient well washed with warm water and soap, then, to anoint it all over with oil, and to slap the oil in with a broad leather strap; then to put the patient to some hard kind of work in the open air and sunshine, that will compel him to expand his lungs, as chopping wood, splitting rails, or sawing with the cross-cut or whip saw. Any kind of labor will do that will cause full and free respiration in its performance, as lifting or carrying heavy weights, or brisk walking; the object being to expand the lungs by full and deep inspiration and expirations, thereby to vitalize the impure circulating blood by introducing oxygen and expelling carbon. This treatment should not be continued too long at a time, because where the circulating fluids are so impure as in this complaint, patients cannot stand protracted exercise without resting frequently and drinking freely of cold water or some cooling beverage, as lemonade, or alternated pepper tea sweetened with molasses. In bad cases, the blood has always the appearance of blood in scurvy, and commonly there is a scorbutic affection to be seen on the gums. After resting until the palpitation of the heart caused by the exercise is allayed, the patient should eat some good wholesome food, well seasoned with spices and mixed with vegetables, as turnip or mustard salad, with vinegar. After a moderate meal, he should resume his work again, resting at intervals, and taking refreshments and supporting the perspiration by partaking freely of liquids. At night he should be lodged in a warm room with a small fire in it, and should have a clean bed with sufficient blanket covering, and be washed clean before going to bed: in the morning, oiled, slapped, and put to work as before. Such treatment will, in a short time, effect a cure in all cases which are not complicated with chronic visceral derangements. The effect of this or a like course of treatment is often like enchantment. No sooner does the blood feel the vivifying influences derived from its full and perfect atmospherization by exercise in the open air and in the sun, than the negro seems to be awakened to a new existence, and to look grateful and thankful to the white man whose compulsory power, by making him inhale vital air, has restored his sensation, and dispelled the mist that clouded his intellect. His intelligence restored and his sensations awakened, he is no longer the *bipedum nequissimus,* or arrant rascal, he was supposed to be, but a good negro that can hoe or plow, and handles things with as much care as his fellow servants.

Contrary to the received opinion, a northern climate is the most favorable to the intellectual development of negroes; those of Missouri, Kentucky and the colder parts of Virginia and Maryland having much more mental energy, being more bold and ungovernable than in the southern lowlands; a dense atmosphere causing a better ventilation of their blood.

Although idleness is the most prolific cause of dysæsthesia, yet there are other ways that the blood gets deteriorated. I said before that negroes are like children, requiring government in everything. If not governed in their diet, they are apt to eat too much salt meat and not enough bread and vegetables, which practice generates a scorbutic state of the fluids and leads to the affection under consideration. This form of the complaint always shows itself in the gums, which become spongy and dark and leave the teeth. Uncleanliness of skin and torpid liver also tend to produce it. A scurvy set of negroes means the same thing, in the South, as a disorderly, worthless set. That the blood, when rendered impure and carbonaceous from any cause, as from idleness, filthy habits, unwholesome food or alcoholic drinks, affects the mind, is not only known to physicians, but was known to the Bard of Avon when he penned the lines—"We are not ourselves when Nature, being oppressed, commands the mind to suffer with the body."

According to unaltered physiological laws, negroes, as a general rule to which there are but few exceptions, can only have their intellectual faculties awakened in a sufficient degree to receive moral culture and to profit by religious or other instructions, when under the compulsatory authority of the white man; because, as a general rule to which there are but few exceptions, they will not take sufficient exercise, when removed from the white man's authority, to vitalize and decarbonize their blood by the process of full and free respiration, that active exercise of some kind alone can effect. A northern climate remedies, in a considerable degree, their naturally indolent disposition; but the dense atmosphere of Boston or Canada can scarcely produce sufficient hematosis and vigor of mind to induce them to labor. From their natural indolence, unless under the stimulus of compulsion, they doze away their lives, with the capacity of their lungs for atmospheric air only half expanded from the want of exercise to superinduce full and deep respiration. The inevitable effect is to prevent a sufficient atmospherization or vitalization of the blood, so essential to the expansion and the freedom of action of the intellectual faculties. The black blood distributed to the brain chains the mind to ignorance, superstition and barbarism, and bolts the door against civilization, moral culture and religious truth. The compulsory power of the white man, by making the slothful negro take active exercise, puts into active play the lungs, through whose agency the vitalized blood is sent to the brain to give liberty to the mind and to open the door to intellectual improvement. The very exercise, so beneficial to the negro, is expended in cultivating those burning fields of cotton, sugar, rice and tobacco, which, but for his labor, would, from the heat of the climate, go uncultivated, and their products be lost to the world. Both parties are benefited—the negro as well as the master—even more. But there is a third party benefited—the world at large. The three millions of bales of cotton, made by negro labor, afford a cheap clothing for the civilized world. The laboring classes of all mankind having less to pay for clothing, have more money to spend in educating their children, in intellectual, moral and religious progress.

The wisdom, mercy and justice of the decree, that Canaan shall serve Japheth, is proved by the disease we have been considering, because it proves that his physical organization and the laws of his nature are in perfect unison with slavery, and in entire discordance with liberty—a discordance so great as to produce the loathsome disease that we have been considering, as one of its inevitable effects,—a disease that locks up the understanding, blunts the sensations, and chains the mind to superstition, ignorance and barbarism. Slaves are not subject to this disease, unless they are permitted to live like free negroes, in idleness and filth—to eat improper food or to indulge in spirituous liquors. It is not their masters' interest that they should do so; as they would not only be unprofitable, but as great a nuisance to the South as the free negroes were found to be in London, whom the British government, more than half a century ago, colonized in Sierra Leone to get them out of the way. The mad fanaticism that British writers, lecturers and emissaries, and the East India Company planted in our Northern states, after it was found by well-tried experiments that free negroes in England, in Canada, in Sierra Leone and elsewhere were a perfect nuisance, and would not work as free laborers, but would retrograde to barbarism, was not planted there in opposition to British policy. Whatever was the motive of Great Britain in sowing the whirlwind in our Northern states, it is now threatening the disruption of a mighty empire of the happiest, most progressive and Christian people, that ever inhabited the earth—and the only empire on the wide earth that England dreads as a rival, either in arts or in arms.

Our Declaration of Independence, which was drawn up at a time when negroes were scarcely considered as human beings, *"That all men are by nature free and equal,"* and only intended to apply to white men, is often quoted in support of the false dogma that all mankind possess the same mental, physiological and anatomical organization, and that the liberty, free institutions, and whatever else would be a blessing to one portion, would, under the same external circumstances, be to all, without regard to any original or internal differences inherent in the organization. Although England preaches this doctrine, she practises in opposition to it every where. Instance her treatment of the Gipsies in England, the Hindoos in India, the Hottentots at her Cape Colony, and the aboriginal inhabitants of New-Holland. The dysæsthesia æthiopica adds another to the many ten thousand evidences of the fallacy of the dogma that abolitionism is built on; for here, in a country where two races of men dwell together, both born on the same soil, breathing the same air, and surrounded by the same external agents—liberty, which is elevating the one race of people above all other nations, sinks the other into beastly sloth and torpidity; and the slavery, which the one would prefer death rather than endure, improves the other in body, mind and morals; thus proving the dogma false, and establishing the truth that there is a radical, internal or physical difference between the two races, so great in kind, as to make what is wholesome and beneficial for the white man, as liberty, republican or free institutions, etc., not only unsuitable to the negro race, but actually poisonous to its happiness.

* * *

JOSEPH RUGGLES WILSON

A Discourse to Be Preached in the First Presbyterian Church, Augusta, Georgia, on Sabbath Morning, 1861

Upon learning of the discussions to be conducted in New York City in July 1845, Pastor Wilson has made special arrangements to circulate this draft of a sermon (in reality given in 1861 and here slightly edited) he plans to deliver to his congregation when he thinks the time is right. His views, as given in this draft, represent the views of the educated, scholarly white Christian clergymen of the time. The document starts with a passage from Scripture.

SOURCE: *Joseph Ruggles Wilson,* Mutual Relation of Masters and Slaves as Taught in the Bible: A Discourse Preached in the First Presbyterian Church, Augusta, Georgia, on Sabbath Morning, Jan 6, 1861 *(Augusta: Steam Press of Chronicle & Sentinel, 1861).*

phebians, VI: 5-9:—"Servants, be obedient to them that are your masters according to the flesh, with fear and trembling, in singleness of your heart, as unto Christ; not with eye-service as men-pleasers, but as the servants of Christ, doing the will of God from the heart; with good-will doing service, as to the Lord and not to men; knowing that whatsoever good thing any man doeth, the same shall he receive of the Lord, whether he be bond or free. And, ye masters, do the same things unto them, forbearing threatening, knowing that your Master also is in Heaven; neither is there respect of persons with him."

I.

Our attention is forcibly arrested by the very first word of this text; "servants." There is no difficulty in ascertaining its true meaning, in the original Greek. It distinctly and unequivocally signifies "slaves," springing as it does in this its substantive form from a verbal root, which means to bind. There are several words, conveying different shades of thought, which Grecians were accustomed to employ in speaking of servants, inasmuch as there are several kinds and degrees of servitude. But no one of them does so emphatically set forth the true and simple idea of domestic slavery as understood in these Southern States, as the word—the word whose plural form opens our text. It refers us to a man who is in the relation of permanent and legal bondage to another: this other having in him and his labor the strictest rights of property. The word is never employed to indicate the condition of a mere hireling. It points out a dependent who is solely under the authority of a master: that master being the head of a household and wielding over his slaves the commission of a despot, whose acts are to be determined only by the restraining laws of Christianity and by general considerations of his own and their welfare: a despot responsible to God, a good conscience, and the well-being of society. I use this word "despot" advisedly. It is the scriptural opposite of "slave," as in the passage from the 1st Epistle to Timothy: "Let as many servants as are under the yoke count their own masters worthy of all honor;" and as in the words taken from the Epistle to Titus: "Exhort servants to be obedient to their own masters"—slaves to be obedient to their despots. In the passage immediately under discussion, the word "servants" has for its antithesis the word which may be rendered "lords," and which, in its lowest signification, means "possessors," "owners," "masters" in a sense sufficiently absolute. As a freedman, in the New Testament sense, is one who is at liberty to go and act and be what he pleases, so a slave is one who goes and acts and is controlled by a superior will. And not only do the New Testament writers use the word, to express the meaning I have shown it to have; this meaning is likewise common to all the ancient authors, whose works in the Greek language are considered classic; men who wrote with strict attention to verbal accuracy, and whose compositions came from their pens at a time when domestic slavery was a universal institution. I have been thus particular in establishing the true import of this word, for a purpose. The time has fully come when all who are interested personally in the subject of Southern institutions—whether masters or servants—should, comprehend their scriptural relation to them—should, know whether or not the holiness of God receives or rejects them—and whether in all our possible contentions for their maintenance we are to have only men for our enemies or, in addition, our Sovereign Ruler also. Now, we have already seen that the Holy Spirit employs words which lie has intended, to be understood, as distinctly enunciating the existence of domestic servitude—that lie has sent to all the world a volume of truth, which is indisputably addressed to men who hold slaves and to the slaves who possess masters—and that, from the connections in which these highly suggestive words occur, He has included slavery as an organizing element in that family order which lies at the very foundation of Church and State. A study of such words is, therefore, a first and an important step in ascertaining the will of God with respect to an institution which short sighted men have indiscriminately and violently denounced, and which wicked men have declared unworthy of the countenance of a Christianity whose peaceful and conservative spirit, as applied to society, they neither respect nor understand.

II.

I am sure that you will bear with me while I take another step in this great argument, and show how completely the Bible brings human slavery underneath the sanction of divine authority, upon other and stronger grounds. In deed, my text compels me to take this course—for, if our domestic servitude be essentially different from that to which the Apostle's exhortations refer, we do but beat the air with empty sounds when we endeavor to apply them to the masters and servants who compose the Christian congregations of this section of our country. If Paul, or rather the great God, speaking by his inspired lips, meant to confine his evangelical teachings to a state of things wholly unlike that under which we live, then this portion of Scripture is to us a dead letter, and can have no influence upon our consciences or conduct. If we preach from it at all, therefore, it must be employed for the practical benefit of hearers now as much as when the Ephesian church opened their ears and hearts to its reception. And, in truth, in the suggestions of this very thought, there is a remote scriptural plea to be found for the divine sanction of slavery. It would seem, that, inasmuch as the Bible was intended for all times and all ages, and not for one period and a single country, the fact that it gives directions as plain and full and forcible for the regulation of domestic service as it does for defining and limiting the marital, parental and filial relations in families, furnishes an inferential proof of the proposition that, everywhere, such service ought to be as universal as such higher and tenderer relations: that no household is perfect under the gospel which does not contain all the grades of authority and obedience, from that of husband and wife, down through that of father and son, to that of master and servant. Accordingly, we do find, as a matter of historical fact, that among all people, during all the periods of time, there have been those, in every family, whom the very law of necessity itself has made servants to the other; servants, if not always in the rigid sense which slavery seems to imply, yet in a sense sufficiently obvious and strict.

Go where you will—visit what family you may, and you will find members of the household, under some law which requires them more than the others, to perform menial services for all the little community. The hireling, the wife, the eldest child, the dependent stranger, may be the voluntary or involuntary doer of offices which must fall to the lot of some one. I need not point you to the manifold illustrations of this idea, which appears in all conditions of human society—even in those which are most favored—even in those from which come the most heated denunciations of a slavery which, existing among us, differs at best from their own more in degree and form than in essential qualities. There must be such inequalities in society; and whenever an attempt has been made to remove them—whenever radicalism has proposed to smooth down all individuals in the family or other community to a common level—as in the experiments of Fourierism, which once excited so much attention in the world,—it was found that a fundamental law had been transgressed, and failure inevitably attended such unscriptural and disorganizing attempts. God has evidently made one to serve another. The simple question is, what must be the nature of this service? The answer is, that its nature depends upon circumstances. And out of this answer springs the interrogation, has God ever shown us that there are circumstances under which involuntary service may be required and yielded on the part of masters and slaves? Has He ever declared this kind of service to be right, and lifted its existence entirely above the charge of sinfulness? Are we at full liberty to carry to Him upon the arms of our faith, our households, and as confidently ask Him to bless our servants as our children? Does this great, beneficial, civilizing institution of slavery live beneath the light of His face, with no fault to be found with it upon the part of His infinite holiness, except when and wherein it may subtler abuse at the hands of the parties concerned? Surely the Bible is clear enough upon this point to satisfy the most sensitive conscience. Light cannot shine with greater brightness than does the doctrine of the sinlessness—nay, than does the doctrine of the righteousness—of an institution, which, besides being sustained and promoted by a long course of favorable providences, besides being recognized as a prime conservator of the civilization of the world, besides being one of the colored man's foremost sources of blessing, is likewise directly sanctioned by both the utterance and silence of Scripture.

III.

Look, first, at the most instructive silence of Scripture upon this subject. An obvious feature of the sacred word, whose office, in the hands of the Spirit, is to convince of sin and conduct to righteousness, is this: it never mentions a grave offence against God without denouncing it directly or impliedly: denouncing it, too, in the face of every human policy for maintaining its existence: denouncing it, that is, without the least regard to present consequences. The Bible could not wink at prevailing error, much less at prevailing crime, least of all at prevailing ungodliness, through any fear of arousing angry opposition against Christianity on the part of such as might hold the civil power, or of such as might direct the sneer of hatred. Christianity came, rather, as necessarily it must have come, as a "sword," to set men at "variance" on the field of a great fight between evil and good. Wherever, therefore, it went in the early ages, it dealt incessant blows at idolatry, for example; blows which are now being repeated throughout the pagan world by an army of missionaries, whom no danger is sufficient to appeal. Under all circumstances, too, falsehood comes under the frown of Scripture truth; so do theft, drunkenness, violence, murder, and a multitude of smaller offenses. In fact, on the deeply colored canvass of God's word, you find such a faithful representation of human guilt through all the turns and pretenses and developments of the sinful heart, as leaves nothing wanting to complete the portraiture of that manifold criminality against which divine wrath breathes one constant stream of fiery condemnation. God will not, must not, cannot tamper with sin, in any of its forms, so long as He remains true to Himself and to His holy magistracy. He can neither connive at it by silence, nor perpetuate it by giving laws for its regulation, nor excuse it by letting down to its weakness His relaxed law. Sin is wrong absolutely—a deep curse to the universe, in itself—and when discovered by the searches of divine truth, whether in the individual heart or in the common practices of societies, must meet with the instant, the spontaneous, the overwhelming displeasure of Jehovah.

Now, in the face of such reflections, it is remarkable, to say the least, that the institution of compulsory slavery, as it existed throughout the Roman Empire, although often referred to in the New Testament, is never once condemned, never once even discountenanced. On the contrary, provision is made for its perpetuation, by means of the rules which are given for its regulation and improvement. So far from Scripture appearing as the destroyer, it appears as the upholder, of an institution, which, under proper management, by Christian people, is represented as an element in domestic completeness, whose presence is a benefit and a blessing. If it be a wrong, it is not so in itself; it can become so only when masters and servants misconceive and abuse their relationship to each other. We are led to understand that if the salt of grace be thrown into this branch of the family union, it will prove an auxiliary to the church and society only second to the parental and filial relationship. And, lest any should imagine that because the slavery of the Roman Empire was essentially different from that which we cherish, the Bible smiled upon that when it could not upon this, we have the amplest testimony of history to show that the two systems exhibited entire agreement in principle, and that they differ only in their circumstances. It is certain that our servile laws are indefinitely milder—every way more humane—than were those which existed when the Savior preached and the Apostles wrote. It is certain, too, that the institution in that ancient empire was far more extensive—more thoroughly domesticated—more perfectly inwrought into the very structure of society—than is the similar institution in this modern republic—and, therefore, was of such an amazing magnitude of proportions as that, if involuntary servitude were in itself an evil thing, then was presented the very best opportunity to strike it down forever with a blow from the hammer of the Spirit. A sin which overshadowed the land, which darkened every household, which hampered the church—surely a sin of such enormity would have been visited with the utmost severity of heaven's fury. But no: that fury nowhere appears in the threats or expostulations of Scripture. Instead, we find a distinct law of permission, and an unequivocal note of favor, extended to it. The Bible would control and sanctify, but not destroy it.

In the days of the Apostles, it is proper for me to remind you, there was a party, whose numbers were scattered throughout the empire, which constituted the "abolition party" of that period. It is known that the Pharisees gave a special prominence to political freedom; joined with them were the Essenes; and binding together the whole, were certain philosophers who inculcated unattainable notions of universal liberty. These persons were in the habit of condemning Roman masters as unjust, impious, and destroyers of a law of nature. They inculcated the same abstract doctrines as those which have proceeded from mistaken philanthropy in our own distracted country, and which, at the time when Paul wrote to the Ephesians, were threatening the world with discord and bloodshed, as now, by the permissive wrath of God again they threaten. It was, therefore, to meet the unholy recklessness of such a destructive spirit, that the Apostles were careful to enjoin the conservation of an institution, which, though, like all other earthly institutions, attended by many circumstantial evils arising from the corruption of the human heart, was nevertheless no more wrong in its essential principles than the relation of husband and wife or father and child. And Paul was not a mere theoretical teacher upon this subject. He practised the righteousness which he enjoined. He once, at least, had it in his power to display the true spirit of Christian love in his treatment of slaveholders. I refer you to his conduct with respect to Onesimus, a runaway slave belonging to that believer in Christ, Philemon. This servant coming providentially under the influence of Paul's preaching, was happily converted. Being converted, what was his duty to his defrauded master? The spirit of Christianity, which now resided in his heart, informed his conscience of the fact that he was the hypocrisy of Philemon, and that while he remained away from his owner's home and authority, he was committing the sin of robbery. He consulted the Apostle. What was his advice? He did not hesitate to urge Onesimus to go at once to his master, confess at his feet the grievous fault he had committed, and beg to be received once more among the number of his slaves. And that the reconciliation between master and servant might be hastened, Paul wrote, (and wrote under the inspiration of God,) a letter of beseeching tenderness to the offended owner, asking him to pardon the faithful fugitive and give him a place in his confidence, and telling him that he would now, with grace in his heart, be a far better servant than ever. Such reasoning, from the implied allowance of slavery by inspired Scripture, is, my friends, conclusive enough upon the point in question. Let neither master nor servant dispute the righteousness, doubt the wisdom, or fear the reproach of the relation which they sustain towards each other. It is not sinful. It is not inexpedient. It is not degradatory.

IV.

But look at God's direct and positive utterances in the premises. I need only point you to them, so clearly do they establish the fact that this part of family order was always familiar to the divine mind in its plans of human government. Domestic slavery is twice clearly acknowledged in the brief law of the Ten Commandments. In the 4th law, with regard to the proper observance of the Sabbath, the rule of righteousness is laid down, which provides for the periodical rest, during holy time, of the "man-servant and the maid-servant," who, together with the other animate property of the household, must suspend labor; and who, together with the other rational members of the family must expend their thoughts in glorifying God. In the 10th law, again, which establishes those social relations of mankind, whose integrity and purity must be maintained in heart if they would be productive of good in fact, and where, accordingly, the desires of men are forbidden to covet neighbor's blessings—in this law, it is made a fatal sin to covet his "man-servant or his maid-servant," just as it is to covet any other of his possessions.

This recognition of involuntary servitude is, we say, thus found imbedded in the very heart of the moral law itself—that law which determines the principles of divine administration over men—a law which constitutes, if I may so speak, the very constitution of that royal kingdom whose regulations begin and end in the infinite holiness of Jehovah, and whose spread through the universal heart of the race is the aim of all Scripture.

But, in addition, hear the express words of the Holy Ghost in the Levitical law—words which embody an explicit provision for the future possession, by the Israelites, of man in property which they did not have at the time these words were spoken: a provision, then, not to regulate what already existed, but to legalize what was, 40 years afterwards, to become a distinct institution:

"Both thy bondmen and thy bondwomen which thou shalt have, shall be of the heathen that are round about you; of them shall ye buy bondmen and bondmaids. And ye shall take them as an inheritance for your children after you to inherit them for a possession; they shall be your bondmen forever." No law can be plainer. No instruction of truth could more convince the Christian that he is standing upon the surest and safest ground, whenever he resists the imputation that he is a sinner while upholding a system of domestic servitude. He can triumphantly say: "I direct you to the law and testimony!"

V.

But my hearers, if you wish for farther conviction, carry your belief of the essential rightness of slavery to the injunctions of our text, which the Apostle publishes for its conservation and perfection. He as much as says, that it is unnecessary to fear that this long-cherished institution will first give way before the enemies who press upon it from without. If slaveholders preserve it as an element of social welfare, in the spirit of the Christian religion, throwing into it the full measure of gospel-salt allotted to it, and casting around it the same guardianship with which they would protect their family peace, if threatened on some other ground— they need apprehend nothing but their own dereliction in duty to themselves and their dependent servants. I mean, simply, that while we ought to allow no malignant interference from any quarter with the institution of which we are God's appointed guardians, and while we ought to be suitably alive to any threat of presumptuous violence which may seek to wrest from us our heaven-given rights in our heaven-allowed property—yet, after all, the wisdom which, lies underneath the spirit of this sensitive watchfulness of our political zeal, and which gives to that zeal its purity and power, is the wisdom to be exercised in making our domestic servitude all that it should become, so as to render it worth the expenditure of every energy of defence. "We must see to it, that masters and servants understand and appreciate their mutual relation, and that they maintain it on both sides as Christians. This is the object of the apostolic exhortations before us, and upon which I will now briefly comment: exhortations which, seeking to purify domestic servitude, do thereby bring it completely within gospel sanctions.

This passage articulates the core of the proslavery theology of antebellum Southern Christianity in the claim that enslaved people are required by God to obey their enslavers' command.

There are certain vices which slavery is apt to engender, in preference to all others. These are founded in indolence, eye-service[1] and hypocrisy. These evils appear in a variety of forms, and are a constant source of irritation and unhappiness. But, so far as the servant is concerned, they are met by one simple injunction, the injunction of obedience to his master. If obedience be sincere, be consistent, be from proper motives, it will remove every vice from the servant's temper and conduct. The Apostle, therefore, presents to the reader those noble qualities of servile allegiance which will elevate it at once to the high point of Christian compliance with rightful authority; the only worthy compliance. He exhorts servants to obey, 1st, with conscientious anxiety: expressed by "fear and trembling." Not, however, so much the fear of man as a reverential fear of God, is to be understood in these words. It is not the servile dread of punishment. It is a careful and painstaking solicitude to do right under all the circumstances of their relation, because the eye of heaven rests upon them and will follow with its displeasure every act or course of wrong-doing.

---

1. "Eye service" meant a slave laboring while in eyesight of the Master or other superior, but not providing good or steady service when out of eyesight.

Obedience must oddly be with "singleness of mind": not hypocritical, not deceitful, not inspired by duplicity or cunning. There must be no double-mindedness, but the giving to the business in hand all the simplicity of an honest purpose. Service is to be yielded upon principle, not with that attempt to please both self and the master which ends in "eye-service," and then only seems diligent and complete when he is present, but breaks down into remissness when he is absent. And to this excellence will obedience attain when, oddly, it issues from the heart which desires "first of all to please Christ. Obey "not as men-pleasers" says the exhortation, "but as the servants of Christ, doing the will of God" in your station, "from the heart; with good-will, doing service, as to the Lord and not to men." The servant is, like the child, to know that the authority under which he has been placed is from above, and that the master rules him as the agent of heaven. He must, therefore, do his whole duty with his thoughts fixed upon that divine upper hand of which the lower one of his owner is but the representative. Disobedience to his proprietor on earth, is rebellion against the law of God, who is the first and principal proprietor of all. And this consideration is required in order to render the service good, elevating and self-rewarding. To serve Him, who is infinitely holy and infinitely great, while giving heed to his temporal and imperfect master, throws into the servant's obedience that element which makes it eminently saint-like, and gives it a place in his Christian experience. So that he goes through his daily duties with this consolation, singing its glad song to his labor: "Whatever good thing any man doeth, the same shall he receive of the Lord, whether he be bond, or free."

What a pleasing scene would the institution of slavery exhibit, were all our servants to yield their obedience in this spirit of the Christian religion! It would commend itself to true philanthropy as containing the best system of labor which is allowable to fallen man. But alas! the bondmen whom we own and employ, while occupying the most favorable position for improvement and happiness that is possible to them, are, as yet, far from being imbued with that love to God, which alone can raise their lot to its highest dignity. We thank God that so many of them are pious—that from so many of their comfortable houses comes the voice of prayer and praise—and that so many of them are conscientious servitors of man for Christ's sake. But we ought to look forward to the time when they will all be what the Bible would make them; a race whose love for the Master above will spread through their rejoicing millions a measure of sanctification which will convert their services into the very first of home-blessings, and their piety into a missionary influence for saving the black man everywhere from the ruin of perdition.

But to accomplish this, their earthly masters have something—have much—to do. "Ye masters, do the same things unto them, forbearing threatening; knowing that your master also is in heaven; neither is there respect of persons with Him." For masters to "do the same things" which their servants are required to do, is for them to "act towards the dependents with the same regard to the will of God, the same recognition of the authority of Christ, the same sincerity and good feeling which has been enjoined upon the slaves them selves." God concedes nothing to the master beyond what the law of love, demands. He does not allow the reign of injustice over this institution any more than over the other departments of family order. Every dictate of humanity does, indeed, render necessary the maintenance of a due subordination of the servant to his proprietor: righteousness in fulfilling the obligations of the relationship does not ask for equality, but rather repudiates it, seeing that the best interests of all parties can be served only on the terms which nature and providence and scripture have fixed—the terms of mastery on the one side and servitude on the other. But, notwithstanding the careful guardianship of the principle of authority on the part of owners, yet must they not forget that they are to give an account to God at last for the right use of their exalted stewardship—the stewardship over souls of immortal men, placed directly underneath their control. They are to endeavor to train up their servants for heaven—as much bound to do this as they are bound to attend to the religious instruction of their own children. **Masters are, for this end, even required to guard their tempers, that they may be guiltless of unnecessary severity in the treatment of their domestics; to "avoid threatening": but to administer a firm, consistent, orderly, paternal government, which will suitably mingle the mercy of punishment with the justice of reward. They must remember to treat their servants as they will expect their own Master in heaven to treat them. They must not neglect discipline, but it must always be the discipline which is dictated by holy principle. In short, the master who would do for his servants up to the full measurement of Bible requirements, will find himself unequal to the task in all its length and breadth, unless he himself become a Christian in heart and practice.** To vital goodness alone belongs the privilege of understanding and administering the whole authority of a masterhood so responsible. And, oh, when that welcome day shall dawn, whose light will reveal a world covered with righteousness, not the least pleasing sight will be the institution of domestic slavery, freed from its stupid servility on the one side and its excesses of neglect or severity on the other, and appearing to all mankind as containing that scheme of politics and morals, which, by saving a lower race from the destruction of heathenism, has, under divine management, contributed to refine, exalt, and enrich its superior race!

In this passage, the measures taken by enslavers to control their slaves are held to be duties assigned by God, ones that require a successful master to be "a Christian in heart and practice."

ACKNOWLEDGMENTS

Decades ago, conversations with two professors, Jim Dunn at Antioch College and Herbert Gutman at the CUNY Graduate Center, first inspired me to ponder how to "cover" American slavery and racism, and nationalistic mythologies, with an engaging and active—rather than didactic and boring—pedagogy. Much later, in 2010, in similar discussions with my visionary provost at Eastern Michigan University, Jack Kay, about our university's need to achieve higher retention and graduation rates *and* deeper intellectual engagement with what Jack called "the hard issues of racism," I ventured that we could create a Reacting to the Past game that would deliver a unifying, engaging college experience for our highly stratified student population (by which I meant not merely to those at EMU, but across the USA). A researcher on hate groups and the son of Holocaust survivors, Jack Kay replied: "Yes! Do so, quickly!" If Jim Dunn, Herb Gutman, and Jack Kay still lived, I think they would like the *Frederick Douglass* game.

Long before publication, this venturesome classroom game has proven itself in scores of college classrooms. Many thanks to the several thousand Eastern Michigan University students who played early versions in my classes and those of colleagues. I am grateful for these students' passion, comments, and their engagement with learning—what I learned from them cannot be overstated. Special thanks to former students James Tatum, Jessica Howell, Taylor Kirchoff, Julie Salvo, Vinnie Massamino, Nikki Rice, Olivia Mateso Mbala-Nkanga, Emma Mayhood, and Justin Payne. To my now-retired colleague-in-arms, Melvin Peters, the David Walker of EMU, my undying appreciation and solidarity, comrade.

I heartily thank my many friends and colleagues in the Reacting to the Past community for their ideas, critiques, and informative conversations: Mark Carnes, Nick Proctor, Bill Offutt, Pat Coby, Sumaiya Khalique, Gretchen McKay, Clare Crowston, Dorothea Herreiner, Paula Lazarus, Justin Carroll, Judith Shapiro, Jon Truitt, my brother Joseph Engwenyu, Denise Spivey, Priscilla Dowden-White, Nik Ribianszky, Jace Weaver, Laura Adams Weaver, Laura Kieran, Lisa Pruitt, Patrick Rael, Larry Carver, Shoshana Brassfield, Mary Strasma, Verdis Robinson, Eleanor McConnell, Debbie Field, Sean Taylor, Fred Hoxie, Sakina Hughes, and many more. Thanks also to Barbara Bair, Victoria Chevalier, Eileen Janadia, and Ericka Terry for sharing their insights with me. Thanks to Kate Levin, Marley Higbee, and Jonas Higbee for the greatest blessings of my life and countless discussions about games, the past, and life in general.

This game could not have been imagined, let alone created, without the rich, detailed scholarship on slavery and abolitionism in the United States and related subjects written in recent decades. My debts to countless fellow historians are immense, but here I just thank a few whose work has been especially valuable to me: David Blight, Edward Baptist, Ira Berlin, my great mentor and teacher Eric Foner, Paul Finkelman, Walter Johnson, Staughton Lynd, Ibram X. Kendi, Andrew Delbanco, Robin Einhorn, and my Columbia grad school classmates, Sven Beckert and Manisha Sinha. The late Harold Cruse, who lived and wrote about twentieth-century Black history and was my professor, greatly shaped my capacity to find meaning in our conflicted past.

Special thanks to another great historian, James Brewer Stewart, Professor of History Emeritus at

Macalester College, for his vital work on abolitionism, for his inspiring work as the founder of Historians Against Slavery, and for accepting my invitation to become coauthor of this game. A superb teacher, Jim Stewart *has game*; he "got" the idea of Reacting immediately, and he made this game complete. (Historians Against Slavery works to end the widespread use of slave labor in our twenty-first century. Check it out at www.HAS.org.)

Learning and teaching history, like making it, is best done collaboratively. Much appreciation to the many collaborating instructors—including many in disciplines other than history—who "ran the game" in their classes and reported back to me on how it went. Apologies to anyone overlooked here, and deep gratitude to all:

Ben Alpers, University of Oklahoma

Karrin Anderson, Colorado State University

Elizabeth Beaumont, University of Minnesota Twin Cities

Ian Binnington, Allegheny College

Megan Boccardi, Quincy University

Betta Borrelli, Georgia College

Suzel Bozada-Deas, Sonoma State University

Corey Brooks, York College of Pennsylvania

Matt Carhart, Minneapolis Community & Technical College

Justin Carroll, Indiana University East

Rachel Cleves, University of Victoria

Perrin Cunningham, University of Colorado Colorado Springs

Laura June Davis, Southern Utah University

Jonathan DeCoster, Otterbein University

Kathy Donohue, Central Michigan University

Priscilla Dowden-White, University of Missouri–St. Louis

Joseph Engwenyu, Eastern Michigan University

Paul Fessler, Dordt College

Debbie Field, Chris Momany, and the Brothers in Action at Adrian College

Billy Fields, University of Alabama

Bridget Ford, California State University, East Bay

Karin Gedge, West Chester University

Elizabeth George, MidAmerica Nazarene University

Hilary Green, University of Alabama

Matt Harper, University of Central Arkansas

Bethany Holmstrom, LaGuardia Community College

Rebecca Hooker, Virginia Wesleyan University

Stacey Horstmann Gatti, Long Island University Brooklyn

Elizabeth Hovey, John Jay College of Criminal Justice

Sakina Hughes, University of Southern Indiana

Daniel Hutchinson, Belmont Abbey College

Kimberly F. Jones, Long Island University Brooklyn

Sara Lampert, University of South Dakota

Peter Levy, York College of Pennsylvania

Alyce Loesch, University of Connecticut

Daniela Mansbach, University of Wisconsin–Superior

Bruce McCluggage and Robin Schofield, Pikes Peak Community College

Eleanor McConnell, Frostburg State University

Elizabeth Medley, Abraham Baldwin Agricultural College

Elisa Miller, Rhode Island College

Jane Murphy, Colorado College

Sylvie Murray, University of the Fraser Valley

Alice Nash, University of Massachusetts–Amherst

Kathi Nehls, Peru State College

Bill Offutt, Pace University

Russ Olwell, Merrimack College

Allison O'Mahen Malcom, Jim Grimshaw, and Abby Markwyn, Carroll University

Dan Ott, University of Wisconsin–Eau Claire

Carolan Ownby, University of Utah

Abby Perkins, Kean University

Jill Peterfeso, Guilford College

Lisa Pruitt, Middle Tennessee State University

Patrick Rael, Bowdoin College

Nik Ribianszky, Queen's University Belfast

Patricia Richey, Jacksonville College

Verdis Robinson, Campus Compact

Sarah Rodriguez, High Tech High, San Diego

Alisa Rosenthal, Randolph-Macon College

April Schultz, Illinois Wesleyan University

Hannah Schultz, Bryan College

Robert Shelton, Cleveland State University

Martha Sledge, Marymount Manhattan College

Gary R. Smith, Central Texas College

Zach Smith, Lansing Community College

Elizabeth Smith-Pryor, Kent State University

Edie Sparks, University of the Pacific

Denise Spivey, Tallahassee Community College

Mary Strasma, Eastern Michigan University

Sean Tayor, Minnesota State University Moorhead

Mark Thompson, California State University Stanislaus

Eleanor Wittrup, University of the Pacific

Kirsten Wood, Florida International University

Matt Wranovix, University of New Haven

Nicole Wyatt, University of Calgary

APPENDIX A: SAMPLE RESOLUTIONS AND BROADSIDE

RESOLUTIONS

In each of the three Meetings, two Resolutions must be brought to a vote by the Chairman. Ideally, the Chairman's draft Resolutions should be short and punchy, not wordy or hard to follow. Trying to write them when the game is in session rarely results in much besides confusion. They must be written out and accessible to everyone before any vote is held. Changes may be suggested, but none added to draft Resolutions without being agreed to by the Chairman, before the vote.

The sample Resolutions that follow illustrate the range of possible Resolutions. No doubt, good Chairmen attuned to their classmates' characters will compose Resolutions superior to these. Resolutions can contain statements unrelated to each other, but to include contradictory statements is pointless.

> *Resolved:* We affirm that the status of all forms of property that exist within these United States is a matter to be determined solely by each state and deplore efforts of abolition societies to violate these rights and to trample on states' rights.
>
> *Resolved:* We admire Horace Greeley's handsome beard; deplore all drinking of alcohol; thank the Lord for the glorious honeybees, with which He provides us a model for a just, orderly society; commend the industrious people of Illinois for their admirable courts of law; and demand an immediate end to the slave trade in Washington, D.C.
>
> *Resolved:* The Constitution is a pact with the devil that upholds the Slave Power over morality and justice and must be disallowed.
>
> *Resolved:* We applaud Mr. Calhoun for his statesmanship and deplore the attacks on him by abolition lunatics like William Lloyd Garrison. Garrison is a threat to public order and must be silenced by lawful authority or by the people directly.
>
> *Resolved:* We praise Edgar Allan Poe and Walt Whitman for their literary creations, just as we praise the editor of the *Evening Post* for publishing distinguished writing, and declare that the apples of Indiana are the envy of all Americans.
>
> *Resolved:* We denounce Douglass and declare his so-called *Narrative* and the Abolitionist Movement to be a pack of lies designed to elevate the inferior race while degrading the supreme white race.
>
> *Resolved:* The Declaration of Independence, written by Thomas Jefferson, remains the fullest expression of the rights of man, relevant for all time.
>
> *Resolved:* Slavery is a positive good that benefits all mankind.
>
> *Resolved:* We condemn slavery as a sin and require the immediate, universal, uncompensated abolition of slavery, with full equality to all people, regardless of color. We thank Frederick Douglass for his truthful *Narrative*.

BROADSIDES

On the next page is a broadside produced by one player in the Douglass game. Broadsides are one of the three types of required work for players in the game and will be mounted in the classroom as posters. Nobody can remove another character's poster or broadside, but players can respond to one by creating their own broadside.

A·N·N·O·U·N·C·I·N·G

◆ AN ORATION ◆

by the *foremost* of our *proud nation's*

Most Towering Intellects

War Hawk : Peace Negotiator : Architect of Whiggery : "The Western Star"

Tireless upholder of the ideals of THOMAS JEFFERSON

Senator Henry Clay on

RACIAL INCOMPATIBILITY, COLONIZATION, & THE RIGHTS OF MAN.

His learned exposition shall include all of the following *and more*:

I. Incompatibility of the Races

The liberty of the descendants of Africans in the United States is incompatible with the safety and liberty of the European descendants.

The Anglo-Saxon, the Irishman, the German and the negro – *their differences considered.* Illustrative examples from the GREAT EMPIRES of Antiquity and the Dark Ages. Explanations regarding the seeds of their decline. The empires of Alexander the Great, Augustus Caesar, and Charles Magnus. The *backwardness and stagnation* of Russia, Austria, and Turkey. The *vitality and productivity* of England, France, and Prussia.

☞ The pressing QUESTION: *Which path shall we follow?* ☜

II. Objections to Colonization Overturned

Constitutional sanctions for slaveholding. Statistical charts and graphs based on information from the United States Department of State, Bureau of the Census. The pleasant shores of sunny LIBERIA. The deplorable situation in HAYTI. Removing the great Indian tribes. Domestic dependent nations considered. The value to the negroes of colonizing Liberia, and to us.

III. Rationality & Peace between Races

The rationality of man. We desire racial self-fulfillment. Our proud past considered.

ALL PROCEEDS TO BENEFIT THE AMERCAN COLONIZATION SOCIETY.   PRINTED BY N. PROCTOR.

APPENDIX B: ADDITIONAL ROLES (used in some classes)

(Note to Gamemasters: full descriptions and role sheets for these additional characters are available through the Reacting Consortium Library. Visit www.reactingconsortiumlibrary.org/ for more information.)

Abolitionist Faction

William Powell, a colored boardinghouse owner in New York City, is a stalwart of the Abolitionist Movement, an active helper for runaway slaves, and a true Garrisonian.

The Reverend Henry Highland Garnet pastors a church in Troy, New York, and is one of the nation's leading Black clergymen. He escaped slavery in Maryland at age nine, and his 1843 speech to the National Negro Convention urged rebellion against slaveholders.

Miss Frances Ellen Watkins is a young Black woman, born free in Maryland, devoted to racial uplift, emancipation, and writing; she's published a book of poems already and will become a famous Black writer (in the future, after she marries and takes the name Harper).

Northeast Ohio Methodist church minister admires the music of the Hutchinson Family Singers and is, like them, a dedicated immediate Abolitionist.

Sarah Grimké grew up in one of South Carolina's wealthiest, most powerful slaveholding families, rejected that legacy, moved North, joined the Society of Friends (Quakers), left it, became an Abolitionist, and asserts the rights of women to speak publicly and advocates full racial equality.

Asa Mahan, president of Oberlin College, converted to abolitionism during the Lane Seminary debates in Cincinnati, and believes the Constitution is antislavery.

James G. Birney, although born into a Kentucky slaveholding family, is an ardent immediate Abolitionist, but he differs sharply with the Garrisonians, who abstain from voting as corrupt. Birney advocates political abolition: he ran for president in 1840 and in 1844 as the nominee of the Liberty Party.

Solomon Northup, a free Negro from New York State who was unlawfully seized and taken into slavery in Louisiana. He miraculously escaped and is now an active Abolitionist.

Charles Sumner, a young Boston lawyer increasingly interested in public issues.

Salmon P. Chase, a Cincinnati lawyer, known for defending fugitive slaves, is a leader of the Liberty Party.

Owen Lovejoy, a pragmatic Illinois Abolitionist and brother of the murdered Elijah Lovejoy.

William Seward, the former governor of New York, a lawyer with political ambitions.

George Thompson, a famed British Abolitionist orator and organizer.

Joshua Leavitt, one of the nation's most articulate advocates of Abolitionists, uses elections and political plans to advance the cause of emancipation and liberty.

David Walker Jr., a son of the noted Black pamphleteer David Walker, is devoted to spreading the truth of his late father's word and acting courageously in the freedom struggle. He compels attention to his father's *Appeal to the Coloured Citizens.* The composite character David Walker Jr. represents the thoughts and goals of a real person, David Walker, who died in Boston in 1830. Walker's ideas remained very much alive among African Americans, for generations after his death. Excerpts from his *Appeal to the Coloured Citizens* appear on page 111 in this game book and are indispensable for all players in the game.

The Status Quo Faction (aka the Proslavery Faction)

The New York City Merchant buys cotton in the South, ships it to manufacturers in New England and England, and provides credit and merchandise to plantation owners. He sees the big picture of the national economy and his class is central to its growth.

Howell Cobb, a Georgia planter, currently serving his first term in Congress.

The New Haven Carriage Manufacturer is a northern capitalist, producing carriages for the elite of both the South and the North. He met Charles Dickens a few years ago.

Mr. A. C. C. Thompson of Delaware, originally from Maryland's eastern shore, a hardworking white man.

Roger B. Taney, U.S. Supreme Court Chief Justice, affirms the Constitution as the supreme law of the land and maintains that the white race is superior to the African race: no Black person has any right in the United States that whites are obliged to respect. For him, this is a matter of law, not prejudice. A native of Maryland, Taney is the first Catholic to serve on the Court.

Hugh Auld is the Baltimore man whom the slave Frederick Bailey lived with for years. His shipbuilding business has failed in the years since Frederick ran away.

Thomas Auld, brother of Hugh Auld, is the legal owner of Frederick, who was inherited by Thomas's late wife. They sent him to work for Hugh, allowing Frederick to leave the eastern shore of Maryland.

The Southern Theologian is a clergyman who expounds the biblical justification for slave owning. (For more on his ideas, see page 158 in this game book.)

The White Lady of South Carolina is a young woman of a slaveholding family who has come to New York, hoping to market a unique manufactured product from Edgefield County. She is accompanied by her slave girl, the Daughter of Dave.

The Colored Slaveholder is one of a very small group of Black people who own slaves. He has a prosperous farm outside of Charleston, South Carolina, owns a handful of slave laborers, and he also owns his wife and children.

John Tyler of Virginia was president of the United States until early this year; he ardently champions a strict construction of the Constitution, abhors abolitionism, and upholds southern traditions, including slavery and its protection, states' rights.

James Trecothick Austin, former attorney general of Massachusetts, publicly praised the people of Alton, Illinois, for killing the Abolitionist editor

Lovejoy, on the grounds that they were an "orderly mob," motivated, like the patriots of the Boston Tea Party, to defend their way of life. He advocates a wide suppression of abolitionism.

Dr. Samuel A. Cartwright of Alabama, a well-trained medical doctor, affirms that he is the chief expert on the diseases of the colored race. Enslavement, in his view, benefits the colored population. (For more on his ideas, see page 151 in this game book.)

Richard Riker Jr. is the son of a politically well-connected New York City family.

Francis Todd of Newburyport, Massachusetts, a merchant and owner of ships, was libeled years ago by an Abolitionist newspaper, which reported that Todd's ship was used to transport slaves from Maryland to Louisiana. Todd advocates suppressing Abolitionists.

Francis Scott Key, the patriotic lawyer who wrote "The Star Spangled Banner," is a federal prosecutor in Washington, D.C., where he has brought cases against Abolitionists for their seditious plots. He is a nationalist, born to a Maryland planter's family.

Richard Mentor Johnson, the eccentric, unpredictable Kentucky slaveholder, ex-congressman, ex-senator, and ex-vice president of the United States.

Senator Thomas Hart Benton of Missouri is a Democrat who advocates for the western states and owns slaves and plantations. He knows, however, that the nation has other concerns too. He passionately backs the union and its expansion.

Nicholas Trist, son of an aristocratic Virginia family and husband to Jefferson's granddaughter, is a distinguished American diplomat who has facilitated the Atlantic trade. Formerly stationed in Cuba, he now seeks a diplomatic appointment from President Polk.

Independents

Horace Greeley, newspaperman, is a gifted writer and sympathetic to social reform; his *New-York Tribune* newspaper always catches the main story and puts it before the public in enlightening ways.

James Gordon Bennett, newspaperman, is the publisher of the most widely read paper in the United States, the New York *Herald*, and the inventor of such journalistic practices as the interview. He deplores abolitionism and servile revolt.

Clement Moore, a New York gentleman, author, and owner of much Manhattan land.

Ralph Waldo Emerson, leader of transcendentalism and giant of American letters.

Henry David Thoreau of Concord, Massachusetts, a graduate of Harvard College, is a social critic and a writer on natural history.

Mrs. Eliza Hamilton, widow of Alexander Hamilton, whose legacy she promotes.

John Chapman, itinerate nurseryman of the western states, and New Church missionary.

Beverly Snow, a noted chef, a mulatto, who ran the Epicurean Eating House for years at Sixth Street and Pennsylvania Avenue, in Washington, D.C.

Dr. Samuel George Morton of Philadelphia, the founder of American anthropology, has measured the cranial capacity of the races of mankind, proving, he asserts, that the African race has innately smaller, inferior brains than does the white race. He doubts that enslaving inferior people is prudent.

Dr. Edward Jarvis of Massachusetts, a capable physician and statistician.

George R. Gliddon, a self-styled expert on Egypt and a popular lecturer.

William Cullen Bryant, newspaperman, edits the New York *Evening Post* and is a man of letters, possessed of great devotion to the public good of the whole United States—and a sharp questioner of all speakers.

Jesse D. Bright, the newly elected U.S. senator from Madison, Indiana, a Democrat.

The Hoosier lives in Pendleton, Indiana, where he owns much land, timber, livestock, a store, and an impressive grist mill on Fall Creek. A man of "property and standing," he brags of his involvement in the mobbing of the colored man Douglass in 1843, when that fugitive dared to attempt to speak in Pendleton, a white man's town.

The Dockworker, a New York City white man who is proud of his race, his nation, and his virile manliness. He dislikes slavery but is grateful that it keeps most colored people out of the North. He violently hates Blacks and upholds white labor over Black.

The Philadelphia Butcher, a proud shopkeeper who is drawn toward independence in all things; he dislikes slavery, but hates Black people even more. He helped burn Philadelphia's Pennsylvania Hall in 1838, a great anti-Abolitionist victory.

Amos Kendall, a Kentucky native who was President Jackson's postmaster general and has been involved in countless inventive activities since 1836.

The Scholar of Alexis de Tocqueville's *Democracy in America*, a learned young man from New Jersey who grapples with Tocqueville's view that slavery is wrong but that an interracial society of free and equal Blacks and whites is unimaginable.

Fanny Kemble, a noted British actress now married to a Georgia plantation owner, Pierce Butler, whose grandfather was one of the signers of the Declaration of Independence. She's lively and entertaining, a sharp questioner, and a devoted mother of two young daughters, whom she misses very much.

Senator Lewis Cass, the Michigan Democratic Party politician who was Andrew Jackson's secretary of war, is an ambitious man from the west. He worries about the growth of abolition, but is comforted by the persistent color prejudice of white voters.

The New York Madam, owner of a successful brothel where prostitutes entertain customers, sees clearly who has power and who merely struts about. She knows that female subordination is based not on innate inferiority, but lack of power. Prostitution, one of the city's largest industries, has allowed her to escape subordination. She is well-read, loves Wollstonecraft, and reasons and talks brilliantly, flaunting convention.

The Morals Reformer is dedicated to ending prostitution and the problems it creates. Her husband, a New York furnishing merchant, supports her dedication to the moral purity cause.

Dorothea Dix advocates what she calls humane and therapeutic treatment for the insane.

John Jacob Astor, now an old man, immigrated to America from Germany as a youth and is currently the richest man in the world and the owner of the Astor House Hotel. He made his first fortune in the fur trade and now owns much New York real estate. Astor is stingy; asks smart, logical questions; and is nationalist, loyal to the United States.

Albert Gallatin, the last living statesman of the Founders' generation, still ponders the nation's heritage, future, and possibilities.

Madison Hemings, a colored man, age forty, is a farmer and carpenter in southern Ohio. His mother, Sally, was a slave of Thomas Jefferson. He claims she was Jefferson's concubine and that President Jefferson is his father.

Margaret Fuller, a member of the transcendentalist circle and the first woman to ever edit a magazine, *The Dial*, asserts the intellectual capacity of the female sex and asks sharp questions. She now writes book reviews for the *Tribune*.

A Brooks Brother, whose family pursues a trade in fine men's clothing and other garments.

James Fenimore Cooper, author of *The Leatherstocking Tales* and other novels, is an influential American thinker on the United States, as shown in *The American Democrat* (1838).

Herman Melville aspires to be a serious writer and man of influence. Having spent years at sea, he currently lives in New York.

Thomas Cole, painter of the Hudson River school; his allegorical *The Course of Empire* is a noted American masterpiece.

George Catlin, a painter celebrated for his works on the Indians and the West.

John James Audubon is best known for his *Birds of America* paintings.

Robert Seldon Duncanson, a young itinerant portrait painter.

Orson Squire Fowler, a well-known phrenologist; lives in New York.

Jared Sparks, the world's first professor of American history, an idealizer of George Washington.

NOTES

1. Edmund Morgan, *American Slavery, American Freedom* (New York: W. W. Norton & Company, 1975).

2. Quoted in Gerda Lerner, *The Grimké Sisters from South Carolina* (Chapel Hill, NC: University of North Carolina Press, 1967), p. 173.

3. Leonard L. Richards, *"Gentlemen of Property and Standing": Anti-Abolition Mobs in Jacksonian America* (New York: Oxford University Press, 1970).

4. "The Constitution empowered Congress to create a uniform system by which immigrants became citizens, and the Naturalization Act of 1790 offered the first legislative definition of American citizenship. With no debate, Congress restricted the process of becoming a citizen from abroad to 'free white persons.'" Eric Foner, *Give Me Liberty!*, Brief 5th ed. (W. W. Norton & Company, 2017), vol. 1, p. 218.

5. For a pithy account of this 1811 revolt in Louisiana, see Edward P. Baptist, *The Half Has Never Been Told: Slavery and the Making of American Capitalism* (New York: Basic Books, 2016), pp. 57–63.

6. Ira Berlin, *Generations of Captivity* (Cambridge, MA: Harvard University Press, 2003), p. 161.

7. Manisha Sinha, *The Slave's Cause: A History of Abolition* (New Haven, CT: Yale University Press, 2016), is a comprehensive history of the abolition movement.

8. Leonard L. Richards, *The Slave Power: The Free North and Southern Domination 1780–1860* (Baton Rouge: Louisiana State University Press, 2000).

9. Eric Foner, *Free Soil, Free Labor, Free Men: The Ideology of the Republican Party before the Civil War* (New York: Oxford University Press, 1970).

10. James Brewer Stewart, *Joshua R. Giddings and the Tactics of Radical Politics* (Cleveland, OH: Case Western University Press, 1970), and "Joshua Giddings, Antislavery Violence, and the Politics of Congressional Honor" in Stewart, *Abolitionist Politics and the Coming of the Civil War* (Amherst, MA: University of Massachusetts Press, 2008), pp. 113–138.

11. Charles G. Sellers, *James K. Polk: Continentalist, 1843–1846* (Princeton, NJ: Princeton University Press, 1966).

12. See Marcus Rediker, *The Amistad Rebellion: An Atlantic Odyssey of Slavery and Freedom* (New York: Viking, 2012), for a superb account.

13. Amy S. Greenberg, *A Wicked War: Polk, Clay, Lincoln, and the 1846 U.S. Invasion of Mexico* (New York: Alfred A. Knopf, 2012).

14. William Dusinberre, *Slavemaster President: The Double Career of James Polk* (New York: Oxford University Press, 2003).